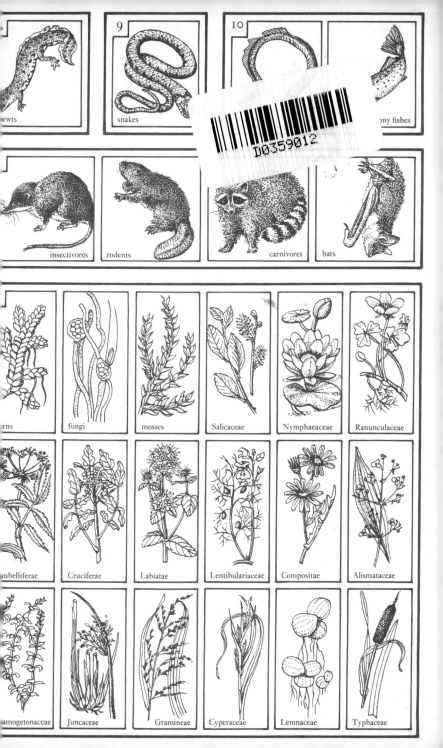

ewts

9 snakes

10

ony fishes

insectivores

rodents

carnivores

bats

rns

fungi

mosses

Salicaceae

Nymphaeaceae

Ranunculaceae

mbelliferae

Cruciferae

Labiatae

Lentibulariaceae

Compositae

Alismataceae

amogetonaceae

Juncaceae

Gramineae

Cyperaceae

Lemnaceae

Typhaceae

THE NATURAL HISTORY OF BRITAIN AND NORTHERN EUROPE

RIVERS, LAKES AND MARSHES
BRIAN WHITTON

Editors JAMES FERGUSON-LEES & BRUCE CAMPBELL

Contributors Franklyn and Margaret Perring (Plants);
Peter Mordan, Edward Easton, Geoffrey Fryer,
Paul Whalley, Frederick Wanless (Invertebrates);
Alwyne Wheeler (Fish); Tim Halliday (Amphibians and Reptiles);
James Ferguson-Lees (Birds); Gordon Corbet (Mammals)

Illustrators Deborah King (Plants); Joyce Tuhill (Invertebrates);
Annabel Milne and Peter Stebbing (Fish);
Hilary Burn (Amphibians, Reptiles, Birds and Mammals).

This book was designed and produced by
George Rainbird Limited,
36 Park Street, London W1Y 4DE
for Hodder & Stoughton Limited,
Mill Road, Dunton Green,
Sevenoaks, Kent

House Editors: Karen Goldie-Morrison,
                Linda Gamlin
Designers: Patrick Yapp, Judith Allan
Indexer: Diana Blamire
Picture Researchers: Karen Gunnell
                Nicholas Matthews
Cartographer: Tom Stalker Miller
Cover Illustrator: Hilary Burn
Endpapers Illustrator: Joyce Tuhill
Production: Jane Collins
                Elizabeth Winder

Printed and bound by
W. S. Cowell Limited,
28 Percy Street, London W1P 9FF

ISBN 0 340 23155 6

CONTENTS

FOREWORD

With increased travel and an expanding interest in Europe as a whole, many books and field guides on its natural history have been published in the last two decades, but most either treat a wide field in general terms or cover a single class or group of animals or plants. At the same time, inspired by the need for conservation, the pendulum is swinging back from the specialization of the post-war years to a wish for a fuller appreciation of all aspects of natural history. As yet, the traveller-naturalist has to be armed with a variety of volumes and, even then, has no means of understanding the interrelations of plants and animals. We believe that this new series will help to fill that gap.

The five books cover the whole of the northern half of Europe west of Russia and the Baltic States, and include Iceland: the limits are shown by the map on pages 70–71, which marks the individual countries, and the various sub-regions with the abbreviations used for them. Four of the volumes deal with (a) towns and gardens; (b) coniferous forests, heaths, moors, mountains and tundras; (c) broad-leaved woodland, hedgerows, farmland, lowland grassland and downs; and (d) coasts, dunes, sea-cliffs, salt-marshes, estuaries and the sea itself. This book is about lakes, rivers and freshwater marshes. Thus, the series covers the whole rural and urban scene.

Each book is divided into two. The first half is an ecological essay about the habitats, with examples of plant and animal communities as illustrations of interrelationships. The second is a field guide of selected species, each illustrated and described, with its habitat, the part it plays in food webs, and its distribution. Obviously there are limitations: about 600 species are illustrated in each book, or around 3000 in the series, but the north European total is probably at least 50,000. Whereas good proportions of the characteristic vertebrates (148 mammals, 364 birds, 18 reptiles, 22 amphibians and more than 100 fishes) are included, some single *families* of insects have more species than the total of these; there are over 4000 different beetles in Britain alone, and probably 8–9000 in the whole of our area, while some 3500 plants are also native or naturalized in north Europe. On the other hand, the identification of many insects and some groups of plants is a matter for the specialist and we believe that many readers will be satisfied if they can identify these at the family level. So our list of invertebrates and plants is selective, but we hope that it will form a useful groundwork from which interest in particular groups can be developed.

All plants and animals are grouped into classes (*eg* Angiospermae, Insecta, Aves), orders (*eg* Campanulatae, Lepidoptera, Passeriformes), families (*eg* Compositae, Nymphalidae, Turdidae) and genera (*eg Aster, Inachis, Turdus*), groups of increasingly close affinity. Each plant or animal has two scientific names, the first of which is the genus and the second the species. These are often considered to be outside the scope of a work of this kind, but many invertebrates and some plants have no vernaculars and, at the same time, such names are invaluable in showing relationships. Consequently, each species is given its scientific name at the first mention in each essay chapter and again in the field guide, where the family name is also inserted in capitals.

The specially commissioned colour paintings which illustrate the field guide are a delight in themselves. It has become customary to illustrate plants and animals in field guides as individual specimens, but here they are arranged in attractive compositions. Scale has had to suffer, but the sizes are always given in the facing descriptions.

Although it is not so immediately obvious, man has had as much influence on the lakes and rivers in industrial northern Europe as on the land surrounding them. This book explores these changes, which include the replacement of the 'sporting' salmon and trout, with their need for unpolluted water, by coarse fish such as pike and perch, or even in extreme cases the disappearance of fish altogether. Windermere, the largest body of freshwater in England and one subject to complex pressures, has been fairly intensively studied and is taken as an example. But, quite apart from the influence of man, the lakes of northern Europe exhibit a variety of conditions, due to their different geological, topographical and climatic situations. In the same way the streams and rivers, rising in the hills, sometimes from small lakes, and flowing into large lakes or the sea, show a great diversity of life, both plant and animal. Recently the term 'wetland' has come into use to cover all sorts of freshwater habitat, but originally it comprehended only swamps, bogs and marshes. The whole range of wetlands, from the Norfolk Broads and the turloughs in Ireland to Iceland's hot springs, all come into the purview of this book; as well as their distinctive plant communities, they are the homes or resting places of a great many birds, ranging from cranes and geese to tiny warblers in the reed-swamps, whose identities tantalize the naturalist.

The ecological essay for each book has been written by a specialist in all or most of the habitats covered by it. Dr Brian Whitton, the author for this book, can claim to be very well equipped for its whole range. He is a senior lecturer in Botany at the University of Durham, and his present research is concerned with streams and rivers and especially with the effects of zinc and lead on the plants and animals inhabiting them. He has a particular interest in the adaptations shown by the lower plants known as algae living in the streams in old mining areas in the Pennine Hills of northern England. For three years he was financed by the European Economic Community to carry out research on lead, zinc and cadmium in the rivers of EEC countries.

JAMES FERGUSON-LEES
BRUCE CAMPBELL

INTRODUCTION

One of the fascinations of lakes and rivers in industrial northern Europe is their range of wildlife. Even in big cities, there is plenty to be seen. Shallow water on wasteland, with its fringing beds of reeds and bulrushes, and sometimes also coots and moorhens, can bring a sense of wilderness right into the urban area. Elsewhere, freshwaters are among the most popular places to spend weekends or holidays. This book is about the plants and animals that live in the lakes, rivers and other wetlands of northern Europe.

Although it may not always be so obvious to the casual observer, man has had just as much influence on these aquatic sites as he has had on the land. Pollution of rivers has led to the replacement of salmon and brown trout by coarse fish, such as roach and pike, or even, in extreme cases, to the loss of all fish. Such pollution may be easy to see, like a large industrial effluent, or it may be more subtle. Fish die in spring in many of the soft-water lakes and rivers of southern Norway and Sweden because the fumes of industrial Britain, Germany and the Netherlands are carried by the wind, and then deposited by rain and snow, making the waters more acidic. Man has drained large areas of wetland and in many parts of Europe one must travel a long way to see well-developed marshes and bogs.

On the other hand, changes brought about by man are by no means all for the worse. In particular, there has probably been an increase in open water. Some such changes were made long ago: for instance, the formation by the 13th century of the Norfolk Broads, due to the cutting of peat; the extensive medieval fish-ponds near Milicz, Poland; the construction of English 'dew-ponds' in the 17th century; and the tremendous spread of canals in lowland Europe during the early part of the industrial revolution. In modern times, the most important developments have been the construction of reservoirs, first for drinking and industrial water, then as parts of hydro-electric schemes and, most recently, to regulate the flow of rivers so that water may be abstracted at sites far downstream.

The problem of language
One problem in describing waters and wetlands is language. For a start, fresh-waters may sometimes be far from fresh in the sense which would appeal to an advertising agent. Below a sewage works they may be, in fact, decidedly

Mývatn is within a volcanic region of Iceland. The richness of its waters makes the lake an important summer feeding ground for waterfowl.

smelly. Freshwaters are simply those which are not brackish or saline. The languages of all the countries treated in this book have a variety of words for their wetlands. Vernacular English is especially rich in such words, which can cause much confusion. Sometimes a particular word corresponds to a particular type of vegetation, and yet this may apply to only one part of Britain: 'carr' refers in East Anglia to forest developing on peat, but in Yorkshire to open marshy areas. 'Marsh' and 'bog' are used generally for many types of wetlands, though the latter usually relates to vegetation dominated by bog-mosses *Sphagnum*. Other common words are 'swamp', 'fen', 'mire', 'moor' and 'moss'. We shall return to this problem when discussing the types of vegetation that develop over peat.

LAKES

Lakes vary so much that it is difficult to give a general impression of their plant and animal life. The summer tourist who spends only ten minutes on the shore of some deep lake in the Scottish Highlands or Norway may see few species. A similar visit to the edge of one of the shallow fertile lakes of the English county of Salop or of lowland Czechoslovakia will reveal a great variety. It is, nevertheless, evident that it takes more effort to see what is present in a lake than in a forest; it also requires more background knowledge to understand why the flora and fauna of one lake differ from those of another, than it does to understand the differences between coniferous and broad-leaved forests. To demonstrate this, let us first look at one particular lake.

Windermere

The two most intensively studied lakes of northern Europe are Windermere, in the English Lake District, and the Plussee, in Schleswig-Holstein, north of Hamburg. The latter is only small and off the beaten track, so Windermere, which is seen by tens of thousands of tourists each year, will serve as our example. It is in fact the largest natural lake in England, although it is only 17 km long and 1 km at its widest. It was formed by glacial action during the Ice Age and so is relatively deep, reaching a maximum of about 67 m. The depth varies, because the lake level changes with the amount of water entering from rivers and streams. Although the range is in most years little more than 50 cm, this is enough to have a marked effect on the development of some plants and invertebrates at the edge.

Much of the shoreline of Windermere is rocky and lacks a fringing bed of emergent vegetation, but sheltered areas with fine sediments have growths of the common reed *Phragmites australis*. Beneath the water, other rooted plants may grow down to depths of about 4 m. Some of these, such as perfoliate pondweed *Potamogeton perfoliatus*, have long, leafy stems which reach the surface, whereas others, such as shoreweed *Littorella uniflora*, have short stems and leaves that do so only in the shallowest waters. In many lakes there is a general zonation of species with increasing depth, but in Windermere this changes from place to place, according to the nature of the sediment. Most of the submerged plants form flowers, but these tend to be inconspicuous. Only the amphibious bistort *Polygonum amphibium* produces a colourful display, with spikes of pink flowers emerging from the surface in late summer.

Most of the bottom-living invertebrates can be found near the edge of the lake among these rooted plants, on stones or in the sediments. Species of snails, such as the wandering snail *Lymnaea peregra* and various ram's-horn

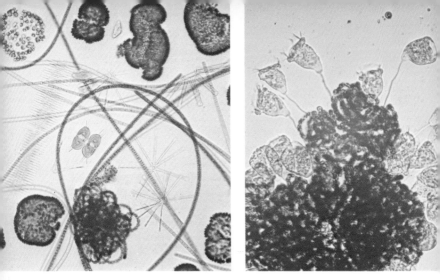

LEFT *Typical algal plankton in a sample from Windermere. The darker colonies and the filaments are blue-green algae, the brighter green structures are green algae, and the delicate shapes are diatoms. The latter include the star-shaped* Asterionella (*scale* × 100). RIGHT *A protozoan,* Vorticella, *attached to a colony of blue-green alga,* Anabaena, *feeds on bacteria* (*scale* × 100).

snails *Planorbis/Planorbarius*, are usually obvious. A range of other invertebrates can be found without much trouble. The river limpet *Ancylus fluviatilis* and lake limpet *Acroloxus lacustris* are both common. Other widespread groups include flatworms (Platyhelminthes), leeches (Hirudinea), mites (Acari), insect nymphs and larvae, and freshwater shrimps *Gammarus*; among these are herbivores, carnivores and omnivores. Some herbivores feed directly on the leaves of submerged plants, but more depend on the films of algae that develop on the leaves or rocks: surprisingly little is known about the relative contributions of these two types of plant materials as foods for invertebrates. Flatworms are carnivores that feed on, for instance, oligochaete worms and larvae of mayflies (Ephemeroptera) and stoneflies (Plecoptera). Freshwater shrimps eat plant and animal materials, both live and dead, including algae, insect eggs and fragments of dead organisms; they are themselves the favourite foods of some fish, such as trout *Salmo trutta*.

Most bottom-living invertebrates are found only in shallow water, but some go much deeper and a few are restricted to deep water. Below 10 m the fauna consists largely of oligochaete worms, pea mussels *Pisidium* and the larvae of non-biting midges (Chironomidae) and of the phantom fly *Chaoborus flavicans*. These mosquito larvae, which may reach 1 cm in length and are almost transparent, are especially interesting. By day they are usually found in the bottom mud, but at night they rise to the surface. They can do this partly because they are active swimmers, but also because they have a pair of air-sacs at each end of the body which help regulate their position in the water. Light evidently plays a role in determining this behaviour because in especially cloudy weather the larvae may remain near the surface by day as well as by night.

Although plants and animals near the edge or on the bottom of the lake may be the most obvious, the tiny organisms suspended in the water form a much greater bulk. This plankton consists of algae, small animals such as protozoa, rotifers, cladocerans and copepods, and also bacteria and tiny fungi. Some rely simply on buoyancy to keep them in the water column, but others can swim actively. Most of the plankton organisms are present the whole year round, but the numbers of each species vary greatly at different seasons. Plankton is usually most evident in summer, as can be seen by holding a glass of lake water against the light. The plankton algae play an especially important role because they make use of the sun's energy to carry out photosynthesis, and thus create new food material for the herbivorous rotifers

Ostracods and copepods are small crustaceans visible to the naked eye. They jerk around in the water column feeding on algae and other small organisms.

and cladocerans. These, in turn, may be eaten by small carnivores, such as fish larvae. The algae are thus the first link in many different food-chains or food-webs.

Most plankton algae are relatively short-lived; they either grow and divide, or are attacked by other organisms. While many species may be eaten by animals, some are also especially susceptible to attacks by bacteria or fungi. On the other hand, one remarkable species, *Melosira italica*, sinks to the bottom after a burst of growth each spring and can survive long periods in the mud. In one case, cells laid down 180 years ago were still alive. This alga belongs to the group known as diatoms, the sculpturing of whose silica walls has long been a fascination to microscopists. Because the patterns on the shells of long-dead diatoms are still clearly visible, and because each species has a different pattern, the zonation of these shells in the bottom sediments of Windermere has provided valuable clues to the history of the lake. In the middle of the 19th century there was an increase not only in the rate at which sediments were laid down on the bottom, but also in the deposition of diatoms, especially *Asterionella formosa*. This was probably one of many changes which took place about 1850 as a result of a growing human population, which led to an increase of sewage in the catchment area and so eventually also in the lake.

Windermere supports both game and coarse fish. The former are mainly brown trout and arctic charr *Salvelinus alpinus*. Salmon *Salmo salar* pass through the lake to spawn in inflow streams. Coarse fish include perch *Perca fluviatilis*, pike *Esox lucius* and eels *Anguilla anguilla*, as well as such small species as minnows *Phoxinus phoxinus*, bullheads *Cottus gobio* and sticklebacks *Gasterosteus aculeatus*; of these, the perch, pike, minnows and bullheads were introduced to the lake. Although trout are sufficiently abundant to make fishing popular, they do not breed actually in the lake: when mature, they enter the inflow streams to spawn and the young return usually within two years. In contrast, the charr does breed in the lake, burying its eggs in areas of gravel; this species lives mostly in deep water, some individuals spawning there in spring, others in shallow water in autumn. Perch and pike likewise both live in deep water for part of the year and then spawn in shallow water: perch lay their eggs on larger plants, especially Canadian waterweed *Elodea canadensis*; pike spawn among reeds. Both these species can be cannibals: perch only occasionally, but young pike are regularly eaten by their older relations.

The status of some of the fish in Windermere has changed markedly over the years. These changes have been documented especially well for several of the larger species, initially in the records and general observations of anglers, but since the 1940s also by a careful programme of trapping. Some are almost certainly the result of man's activities, though others might well have taken place even without him. Over the past century, for example, trout and charr have become less abundant and, until recently, pike and perch more numerous: it seems likely that these are further signs of the increased effluent.

Man has also had more direct effects on the pike and perch populations. Since 1944 the larger pike have been selectively removed by netting in shallow bays with the aim of favouring the trout and charr. A similar decrease in average size and total numbers was brought about among perch during the 1939–45 war when they were caught to supply a small cannery: the population was reduced to about one-third and never fully returned to pre-war numbers. Moreover, since 1976 the majority of perch have been killed by a disease which has spread rapidly through the lake. No one is at present sure what long-term effect this will have on the other fish.

A number of species of waterfowl spend all or part of the year on Windermere. Mute swans *Cygnus olor*, shelducks *Tadorna tadorna* and mallard *Anas platyrhynchos* are present at all seasons, though the mallard are supplemented by others from continental Europe each winter. Red-breasted mergansers *Mergus serrator* are also mainly resident, having spread from farther north in Britain since about 1950. Other winter visitors include coots *Fulica atra* and cormorants *Phalacrocorax carbo* from various places, tufted ducks *Aythya fuligula* from Iceland, pochards *A. ferina* from eastern Europe and goldeneye *Bucephala clangula* from Norway and Sweden. Most of these birds feed on such animals as snails and small fish, but the mute swans, pochards and coots eat mainly plants. Coots may feed in large flocks of several hundred, which can cause considerable local damage to the submerged plants.

Regular counts have been made of the waterfowl since 1947, and it is clear that, as with the fish, obvious decreases and increases have taken place. Mute swans and shelducks have decreased, apparently because of greater disturbance by tourists in summer. There has, however, been a general rise in the numbers of most waterfowl, probably due to shooting being stopped and the succession of mild winters during 1963–78. A large increase in the mallard population is due to the release of hand-reared stock on some of the small lakes in the region, and wildfowlers have now also introduced greylag geese *Anser anser* to the lake.

Numbers of several species of gulls *Larus* spend much of the year on Windermere, many of them probably from breeding colonies on the Pennine moors or the coast, especially Walney Island.

Why lakes differ

No two lakes have quite the same biology. Each is influenced by slightly different combinations of key factors, such as geology, topography, climate and man. The geological formation underlying the basin determines the kinds of minerals and sediments flowing into it. Some of the upland lakes in granitic regions of Scotland and Norway have such low levels of dissolved minerals that their waters can be used to fill a car battery. In complete contrast are the calcareous lakes with very hard waters in, for example, Co. Clare, Ireland. Not surprisingly, the flora and fauna of these extremes are quite different. The shape of a lake basin also has a major influence on its biology: for

Wastwater in the English Lake District illustrates the scenery typical of an oligotrophic lake.

instance, green plants can grow only where light penetrates, so those with roots are restricted to shallow waters. In general, lakes that are shallow and have a high proportion of shoreline to the total area of water tend to be the most productive; they are also more likely to be affected by the activities of man. Deeper lakes, like Windermere, tend to be less productive.

Topography and climate combine to determine two important differences among lakes in northern Europe, one apparent in winter and the other in summer. Lakes near the Atlantic coast never form an ice cover, or do so only rarely for a few days at a time. On the other hand, many lakes in the centre of the Continent have an ice cover for long periods, and this influences the growth of organisms in various ways. It forms a barrier between the water and the winter storms and so prevents the disturbance of animals and plant-roots in the sediments of the shallows. At the same time, the ice also prevents any oxygen from reaching the water below: at latitudes or altitudes with pro-longed severe weather, fish may be absent from a shallow lake simply because it loses its oxygen by late winter. In the fish-ponds of eastern Europe, holes have to be maintained in the ice to prevent this; the most dangerous time appears to be when the ice is breaking up in spring, because the thin layer of

An eutrophic lake, Crose Mere lies in rich farming country in Salop.

oxygenated water just beneath it becomes dispersed throughout the lake, and there is nowhere with sufficient oxygen for the fish. Many invertebrates can, however, survive long winter periods without any oxygen: this has been shown in Sweden, for instance, for leeches and for the larvae of dragonflies (Odonata) and chironomid midges.

Although not so immediately obvious, there is an equally important difference between lakes in summer, but this is not evidently geographical in origin. In some cases the upper part of the water mass becomes much warmer than the lower: in fact, the lake splits into two distinct zones, with a narrow transition known as the thermocline. Any diver will be familiar with this sharp change in temperature as he passes suddenly from warm to much cooler water. Most deep lakes and many shallow ones form such a thermocline, but in others the action of wind stirring up the water prevents the separation of the warm upper layer. The Derwent Reservoir, for example, which is the third largest man-made lake in Britain, hardly ever develops a thermocline, because winds are funnelled down its valley and keep the water mixed; as a result, the temperature of the water at the edge of the reservoir seldom rises above 14–15°C as opposed to the 18–20°C of other waters at a similar latitude with a thermocline. This is a big difference, not only for the swimmer, but also for plants and invertebrates in the water. In central Europe, temperatures of shallow lakes with a thermocline may reach 25°C or even higher, providing for a few weeks of the year a sub-tropical environment.

In autumn, lakes which form a thermocline earlier in the year undergo a reverse change, known as the autumn overturn: the upper layer cools and then, often on a windy night, starts to sink until all the water becomes mixed. This is one of the most important events in the annual cycle of change. Sediments, nutrients and organisms near the bottom are all stirred into the water column. In Windermere, for instance, the diatom *Melosira italica*, which has been resting on the bottom, again reaches the light and starts a fresh burst of growth.

Lakes rich and poor in nutrients
Many lakes have shown obvious changes in nutrient level since the early 1950s. Examples could be given from almost any part of Europe, but among those where the changes have been most carefully studied are Loch Leven in Scotland, Lingby Sø in Denmark, Lake Mälaren in Sweden, and some of the Polish Mazurian lakes, such as Lake Sniardwy.

Microscopic algae may become so abundant that they colour the water, especially if they are concentrated at the surface. These 'blooms' may appear rapidly because the cells of some of the species involved contain tiny cylinders of gas, which make them highly buoyant; indeed, in still weather the appearance of the water may change almost overnight. The Shropshire meres are one area where such blooms are familiar: there, the sudden covering of one of the lakes with a blue-green scum is known as 'the breaking of the meres', by analogy with the breaking of wort in beer-making. Although these water-blooms have become much more frequent, there are also old records, and in various parts of Europe legends grew up relating to them: the occurrence of a red bloom at Finchampstead, Berkshire, supposedly forewarned of the death of William Rufus in 1100. The blooms are unpopular, not just because people find them offensive to look at; some of the species involved may be poisonous to fish, farm animals and also man, if he is foolish enough to drink the water, which is rather unlikely as the blooms often decompose quickly and give rise to most unpleasant smells.

What has led to the great increase in water-blooms in recent years? The answer is the increased levels of plant nutrients which have been reaching the lakes, from sewage effluents and run-off of agricultural fertilizers. One particular culprit in the 1960s was detergents with a high content of phosphate.

Not only man has suffered as a result of the formation of these dense algal populations. Other recent changes in lakes have been ascribed to them, in particular the decreases of submerged plants, such as pondweeds and water-milfoils *Myriophyllum*, and of mayflies, dragonflies and other insects. Often the cause is simply that the algae in the plankton form a water-bloom, but sometimes the development of a heavy cover of algae on the leaves and stems of submerged plants may also be important. In each case, the end result is the same: so much of the light is absorbed by the algae that not enough reaches the larger plants to let them grow.

Large submerged plants provide food or homes for many animals, so their loss may have many other effects. Loch Leven provides various examples. Since about 1950 there have been marked decreases in pondweeds and other submerged plants, resulting from the increased algal blooms. The lake is one of the best sites in Europe for waterfowl, so the ups and downs of its bird population have been followed for many years. For instance, since 1880, wintering greylag geese and pink-footed geese *Anser brachyrhynchus* have gradually increased and bean geese *A. fabalis* have now disappeared. While these changes correspond to those elsewhere and do not appear to be related to particular events at Loch Leven, others are almost certainly the result of the loss of submerged plants. Examples are the virtual disappearance of a large summer flock of mute swans, the loss of concentrations of coots, and reduced summering by pochards; all of these birds are heavily dependent on submerged plants for food.

Since submerged plants can provide homes for snails, insect larvae and fish eggs, anything which feeds on these also suffers. On the Loosdrecht broads near Amsterdam, enrichment of water from the heavily polluted Vecht led to the loss of dense beds of the alga known as stonewort *Chara*. The animals living on and among the stonewort also vanished, in particular the zebra mussels *Dreissena polymorpha*. As a result, the many thousands of diving ducks that normally remained through the winter also disappeared. Lakes like Loch Leven and the Loosdrecht broads with high levels of plant nutrients and dense growths of algae, often leading to the formation of water-blooms, are termed 'eutrophic'. In contrast, lakes with low levels of nutrients and clear waters are termed 'oligotrophic'. Most lakes fall between these extremes, but recognition of the two types is helpful.

Deep, upland lakes in granitic regions of Scotland and Norway provide the best examples of oligotrophy. Their waters are low in dissolved minerals, planktonic algae are sparse, and sufficient light penetrates the water for rooted plants to grow at much greater depths than in Windermere. Many groups of invertebrates are represented by far fewer individuals or are absent, but a few are more abundant, especially mayflies and stoneflies. Game fish such as trout and salmon, and locally also charr, powan *Coregonus lavaretus* or vendace *C. albula*, are the only large species present.

Eutrophic lakes provide a contrast in every feature. Typically they are shallow and in flat lowland country, such as the Shropshire meres and many lakes of the north German plain and Denmark. Plants other than plankton algae may be absent, insufficient light reaching any part of the bottom for them to grow; those rooted plants which do occur in eutrophic lakes are present only at the very edge, and their roots or other structures in the mud

A dense algal bloom at the edge of a lake. The cells float at the water-surface because they contain gas vacuoles.

store plenty of food in winter for the shoots to grow up to the surface again next spring. Most of the mayflies (except *Cloeon dipterum* and often also *Caenis*) and stoneflies are absent, but some species of chironomid midges may be abundant. Other invertebrates which often occur in large numbers include leeches and the water-lice or hog-slaters *Asellus*. Game fish are absent, and highly eutrophic lakes may even lack coarse fish. In very large lakes one part may be much more eutrophic than another, and then it is especially easy to see the differences. The eastern end of Lake Mälaren, for instance, is much less rich in nutrients than the western. Towards the east edge, crustaceans are predominant among the bottom fauna, and vendace among the fish; in contrast, the bottom fauna at the west end consists of chironomid midges and oligochaete worms, and the zander *Stizostedion lucioperca* is the main fish.

Some of the most dramatic examples of eutrophic water are found in cities, such as St James's Park Lake in the centre of London. Here six hectares of shallow, nutrient-rich water support a dense bloom of algae which lasts right through the summer. In June 1969 the lake was a bluish-green colour due to the alga *Oscillatoria agardhii*; in some areas the water emitted a foul smell. Dead birds were first observed during the last week of that month, and by the middle of November some 400 of the original population of 1000 ducks and geese had died, as well as various other species. It was found that at least some deaths were due to botulism, caused by a highly toxic product of the bacterium *Clostridium botulinum*, which can develop in muds completely free of oxygen and rich in decaying organic matter. Relatives of the alga forming the bloom are also known to be very poisonous, but in this case it is likely that botulism was the main culprit. Because of this danger, the lake is now drained and cleaned every few years. Botulism is most prevalent in warm weather, and the disease was widespread in western Europe during the long, hot summers of 1975 and 1976.

When lakes become eutrophic, the resulting series of changes includes obvious losses of particular species or even whole groups of plants and animals. Nevertheless, the abundance of plant and animal matter usually increases and, unless conditions are extremely eutrophic, the total numbers of species present may stay as high as they were. The main difference is that smaller organisms increase in importance: although St James's Park Lake lacks any large plants, in early summer one drop of water may contain a hundred different species of microscopic algae.

Control
The drainage and subsequent removal of bottom mud to control biological changes in St James's Park Lake are drastic and rather expensive, though also used for some small, shallow reservoirs. Lake Trummen, near Växjö in southern Sweden, was brought back to a healthy condition in the early 1970s by pumping all the black mud and some underlying sediment from the bottom while it was still full of water; this operation was particularly successful because it was achieved without the mud becoming stirred up into the water column.

Where a high level of phosphate is responsible for forming a dense bloom, the most effective prevention is usually to reduce the amounts entering the lake. This has been achieved in part by lessening the quantities of phosphate in many detergent packets bought by households, but in some cases that is just not drastic enough. Another solution is to remove much of the phosphate from the sewage effluents, a very expensive process unless, as in Norway, cheap electricity is available from hydro-electric power. In some lakes which are key sources of drinking water, the risk of a bloom is so great that phosphate has to be removed from effluents in spite of the cost. Such treatment is given, for instance to the effluents entering the rivers which feed Lough Neagh, the large, shallow lake which is the main water supply for Northern Ireland.

There are other, quite different approaches to stopping the formation of blooms. One is to prevent the entry of the nutrient-rich water by diverting it downstream of the lake. Large-scale operations of this sort have been carried out in North America and smaller ones in Europe. The eutrophic features of Lake Bikczwe in Poland have been reduced by building a ditch to separate it from the surrounding farmland; sewage effluents were diverted in 1969 from the highly eutrophic Lake Norrviken in central Sweden and sent by tunnel to a treatment plant near the coast north of Stockholm. The one problem with such schemes is that the nutrients in the water still have to go somewhere: in the cases of Lakes Bikczwe and Norrviken, most presumably eventually reach the Baltic Sea, which has itself undergone changes rather similar to those in lakes as they become eutrophic.

REED-SWAMP AND FEN

A mere fraction of the former marshlands of lowland Europe now remains. Some of the losses are natural ones that have taken place since the end of the last glacial period, but man has been the chief agent: he has drained such areas ever since he began intensive agriculture, and the process continues. Only in the north of Sweden and Finland, and in parts of Poland, are there extensive marshlands in anything like their natural state. Drainage is important to the farmer to prevent crops from becoming waterlogged in winter, and the soils left behind are frequently very fertile. Yet those areas of marsh which do remain are often strikingly rich in plant and animal life, so it is not surprising that the naturalist who wishes to conserve these communities often comes into conflict with the farmer.

Reed-swamp

Reed-swamp is tall vegetation at the edges of many lakes, which is dominated by such species as common reed *Phragmites australis*, the bulrushes *Typha latifolia* and *T. angustifolia*, and the common club-rush *Scirpus lacustris*. At Windermere, for example, there are small patches of common reeds in sheltered bays. In the shallow lakes of Poland, southern Czechoslovakia and many other parts of Europe, however, the reed-swamp often forms a distinct zone round much of the shore-line and sometimes reaches 100 m or more in width.

Just as some of the most notable 'lakes' in England are man-made, such as the great modern reservoirs and the many gravel pits, so the reed-swamps of Leighton Moss (Cumbria), Minsmere (Suffolk) and Stodmarsh (Kent) have arisen due to flooding for various reasons of low quality farmland. But, in general, apart from such areas as the Norfolk Broads, Britain seems poorly off for reed-swamp, especially when compared with a single river in northern France, for example the Somme.

Reed-swamp is limited on the landward side by the summer water-table; there is no sharp change in the vegetation, but typical reed-swamp occurs only where the summer depth is at least some 20 cm. Its encroachment into the open water is clearly affected by the formation of the lake: a gently sloping shelf permits the development of a wide zone. The common club-rush often reaches farthest from the shore and, where everything else is favourable for it, this plant may occur in water as deep as 2 m. Where it is absent, the common reed usually extends the farthest. The nutrient composition of the lake also affects the extent of the reed-swamp, the outer boundary generally spreading into deeper water when conditions are rich. This trend can, however, be reversed if the water is too eutrophic. A survey of the Bastrup Sø, at the upper end of the Molleaa river-system in Denmark, over a period of 60 years, showed that there had been a great decrease in the area of reed-swamp, the common reed and club-rush and the lesser bulrush all being affected.

A narrow fringe of reed-swamp occurs also along the banks of many lowland rivers. When the water level is low, conditions there are little different from a lake reed-swamp, with organisms typical of stagnant waters, such as duckweed *Lemna* and pond-skaters (Gerridae), living on the surface. When the level is high, conditions are quite different: water flows right through the fringe of river reed-swamp, flooding birds' nests in summer and washing away old plant remains in winter.

Birds

Many of the plants and animals of reed-swamp are widespread throughout Europe, though not necessarily present at every site. Numerous birds nest and roost in the thick cover provided by reed-swamp. Some feed there as well, on plants or animals, while others, generally the larger species, fish or hunt in or over the open water, fens and riparian marshland.

Perhaps the best known is the grey heron *Ardea cinerea*. Although in parts of northern Europe, especially in Britain, it nests in trees, often several kilometres from water, it does also build in reed-swamp, and by the Naardermeer, near Amsterdam, it shares a tree colony with cormorants *Phalacrocorax carbo* in fen woodland adjacent to the reeds. The grey heron has been the subject of one of the longest-running censuses, begun in England and Wales in 1928. The total has generally varied around 4000 nests, dropping to 2250 after the cold winter of 1962/63 and rising again to 4925 by 1973. Although high residues of organochlorine pesticides have resulted in deaths of grey herons during the breeding season, the population as a whole does not seem to have been greatly affected.

Related birds of the reed-swamp are the purple heron *Ardea purpurea*, the bittern *Botaurus stellaris* and little bittern *Ixobrychus minutus*, and the very local spoonbill *Platalea leucorodia*. At the other end of the size scale are the bearded tit or reedling *Panurus biarmicus*, which has spread eruptively in many countries of northern Europe in recent years; the penduline tit *Remiz pendulinus*, another increasing species, which nests not low down like the bearded tit but in the terminal twigs of drooping branches; and several warblers of the genera *Locustella* and *Acrocephalus*, some of which may be associated with particular plant species. For example, in a study of Opatovický Pond, near Třebon, Czechoslovakia, most nests of the reed warbler *Acrocephalus scirpaceus* occurred in common reeds, while almost all those of the great reed warbler *A. arundinaceus* were in bulrushes. Both these warblers are favoured hosts of the cuckoo *Cuculus canorus*.

Natural pool and marshland in Finnish Lappland.

Typical medium-sized birds of the reed-swamp are the water rail *Rallus aquaticus*, the spotted crake *Porzana porzana* and two smaller relatives, the little crake *P. parva* and Baillon's crake *P. pusilla*. These are normally identified only by their calls and are as secretive as coots *Fulica atra* and moorhens *Gallinula chloropus*, members of the same family, are often conspicuous – though moorhens can at times be remarkably unobtrusive. So can the grebes (Podicipedidae), five species of which breed in the region, in reed-swamps or emergent aquatic vegetation.

The marsh harrier *Circus aeruginosus* and Montagu's harrier *C. pygargus* are birds of prey which breed in this habitat, sometimes also nesting in fields of corn. In winter the hen harrier *C. cyaneus*, mainly a moorland nester, replaces the Montagu's, which is a summer visitor to the region. Harriers also hunt over open marshland, the feeding place of white storks *Ciconia ciconia*, which in northern Europe nest predominantly on buildings. Marshes are also the feeding and breeding places of many waterfowl, of the graceful black tern *Chlidonias niger*, and of various waders, of which the richly caparisoned male ruffs *Philomachus pugnax* displaying in mock combat are the most spectacular.

In addition to their resident birds, reed-swamps provide roosts, notably after the breeding season, for species as diverse as swallows and martins (Hirundinidae), wagtails *Motacilla* and starlings *Sturnus vulgaris*, sometimes amounting to thousands of individuals. These gatherings, in turn, attract birds of prey, such as hobbies *Falco subbuteo*.

Formation of peat

On the landward side of reed-swamp, dead plant remains are neither washed away nor decayed as fast as they are produced. Thus, each successive year there is a slight increase in the amount of undecayed material round the bases of the plants, and the deposition of this over many years leads to the formation of peat. Peat tends to develop at most sites in northern Europe where soils remain waterlogged right through the summer, including not only lakes, but also river and stream basins and around springs.

No English vernacular word properly covers all the types of wetlands where peat is formed, but 'mire' is sometimes used for this purpose. Unfortunately there is no simple way of classifying all the types of mire vegetation. The situation is easier to understand by recognizing two key factors – the source of water and its mineral composition. At one extreme, the vegetation may be entirely dependent on rain for replenishment of its nutrient supply, the plants growing so far above the ground water-table that they receive nothing from it: such mires are poor in species and dominated usually by bog-mosses *Sphagnum*. Mires where the vegetation receives additional nutrients from the ground water have more species, particularly if the water is laterally moving (as below seepage lines) rather than relatively stagnant. The situation is complicated by the major influence of the amounts of calcium and of nutrients such as phosphate in the water on the composition of the vegetation. Mires where the water is highly calcareous but the levels of phosphate are relatively low are usually the richest of all in numbers of species. The various types of mire vegetation other than those covered by bog-mosses are often known popularly as 'fen', especially in East Anglia, and the word is used here in this sense.

Fen and Schwingmoor

Where fens develop around a lake, the increasing amount of peat brings about other changes. As peat is laid down at the edge, so the fen vegetation slowly expands into the lake. If the angle of the slope leading to the bottom is gentle, then the vegetation changes gradually into reed-swamp; as peaty sediments accumulate in this reed-swamp, it too can extend still farther into the water. If the angle of the slope is steeper, the pioneer community which gradually encroaches into the lake may be rather different: although in direct lateral contact with the main body of the fen, the vegetation spreads farther and farther over the surface, forming a floating mat known in German as *Schwingmoor*, a reflection of the fact that, if one jumps up and down, the whole mat swings up and down too. (Although such mats are strong, it is wise not to jump too near the edge, because they often form over water many metres in depth: a good example is the Chartley Moss National Nature Reserve in Staffordshire, where the mat lies in some places over more than 10 m of water.)

Except in the far north of Europe, natural fen is colonized by shrubs and eventually also by trees. In East Anglia, willows *Salix* and alders *Alnus gluti-nosa* are the typical tree colonists, but over much of Europe various conifers are more important. In undisturbed fen the trees usually get bigger farther from the open water, especially round a Schwingmoor; this is due in part to the fact that the trees can start growing only when the peat is formed, so the older the peat, the older the trees. The sheer weight of a tree, however, may also be important: if it grows too big too quickly, it sinks gradually into the floating mat. In Moravia and some other parts of central Europe where elks *Alces alces* are common, these animals graze tall fen and reed-swamp in summer, thus keeping the vegetation in a relatively open condition. (The suggestion has even been made that elks should be introduced to some fenlands in Britain, as no other large European mammal grazes the wetter areas.)

Most of the larger herbaceous fen plants such as the common reed and hemp-agrimony *Eupatorium cannabinum* are common throughout Europe, though some of the smaller species are more restricted. For instance, species of orchids which are rare or absent in fens in western Europe may be frequent in the fens of central Europe.

Influence of man

Although the lushness of much fen vegetation makes it appear natural, man

has often played a major part in determining its composition. In the past, many areas were subject to a regular programme of cutting (sometimes also of deliberate flooding) and this still takes place where thatch is required for houses: parts of England, Ireland and Poland all provide examples. In East Anglia, the great fen-sedge *Cladium mariscus* is harvested every four years and the common reed usually every two years. The fen-sedge, which is used for the ridges of thatched houses, is unusual among fenland species in that, where it is present, it is often overwhelmingly dominant; in general, this species is more abundant in Britain than in central Europe, thriving in fens poor in nutrients. As nutrient levels increase, common reed takes over, to be replaced at the highest levels of all by reed sweet-grass *Glyceria maxima*.

August in Wicken Fen, Cambridgeshire. Willow carr overlooks common reeds and water-lilies.

PONDS AND POOLS

Ponds and pools differ from site to site just as much as lakes. Ponds have been formed as a result of a whole range of activities: they may have been dug to water cattle, to farm fish, or to grace the gardens of some large house; they range from simple, plastic-lined depressions in suburban gardens to extensive shallow areas resulting from the removal of sand and gravel or deep pits from quarrying or subsidence. The word 'pool' is often restricted to small natural bodies of water, but in much of lowland Europe it is hard to distinguish what is natural and what results from man's efforts.

The classic examples of water bodies originally formed through man's activities but for long regarded as natural are the Norfolk Broads, discussed later among the 'case-studies', but the 'flashes' and 'ings' of northern England, resulting from industrial subsidence, are hard to distinguish from natural pools with fringes of marsh vegetation; they are attractive to a variety of water-birds for breeding, wintering, and resting on passage. Gravel extraction in the river valleys of eastern England has led to the creation of many wet pits, some large enough to qualify as 'lakes', which have replaced the original marshes. Many of these are now stocked with game and coarse fish, or devoted to forms of water recreation varyingly incompatible with wildlife; but at others compromises of usage have been agreed and some are now important refuges. In the working stage, gravel pits are notable as breeding places for the little ringed plover *Charadrius dubius*, no doubt owing to their resemblance to the riverine shingle beds frequented by this species in continental Europe. Gravel pits proceed through rapid vegetational successions, attended by changing bird communities, which have been well studied in the Huntingdon area. One habitat rich in plants, invertebrates and birds, which has virtually disappeared, is the old type of sewage farm with its sludge beds. These have been replaced by sprinkler systems, which have many associated animals. Over a period, however, the most famous sewage farms, such as Cambridge, Northampton, Nottingham, Reading and Wisbech (the last still relatively unspoilt), were household names to British ornithologists.

Although the only character common to all ponds and pools is their small size in comparison with lakes, certain biological features are also widespread. During their early stages, shallow lowland ponds often undergo rapid changes. Where the bottom is silted, they may develop floating masses of algae, which are often blue-black in colour and appear sufficiently repulsive to cause dismay to the architects of large ornamental ponds. They need not worry, however, because these floating algal masses usually disappear by the second or third year. Often stonewort *Chara vulgaris*, a much larger alga looking superficially more like a flowering plant, covers the bottom for the next year or two. Sooner or later flowering plants also invade and spread, and the pond takes on a mature appearance with submerged pondweeds *Potamogeton* and, for example, arrowhead *Sagittaria sagittifolia*. If the edges are at all marshy, a fringe of emergent species such as bulrush *Typha latifolia* and reed canary-grass *Phalaris arundinacea* will also develop.

The sequence is, of course, often very different from that of floating scum to stonewort to submerged pondweeds. Chance plays an important role in the colonization of ponds, especially where they are small or distant from others. Many of the common flowering plants in ponds reproduce easily from small broken fragments: if such a piece is introduced, by accident or design, it may grow rapidly and choke the site for its first few years. This is often the case with Canadian waterweed *Elodea canadensis*, which is an especially vigorous spreader.

Most of the plants and animals of ponds and pools are found also in lakes, but some are more typical of the smaller bodies of water. Organisms living on or at the surface occur where the water is sheltered from wind disturbance, a condition more likely to be found in a pond than an open lake. The development of a surface community of plants may itself have a marked effect on the rest of the pond. The duckweeds *Lemna* and *Wolffia* or the water fern *Azolla filiculoides* may cover so much of the surface that little light penetrates.

Several species of water-bugs (Hemiptera) are surface-dwellers. Pond-skaters (Gerridae) have legs with pads at the end which actually support the animal on the water. The water measurer *Hydrometra stagnorum* similarly never penetrates beneath the surface: if it is pushed below, air is trapped among the hairs and gives it a silvery appearance; on release, it again rises. Among beetles (Coleoptera), the whirligig *Gyrinus natator* also lives on top of the water, but its flattened legs penetrate just below the surface and are used as paddles; this species can dive to avoid danger and, in doing so, it carries a supply of air trapped under its wing-cases and attached to the end of its abdomen. The great diving-beetle *Dytiscus marginalis* is similarly depen-dent on atmospheric air, but spends more of its time underwater than the whirligig. The great diving-beetle can swim especially powerfully, but it must still visit the surface to renew its air supply: it carries enough air to float up naturally, and to stay below it must either swim or cling to a plant stem or other submerged object. Many pond and lake animals are, of course, truly aquatic in the sense that they take all the oxygen they need from the water, either through the skin like freshwater limpets *Ancylus/Acroloxus* or through elaborate gills like fish.

Tiny ponds may undergo rapid changes even when they have been in existence for many years. This is because the volume of water is so small that relatively minor events can cause marked changes in its properties: an old fertilizer bag may still contain enought nutrients to lead to the development of a miniature water-bloom. Small ponds are especially prone to suffer from

Winsford Flashes are large areas of water resulting from industrial subsidence in Cheshire.

a temporary lack of oxygen; for instance, the temperature of the water may change rapidly in winter, leading to the formation of ice and the consequent disappearance of oxygen. In summer, too, the decomposition of a dead bird in a small garden pond may result in the loss of so much oxygen that even the hardy goldfish *Carassius auratus* die.

Lack of oxygen may also be a problem in deeper ponds, such as some sand-pits in the Netherlands, but for rather different reasons. If the pond is sufficiently sheltered, it may develop a thermocline in summer just like a lake. The oxygen in the lower part is then often used up by late summer, especially if a lot of dying plant material settles down from the top. As a result, the bottom fauna is poor, and any attempt to stock the pond with fish leads to such slow growth that the angler loses interest.

Some ponds and pools are full of water only intermittently. Certain species, such as the fairy shrimp *Chirocephalus diaphanus*, are especially characteristic of this type of environment. Sometimes the filling, drying and refilling cycle may depend largely on the amount of recent rain, and so in western Europe the ponds may be full at any time of year. This occurs, for instance, in the tiny pools on limestone pavement of The Burren in Ireland and in parts of Scotland and northern England. There the flora and fauna are adapted to withstand frequent wetting and desiccation: most species are rapidly activated when the pool fills and become dormant again as the water evaporates. Characteristic organisms here are lichens, the alga *Nostoc*, tiny nematode worms and rotifers. A few mosquito larvae occur in such sites, but they are much more abundant where the formation of pools takes place regularly once a year, as in the larger depressions on the Irish limestone known as 'turloughs', and especially in arctic Norway, Sweden and Finland. Pools form everywhere in this northern region when the snow first melts, because the ground is still frozen.

The loss of ponds in recent years has probably been greater than that of any other type of aquatic environment. They are drained when pasture is turned to arable land. They are drained in urban areas because land is needed or because they are thought to be dangerous or untidy; in fact, ponds seem to be popular with planners only when they are inside parks and ornamental gardens. Plants and animals for which ponds are an important home have therefore declined rapidly. This applies especially to the common frog *Rana*

An adult common gnat emerges from the pupal case to a terrestrial existence.

temporaria, although the demands for teaching biological dissection and the effects of pollution have also contributed to its decrease. From records collected in the 1930s and 1940s, it was estimated that a density of ten adult frogs per hectare was a fair average for Britain; by the 1970s, the population in some parts had fallen to probably less than 1 per cent of this figure. Other amphibians have also suffered. A recent survey of an area of chalk uplands in southeast England showed that frogs and common toads *Bufo bufo* were both extremely uncommon and found only in places largely undisturbed by farming. An important cause of their rarity was the loss of dewponds, the shallow pools dug out by farmers several centuries ago for watering their livestock. Newts *Triturus* were more widespread, although restricted to ponds surrounded by scrub.

RIVERS AND STREAMS

A typical river

No one river has received the same intensive study as have Windermere and the Plussee among lakes, so flowing waters are introduced here by considering a generalized river. We can then see how those in various regions differ from it. Many rivers rise in mountain areas, with numerous small streams gradually joining to form the main flow. As this moves towards the sea, it carries more and more water and the speed of its current becomes less and less. Many of its other features, including key aspects of its biology, are a consequence of these obvious changes.

The fast currents of the upland stretches, especially noticeable at times of flood, can move large pebbles or even boulders, but most of these are eventually fixed in one position, to be moved again only by the highest waters; as a result, the beds of the upland stretches are often stable for months during summer and may develop conspicuous growths of algae, mosses and liverworts. The middle stretches of the river have lost some of their speed, but still carry many small particles in suspension, and the gravel which often forms the bed there is rolled around all too frequently for the plants which try to grow. Films of algae do develop on the gravel, especially in spring, but the vigorous rolling tends to disturb them and they simply float up into the main current; on the other hand, a few flowering plants are successful in the middle river, especially the water-buttercup *Ranunculus fluitans*. Finally, in the downstream stretches, many of the smaller particles settle out, too, and the bed becomes silted; submerged flowering plants can grow here, including pondweeds *Potamogeton*, water-starworts *Callitriche* and water-milfoils *Myriophyllum*. If the water is shallow, these may extend almost from one side to the other, but in large rivers they form a fringe along each bank. Shallow rivers often have a strip of reed-swamp separating the submerged vegetation from the terrestrial species on the bank; the plants at the side may therefore show a rather similar zonation to that in Windermere.

Because there is such an obvious relationship between many of the organisms and the various physical features of rivers, attempts have been made to recognize distinct river zones which can be applied throughout Europe. Most of these have made use of animals, especially fish, rather than plants. This is not just because more people can identify fish, but rather because, while plants are static, fish move and so reflect the features of much wider areas of river bed. Although many fish are well distributed through northern Europe, not all of the key species which have been used to recognize these zones are represented in all rivers. Nevertheless, the following simple

ABOVE *The Teign, Devon, in high flow. The variety of vegetation on its banks includes, in the foreground, Indian balsam.* RIGHT *Giant hogweed often grows by lowland rivers and to heights of three metres. The leaves and stems may cause serious rashes.*

division into four broad zones of fish species can be applied in many cases: (1) brown trout *Salmo trutta*; (2) grayling *Thymallus thymallus* or minnow *Phoxinus phoxinus*; (3) barbel *Barbus barbus* or chub *Leuciscus cephalus*; and (4) bream *Abramis brama*. Zones (1) and (2) correspond very roughly with the upper and middle stretches described earlier, and (3) and (4) with the lowland stretch.

Many of the groups of invertebrates which have been studied from river source to mouth also show a distinct zonation of species: the classic examples are flatworms (Platyhelminthes), non-biting midges (Chironomidae), mayflies (Ephemeroptera) and stoneflies (Plecoptera), but this applies even to, for instance, water-mites (Hydracarina). All these animals move over much shorter distances than fish, so a particular species reflects the conditions on only a small area of river bed. Rivers are a mosaic of different plant and animal communities, and any classification into zones based on groups other than fish requires the recognition of a range of key organisms rather than single species.

How rivers vary

The effects of local rock formations, such as steep banks or waterfalls, may be obvious in determining how particular rivers differ from the generalized

pattern, and these in turn can influence the development or distribution of plant and animal populations in the river. The most important effect of geological structures is, however, on the water composition. Waters rising among chalk or limestone are hard, and in extreme cases, such as the Caher in Co. Clare, western Ireland, the lime may be deposited again on the bed as the river flows downstream. Hard-water rivers include some of those best loved by the trout angler, like the Blackwater in Co. Meath, eastern Ireland, and the Itchen in Hampshire, England. Just as with lakes and fens, the flora and fauna of hard-water rivers tend to be richer than those of soft waters.

Topography has an obvious influence on the rate of descent to the sea. Many rivers rising in low hills are so slow-flowing that they lack both the trout and the grayling zones. Local topography is also an important factor affecting floods: heavy rain falling on steep hillsides tends to drain rapidly into streams and rivers, while gentle slopes develop soils or peat which are more able to absorb the water and act as a buffer against flooding.

Winter climate causes as big a difference between the rivers near the Atlantic coast and those in central Europe as it does between lakes in the two regions; this is true especially of the fast-flowing upland stretches. In central Europe there is a marked annual cycle in the amount of water passing down the river: flows are low in winter, when the upland areas are covered in snow and many of the small streams are frozen; in spring the snows melt, bringing heavy floods if the process is at all rapid, and floods throughout the rest of the year seldom reach the same height. The scouring effect of ice also has an important effect in upland streams and small rivers, removing mosses and many of the algae. In contrast, rivers nearer the Atlantic are subject to more irregular flooding, which is as likely in mid-summer as in spring. The effect of floods on fully grown plants is much more devastating than on those only just starting to develop from their basal structures buried in the river bed; indeed, a major flood in summer may remove so much plant material that it takes several years for the vegetation to recover.

The profound influence of man is obvious when one stands by some lowland rivers, such as the Trent, Meuse or Rhine. The water looks murky, there are no fringes of submerged flowering plants, and certainly no trout; this is due to the heavy load of suspended matter and the range of toxic materials carried by these rivers. In many other cases, however, man's effects are not so immediately obvious, even though they may be almost as great. Frequently the results are increases in the amounts of plant and animal material and also changes in the types of species present. A river may become eutrophic through sewage effluents or fertilizers just as much as a lake. In shallow, fast-flowing rivers the enrichment of the water leads to massive growths of pollution-tolerant plants, while in long, slow-flowing stretches the growth of plankton algae may develop into blooms. The effect on plant growths is compounded in many rivers by the clearing of trees from the banks, which lets more light reach the water.

River plants

The flowering plants of the downstream stretches of rivers include the same general groups found in lakes. There are small species on the bottom, like the Canadian waterweed *Elodea canadensis*, and larger ones rooted in the bottom mud but with long, leafy stems reaching the surface, like many pondweeds *Potamogeton*. Emergent species live in shallows at the edge, their shoots partially underwater and partially above. Many plants of rivers and lakes are in fact the same, though they may be commoner in one than the other. The relatively fast-flowing stretches of rivers do, however, include several submerged species which are seldom, if ever, found elsewhere. This is especially true of the water-buttercups *Ranunculus*, which are among the few large plants successful in the grayling or minnow zone of rivers.

For various reasons, the distributions and behaviour of the submerged flowering plants of rivers are less well understood than those of the flowering plants of any other European habitat. Many of the species have inconspicuous flowers and so have not attracted the amateur naturalist. The most important groups, pondweeds, and water-crowfoots and water-buttercups, produce numerous hybrids. The biggest problem, however, is simply the extra trouble needed to collect submerged plants. It is impossible to take reliable records from a river-bank or bridge. The botanist must make the same kind of effort as the angler does to catch his fish: the only solution is to reach the plants by wading, boating or, best of all, using a mask and snorkel tube.

Two water-buttercups growing in rivers in northeast England provide an interesting comparison in a situation that is simpler there than elsewhere, as they are the only aquatic *Ranunculus* present. Both are abundant enough to colour some stretches white in June when they are in flower. Their general appearance is similar, but they differ in key aspects which influence their whole behaviour in the Wear and Tees.

The water-buttercup *R. penicillatus* var *calcareus* forms long shoots that flow with the water; these develop roots at intervals along their length. If the river is low in summer, each rooted region of the stem becomes fixed to the bed and a whole series of new plants may arise, in much the same way as the creeping buttercup *R. repens* can spread on damp patches on a lawn. The area of river bed covered by one plant at the outset may therefore increase greatly in a couple of years, and the positions of individual plants are always shifting. Further, the new, small, rooted plants and even detached pieces of stem are all capable of starting entirely new plants if they are swept up by floods and then deposited again downstream, so this species can expand its range very rapidly. It was first seen in the Wear only in 1970, but by 1976 it was probably the most abundant plant there. This river has been undergoing many changes since about 1960, as a result of decreased pollution from the coal industry, but the expansion of *R. penicillatus* has been the most dramatic of all.

The other species of water-buttercup, *R. fluitans*, is quite different in its behaviour. It does not develop numerous tufts of roots along the green stems; instead, its spread takes place mainly underground and the increase in the area occupied by a single plant is much slower. On the other hand, this species does seem to be more resistant to erosion by flood and a single plant may last at one spot for many years. It is not clear whether it spreads from site to site mainly by rooted fragments disturbed in floods, or whether growth from seeds is also important.

Farther downstream, in the barbel or chub zone of the river, a whole range of submerged plants can occur. Pondweeds are almost always present, the species differing according to the conditions of the river, especially the nature of the bottom mud and the extent to which the water has been influenced by pollution. The large, fine-leaved, fennel pondweed *Potamogeton pectinatus*, which produces vast growths at some sites, is almost always an indicator of marked sewage pollution; it can also tolerate slightly brackish conditions, and in many rivers extends farther downstream than any other flowering plant. Water-starworts are usually at their most abundant in hard waters.

A feature of the submerged plants of both rivers and lakes is that they appear to be relatively free from grazing by herbivorous animals, in marked contrast to plants growing on dry land. Certainly some submerged plants are attacked by many insects and eaten by such animals as snails (Mollusca) and crayfish (Decapoda), but most of the smaller herbivores appear to restrict their grazing to removal of the algal films that develop on the submerged leaves. Careful experiments are still needed, however, to be quite sure what effects animals have on submerged plants. For instance, small beds of Canadian waterweed come and go in rivers: their disappearance may be due to some animals having eaten or removed whole plants.

The fringes of emergent plants at the edges of lowland stretches of rivers may include the same species as the edges of lakes or the wetter parts of fens. There are, however, some which are particularly successful if the water-level fluctuates a lot: examples are the branched bur-reed *Sparganium erectum* and the common spike-rush *Eleocharis palustris*. If the river has steep sides which are normally well drained, but occasionally drowned by floods bringing water rich in nutrients, the banks may be covered by two striking annual plants, both introductions to Europe: the Indian balsam *Impatiens glandulifera* and the giant hogweed *Heracleum mantegazzianum*.

River animals

None of the freshwater mammals of northern Europe is confined to rivers, but the best place to see some of them is from a river-bank. In lowland regions, perhaps the species most likely to be encountered is the water vole

Mayflies swarming at sunset.

Arvicola terrestris, usually as it swims from one bed of reeds to another; it lives in holes in the bank, just below or just above the level of the water. Mostly it is a harmless vegetarian, feeding on the stems of reeds and other emergent plants, but in the Netherlands it has gained a bad reputation for turning, in late autumn and winter, from reeds to flower bulbs. In many lowland rivers, however, the common or brown rat *Rattus norvegicus* is as likely to be seen as the water vole; it also swims and dives easily, and the catholic nature of its diet is all too well known. Although it can survive away from man, it becomes more obvious where he leaves his rubbish.

Bats (Chiroptera) are regularly seen hunting for insects over slow-flowing rivers and sheets of freshwater. Although Daubenton's bat *Myotis daubentoni* and the much larger pond bat *M. dasycneme* are traditionally associated with water, records by bat detectors have shown that the ubiquitous pipistrelle *Pipistrellus pipistrellus* occurs more frequently over the River Thames than Daubenton's. The greater horseshoe bat *Rhinolophus ferrumequinum* often hunts the river-banks, and both Natterer's bat *M. nattereri* and the barbastelle *Barbastella barbastellus* occur in river valleys. The summer habitat of Daubenton's bat is woodland close to water, and the colony, which may number several hundred males and females, emerges late in the evening to chase moths and mayflies.

The favourite mammal of most naturalists is, unfortunately, all too rarely seen in most parts of Europe. The otter *Lutra lutra* can live along any of the four river zones, by the side of a lake or on the sea-shore. Although it is potentially to be found in most areas of water, it is now generally rare, and often extinct in lowland regions: pollution, weed cutting and bank clearance, hunting, disturbance by anglers and the introduction of the American mink *Mustela vison* have all been blamed, but along most rivers it is probably a combination of several factors. Although water pollution is often quoted as a major cause of the decline, it is not clear whether any substance is particularly harmful to the otter, or whether pollution simply reduces the food supply. The destruction of fringes of reed-swamp and marsh plants on riverbanks decreases the number of suitable hideouts, and probably again reduces food. The effects of hunting and general disturbance are obvious. Otters are unpopular with many anglers, because fish usually form the bulk of their diet, although they also eat freshwater crayfish (Astacidae), small birds, and other animals of similar size; the choice of food seems to depend on the prey available and the ease with which it can be caught. The fate of otters has been studied in some detail in Norfolk, the Netherlands and Sweden. The population in Norfolk has declined rapidly and is now split into isolated areas, each of which holds few, if any, reproducing otters, which have little chance of coming into contact with other groups; there are still some in the Norfolk Broads, but, although topography and vegetation are at their most favourable there, boats and anglers also cause much disturbance. In the Netherlands, the otter population reached a low of 30 pairs in 1942; it was then completely protected and by 1970 had increased to about 300 pairs. In England and Wales the otter was given wider protection from 1 January 1978 under the Conservation of Wild Creatures and Wild Plants Act 1975, and several conservation projects are in progress. In Scotland, where numbers are higher, the Forestry Commission has declared its extensive land holdings to be otter sanctuaries. These overdue measures will all take some time to show results.

The zonation of breeding birds along a river system roughly follows that of the fishes, but is directly related to suitable nest sites. Thus, the dipper *Cinclus cinclus*, which is found along mountain torrents up to 2500 m may also nest on lowland stretches where man provides the right conditions at weirs or mills. This is also true of the grey wagtail *Motacilla cinerea*, which sometimes even uses old dippers' nests. In contrast, the ring ouzel *Turdus torquatus* is generally restricted to highland areas. Two birds of wide preferences, the wren *Troglodytes troglodytes* and white/pied wagtail *Motacilla alba*, may also be characteristic of steep highland streams. Where gradients are less, common sandpipers *Actitis hypoleucos* and red-breasted mergansers *Merganser serrator* appear. Unique to Iceland in our area, the harlequin duck *Histrionicus histrionicus* nests on islets on the swiftly flowing braided rivers, especially the Laxa draining Mývatn, which has one of the greatest concentrations of breeding wildfowl in Europe.

In Britain the oystercatcher *Haematopus ostralegus* penetrates far up the valleys, nesting on shingle beds as well as riparian fields and moorland. Lower down, shingle attracts ringed plovers *Charadrius hiaticula*, common terns *Sterna hirundo* and, especially in Iceland, arctic terns *S. paradisaea*. Lower still are found the little ringed plover *Charadrius dubius* and little tern *S. albifrons*. In wooded valleys the goosander *Mergus merganser* may overlap or take over from the merganser; the goldeneye *Bucephala clangula*, also nesting in tree holes, is another duck of woodland or tree belts near water. Colonies of grey herons *Ardea cinerea* may be found close to rivers but are often several kilometres away, the great birds flapping to and fro when fishing for their young.

Where suitable sandy or peaty banks appear there may be colonies of sand martins *Riparia riparia* at quite high altitudes, but the kingfisher *Alcedo atthis* is predominantly lowland, though it may nest alongside the dipper, for example, on the borders of England and Wales. River-side meadows attract a number of waders, such as redshank *Tringa totanus*, curlew *Numenius arquata*, black-tailed godwit *Limosa limosa* and snipe *Gallinago gallinago*, which prefer relatively dry ground for nesting but feed in the marshy areas.

Crayfish are easily overlooked, because they tend to be nocturnal. In the laboratory they will eat animals, including other crayfish caught during moult, as well as plants and detritus, but little is known about their choice of food in rivers and streams. Over large areas of France, Germany, Poland, Finland and Sweden, one of the European species, *Astacus astacus*, has been

Brook lampreys spawning in a New Forest stream in April. The male secures the female by clamping his sucker-mouth behind her head.

wiped out by a fungal plague, *Aphanomyces astaci*. Finland in particular has suffered, because there the export of crayfish was at one time of some importance. Pockets of healthy animals are left in all these countries, but only in Norway are crayfish still widespread. The plague was apparently brought to Europe with resistant species of crayfish from North America. As the disease has not yet spread among the British crayfish *Austropotamobius pallipes*, it therefore seems an unnecessary risk to continue importing North American stock from mainland Europe to crayfish farms in Britain.

The fish fauna of many rivers is very much a reflection of man's activities. Angling is everywhere such a popular sport that there are always people willing to slip a few fish from one river to another where a species is absent. As a result, the ranges of certain freshwater fish have been extended, the case of the zander *Stizostedion lucioperca*, described later, being especially marked. Regular stocking takes place in some rivers, usually with brown trout; these fish may or may not breed there, so the population present can be either

A caseless caddisfly larva has spun its net on the surface of gravel-stones with the 5-centimetre-wide mouth facing upstream. The larva seizes invertebrates trapped in the net.

entirely artificial or a mixture of wild stock and others from the fish farm. A pollution disaster may lead to the destruction of all fish in a stretch of river, and complete restocking may then be essential. All these happenings mean that the fish populations of lowland rivers may show marked changes from year to year. Differences are also apparent from season to season because such fish as the brown trout may move upstream to spawn, while the sea trout (a variety of the same species) and salmon *Salmo salar* migrate as smolts to the sea, where they grow to sexual maturity and return to freshwater to spawn, and eels *Anguilla anguilla* travel much greater distances to breed in the western Atlantic.

Streams
The flora and fauna of small streams show much greater variety from site to site than those of large lowland rivers. Streams rise in contact with many different types of rock or soil, which in turn lead to waters of different mineral

composition and with a variety of substrata. Farther downstream, all the waters become mixed, hard with soft, peaty with clear. The mineral composition has more direct effect on the algae, mosses and other plants than on some of the invertebrates, but these are affected by the kinds of plants growing in the stream. Most invertebrates can tolerate hard water, but some require a minimum amount of calcium: for example, certain snails and the freshwater shrimp *Gammarus pulex* are common in small, lime-rich streams.

Small streams are much more susceptible to changes in rainfall and air temperature than big rivers. Organisms which live all the year round in streams may have to withstand floods, low flows and sometimes even temporary desiccation; they also have to endure high and low temperatures, and perhaps also scour by ice in winter. Farther downstream, the daily and seasonal changes in temperature become less and less. Sometimes, however, at the very source, the water comes from deep underground reserves, and temperature, flow and mineral composition may change little during the whole year. This applies to many of the streams in southern England which produce the best beds of water-cress *Nasturtium officinale*, their waters rising from springs originating deep in the chalk strata. Springs, especially those in chalk or limestone regions, generally have an abundant growth of plants just below the source; they are also good places to look for small invertebrates.

The invertebrates of streams include both herbivores and carnivores, just as in lakes. Snails, mayfly nymphs, small stoneflies and the larvae of some caddisflies (Trichoptera) are herbivores, scraping algae from the rocks or the leaves of mosses and flowering plants. Flatworms, leeches (Hirudinea), the larvae of many beetles (Coleoptera) and large stoneflies are carnivores. Decomposing vegetation and detritus originating from outside may also be important, and in many streams this is a principal source of food for invertebrates: freshwater shrimps and small stonefly nymphs, for instance, typically feed on fragments of dead leaves. Some of the animals feeding on detritus occur also in still waters, particularly ponds, but one special type of particle-feeder is characteristic of streams: these are animals which feed on fragments of living matter swept down with the current. They use various means for trapping the particles. For instance, some of the caseless caddisfly larvae, such as *Hydropsyche*, spin conical silken nets attached to pebbles; the force of the current keeps the net open, and the larva, which lives at the end of it, merely has to clean the trapped particles from the surface.

Streams below glaciers are especially inhospitable for most organisms, but some invertebrates are well suited to live even there. A study of streams at the mouths of glaciers in northern Scandinavia showed that chironomid midges were usually present, even though temperatures did not rise above 1·5°C. Because algal growth is negligible, the larvae feed on particles which have been blown on to the glacier surface, preserved there and then released into the stream as the ice melts.

POLLUTION

Pollution is not new. Man has no doubt got rid of his waste into streams and rivers since neolithic times. There are reports of mine-wastes killing fish in the 18th century, and numerous rivers suffered ever-increasing pollution during the 19th century as a result of the industrial revolution. Pollution of the Thames by sewage was already so bad 150 years ago that the last record of a salmon *Salmo salar* was in 1833. Towards the end of that century, the health hazards of pollution became clearly recognized, though steps to reduce the risks were often slow. It is, however, only since the 1939–45 war that we have learned to understand the detailed effects of different types of pollution on the communities of plants and animals in freshwaters. Recent history may be described loosely as a period of recognition and reduction of the effects of some types of pollution, while at the same time the influence of others may be getting worse.

Sewage effluents

The most widespread sources of pollution are sewage effluents. Their immediate impact on a river depends very much on how effective their previous treatment has been. If the effluent is still in a raw condition, many of the processes of breakdown of organic matter which would normally take place inside the treatment plant occur instead in the river. Massive, rather unpleasant-looking grey flocs of 'sewage-fungus' are a sign that the treatment of the wastes before they entered the river was not all that it should have been. The flocs in fact contain only a small amount of fungus, and are really a complex community dominated by bacteria and small invertebrates. The bacteria which form the flocs are harmless to man, but pathogenic organisms may also reach the river. Surprisingly little is known about how and when harmful bacteria, viruses and other microscopic organisms survive in rivers and lakes. Sometimes, children may swim in the water day after day without unpleasant effect; on other occasions, a single brief dip may lead to trouble. Areas where common or brown rats *Rattus norvegicus* are numerous are particularly dangerous, as they can spread the killer disease leptospirosis, caused by a bacterium transmitted in rat urine.

The growths of bacteria in the water use up a lot of oxygen when breaking down the waste organic materials. Different degrees of reduction in the amounts of oxygen bring about a well recognized series of changes ⸱ ᵗʰᵉ invertebrates on the river bed and the fish in the water. If the ox to very low levels, red chironomid larvae become abundant, a high pollution. Oxygen is used up faster in summer, and then ⸴

kills of fish in stretches of river where normally they are healthy. Recent years have, however, seen a marked improvement in the quality of the effluent from many large sewage works. There is just as much sewage, if not more, but treatment is more thorough: the effluent enters the rivers already decomposed to the nutrient elements used for growth by green plants. As a result, the river may become choked with water-weeds instead of sewage-fungus.

The Thames

The pollution of the Thames became severe during the 1800s. 1851 was the Year of the Great Stink when the Houses of Parliament were forced to hang disinfectant-soaked sheets over the windows to dispel the appalling stench of hydrogen sulphide rising from the anoxic waters of the river. Victorian London's expanding population was overloading the Thames with raw sewage and turning it into little more than a sewer. It was not even an efficient outlet to the sea since the Thames is tidal through London. By the 1950s, the only fish capable of surviving was the eel *Anguilla anguilla*, because it can gulp air at the surface. The few remaining mallards *Anas platyrhynchos* and mute swans *Cygnus olor* owed their survival not to a teeming riverlife but to grain spillages from the wharves. It had become clear that stiff legislation was needed to enforce a cleaning programme and to encourage the revitalization of the Thames.

Ten years later, the effects of the clean-up were clearly showing in the return of animals driven out more than a century before. Fish and birds are indicators of less noticeable changes in the water and in the plant and animal communities. From 1963, sea trout *Salmo trutta*, the migratory form of the brown trout, were once again passing through and beyond London on their way upriver from the sea; this encouraged great excitement at the prospect once again of seeing salmon from London Bridge. Masses of red, wriggling *Tubifex* worms proliferate in anaerobic muds and provided almost the only source of food along the tidal Thames during the height of its pollution. Several species of ducks, including mallard, teal *Anas crecca*, pintail *A. acuta*, pochard *Aythya ferina* and shelduck *Tadorna tadorna*, and dunlins *Calidris alpina* fed on them. As the clean-up proceeded, a decline in their densities was to be expected and has occurred in some cases. On the other hand, the spread up-river of the green algae *Enteromorpha*, where they now coat river walls and pilings, has provided new grazing for mallards, coots *Fulica atra* and moorhens *Gallinula chloropus*. But the importance of the Thames to wildlife and to the naturalist lies not only within its waters, but in the associated wetlands radiating northwards to Foulness and southwards to the Isle of Sheppey. This area is most attractive to wintering wildfowl and waders from the Baltic lands and Russia.

Parys mountain, Anglesey, is an old copper mining area where the water is highly acidic and the [on]ly tolerant land vegetation is heather and gorse. The water at the edge is brown due to iron oxide.

Mine-wastes

Ores have long been mined from numerous sites in northern Europe, in some cases even before Roman times, and the effects of mining on rivers may go on long after the work has ceased. Some types of mining are harmful by any standard: coal particles, for instance, smother plants and choke fish. High concentrations of toxic metals, like zinc, copper or lead, can kill fish and some invertebrates.

The River Geul, which flows from Belgium into the southern Netherlands, drains an old lead-mining area. Zinc is a metal associated with most lead ores, and the meadows in the flood zone of the river used to have a flora characteristic of places rich in zinc, such as the zinc violet *Viola calaminaria*. Most of this appears to have gone now, perhaps because of the large amounts of sewage effluent entering the river in Belgium or perhaps because of the fertilizer put on the fields in the Netherlands. It is doubtful whether this community existed there before the lead mines were opened, although elsewhere in Europe ores rich in zinc reach the surface naturally.

The Harz Mountains are one of the best known lead-mining areas and some ore is still removed. There many of the streams, the main river (the Innerste), a reservoir and even the drinking water (in 1977, at least) are rich in zinc. The most metal-rich streams still carry plants and animals, though the number of species is many fewer than might occur elsewhere. The hardiest include a moss *Dicranella varia*, the creeping bent *Agrostis stolonifera*, several rushes (Juncaceae) and sedges (Cyperaceae), and various tiny invertebrates, such as rotifers and nematode worms. Similar species occur at other sites rich in zinc elsewhere in Europe, and many of them seem to have become adapted to withstand this peculiar environment.

One type of pollution resulting from mining activity is notorious. Acid mine-drainages are a problem because, once they have started, they are particularly hard to stop. This type of pollution can arise where coal, pyrites or other mined ores are sulphur-rich. The drainages are really dilute sulphuric acid formed underground from the sulphur in the ores mixing with water and oxygen; the only way to stop such a drainage forming is to prevent the three coming together, generally a difficult task. The streams at source usually have clear waters, though they may be yellow or brown due to dissolved iron. As in the streams rich in zinc, only a few plants and animals can grow here, mostly algae, mosses and rotifers. Where pools form, there may also be a few flowering plants, such as the bulrush *Typha latifolia*, and insects, such as chironomid larvae and pond-skaters (Gerridae). The drainages often contain dead earthworms (Lumbricidae), these animals being killed rapidly by the water which perhaps first attracted them.

A dramatic example of acid mine-drainage pollution occurs in southeast Ireland. A number of little streams drain old mine-workings and eventually these waters reach the Avoca. Within a very short distance, the river changes from being a favourite of anglers, with plenty of insect larvae, algae and moss, to one with no fish and almost devoid of any other form of life. Instead, it is coated with a crust of iron oxide which is deposited when the drainage waters meet the main river. Acid mine-wastes are locally a problem elsewhere in Europe – for example, by various coal tips in Britain, in old lignite mining areas in Denmark, and in the pyrites mining region of northern Norway – but their effects are trivial compared with those in parts of the northeastern United States. A much more serious matter for Europe is that of acid rain.

Acid rain

Acid fumes, arising initially from the combustion of fossil fuels, perhaps particularly in industry but also in the domestic sector, are transported long distances by the wind, and then finally brought down to the ground again, mostly by rain and snow. This fall-out has little effect on lakes and rivers where the rocks contain lime to neutralize the acid, but where the rocks are lime-free the situation is very different: the water is then so poorly buffered against any change that the acid rain makes the lakes and rivers acid too. The effect is most evident in southern Norway, Sweden and Finland.

In Norway, it was first noticed during the 1920s that some waters were becoming more acid and that at the same time fish populations were declining or disappearing altogether; more recently, salmon have gone from several rivers and hundreds of lakes have lost their fisheries. The situation is similar in southern Sweden and, to a lesser extent, in Finland. The effect of the precipitation is particularly pronounced in spring, when melting snow brings a flood of acid water into the streams and rivers. Many studies have shown that this is the most dangerous time of the year for fish: observations during May 1975 on the Tovdal, in southern Norway, showed thousands of dead brown trout along a 30-km stretch. Other changes take place too: as lake water becomes more acid, the numbers of species of algae and tiny animals in the plankton become fewer, as do the invertebrates living on the floor of the lake, but the growths of bottom-living mosses may actually increase.

It seems likely that the flora and fauna of the moors on the millstone grit in West Yorkshire have suffered marked changes since the growth of industrial Lancashire early in the 19th century, though probably not as great as those in Scandinavia. As the first changes would have taken place so long ago, no one seems to worry much now. In southern Sweden, however, where views on the subject are strong, fish populations are maintained by the expensive process of adding annual doses of lime. The international arguments have recently become even more difficult because it is realized that some of the acid fumes come all the way from North America.

There are three further complications. First, rain brings down not only acid, but also metals like zinc and lead. Second, the distance from the sea seems to be of some importance, because common salt (sodium chloride) in the rain helps to reduce the harmful effects of acid water on fish and other animals: the farther from the sea, the less the salt in the rain. Third, a major complication in the disappearance of salmon and trout fisheries in Scandinavia is the use of modern methods of forest and agricultural management, which in turn affect the through-flow of water and so alter the aquatic system.

Mercury pollution

Concern about many different pollutants reached a peak in the 1960s. Indiscriminate use of highly toxic substances during the previous decades had gradually led to more and more harmful effects on animal life. These effects were in many cases especially evident in lakes and rivers, which have a natural tendency to accumulate substances from inflow waters. People also assumed that, if waters were good places to dispose of sewage wastes, they ought to be equally good for getting rid of other unpleasant materials. Unfortunately this has proved to be far from true for certain substances, especially mercury. The distribution of this metal and its effects in natural environments have been followed in detail in Sweden.

The sources of the mercury which eventually reached the rivers and lakes in Sweden were largely industrial, the metal either being released directly into the water through effluents or into the air and then brought down again in rain. Of about 140 tonnes of mercury imported into Sweden in 1963, some 25 tonnes were used as fungicides for the preservation of wood pulp; the importance of the wood pulp industry seems to have been the main reason why levels were especially high in Swedish waters.

The most serious aspect of mercury pollution is its accumulation in fish. In Sweden, fish from a number of lakes and from extensive areas of both the east and west coasts are now forbidden to be offered for sale. Like those of organochlorine pesticides, the levels of mercury increase as they pass up the food-chain, in this case from plant to insect larva to fish; they are especially high in pike *Esox lucius*, which feed on other fish and so have an even greater opportunity to concentrate the metal. Fish high in mercury were reported from Lake Vänern, the largest lake in Sweden, which has an important fishery reaching 1000 tonnes a year; not surprisingly, fish are also significant in the local human diet, and a study reported in 1967 showed just how much mercury could be accumulated as a result. A 60-year-old fisherman had the highest levels: his daily consumption of fish amounted to 0·75 kg, mainly pike and burbot *Lota lota*, and this unfortunate enthusiast had 50 times as much mercury in his blood as someone who never ate fish at all. As a result of control measures, the levels of mercury in Swedish lakes and rivers appear to be dropping, but the problem has by no means been entirely solved.

Seepage from a tip in an opencast coal mining area, Westfield, Fife. The bright green filamentous Hormidium *is one of the few algae to thrive in such acidic conditions.*

MANAGEMENT OF WATER

One of the most important factors over the past century has been the gradually increasing management of water for drinking and industrial purposes. Sometimes management involves little more than the control of quality in an upland lake, but in other cases it means the creation of reservoirs where there was previously no standing water at all.

In many lowland areas the simplest way to get water is to pump it up from deep strata. This may, however, lower the whole water-table and lead to small springs in calcareous regions drying out. Also, if too much deep water is used, there is a risk of brackish or polluted water becoming mixed with the clean water. In some areas, such as southeast England and the Netherlands, just about as much of this deep water is now taken as is possible, and any further expansion of supply will have to come from elsewhere.

Reservoirs
Some cities near hilly regions are fortunate enough to receive their water by pipe from clean upland areas, either natural lakes or reservoirs formed by damming up valleys. This is the situation with much of the supply for Manchester and Liverpool; the main aim of management there has been to keep the upland water as clear as possible. Holiday camps that might turn an oligotrophic lake into an eutrophic one are most certainly discouraged, but in Britain there has been a recent tendency to open reservoirs and such waters for boating, angling and also visits by naturalists. Since the reservoir water has to be treated anyway, the strict prevention of access was always rather ludicrous, particularly as gulls *Larus* and other birds may equally be a source of bacteria harmful to people.

The edges of upland reservoirs often appear ugly, because there is little to see but mud or rock. The water level fluctuates according to demand, and a closed cover of vegetation seldom develops in conditions where plants are sometimes submerged and sometimes exposed. The combination of floods in winter and spring and desiccation in summer and autumn is particularly unfavourable to most species, although the plant communities of the Irish turloughs have adapted well to such fluctuations.

The few plants that can take advantage of the combination of submergence and exposure may sometimes be very abundant. Some annuals, such as the marsh cudweed *Gnaphalium uliginosum*, thrive where the mud is exposed all through the summer. A tiny alga, *Botrydium*, with green vesicles about 1 mm across, often covers the mud a couple of weeks after it is first exposed, especially in areas rich in lime and organic matter. Perennial flowering plants that can tolerate alternating submergence and exposure during summer include the common spike-rush *Eleocharis palustris*, mare's-tail *Hippuris vulgaris* and amphibious bistort *Polygonum amphibium*. The last two species are truly amphibious in that the appearance of the plant, including the shape of the leaves, differs according to whether it is growing on land or submerged.

Many urban areas far from upland regions are supplied by quite different types of reservoirs. London's are scattered round the north and west sides of the city. Much of the water pumped into them is rich in nutrients, as it is taken from such rivers as the Thames and the Lea which are greatly influenced by sewage effluents. As a result, the reservoirs are very productive and steps have to be taken to prevent the development of algal blooms. Until the early 1960s, this was achieved by adding copper sulphate to the surface when it was thought a bloom was about to begin, but this method was expensive and perhaps harmful to more than the algal bloom. A quite different technique is used now, involving air 'guns' which draw up the water from the lower part of the reservoir, thus mixing the whole water column and preventing the formation of a thermocline. Algae which once could accumulate at the surface can no longer do so, and the whole composition of the plankton has changed to one much more easily treated at the waterworks.

The London reservoirs provide a valuable refuge for waterfowl and other aquatic birds. The body responsible for water management has in recent years become more tolerant of sailing and this in turn has had some effect on bird life. An interesting study has been carried out on the influence of sailing at the Brent Reservoir, where there is a small area of canary-grasses *Phalaris* at the side. Moorhens *Gallinula chloropus* and coots *Fulica atra* both take little notice of boats, allowing them to approach as close as 50 m. Little grebes *Tachybaptus ruficollis* merely keep close to the marshy banks when sailing takes place, but the great crested grebes *Podiceps cristatus* are much more sensitive to disturbance and have ceased to breed there since sailing started. Temporary drainage, however, led to an increase in the area of canary-grass marsh in 1975–76 and the great crested grebes took refuge there. The use of reservoirs by birds for breeding depends to some extent on the existence of islets and marshy areas not accessible to boats.

Rivers

Not every reservoir in upland areas is used to feed pipes taking the water to where it is needed. The quite different approach of river regulation has become popular in recent years. The water is held in a dammed valley, and is released as necessary from the dam into the river below, the amounts being greatly increased when the flow in tributaries downstream of the dam is low. Floods are reduced in the lowland reaches because water from part of the catchment is trapped in the reservoir. On the other hand, flows are never very low because of the water released from the dam. Regulation of rivers has been shown in some parts of the world to have marked effects on their biology, such as an increase in the amount of vegetation, but it is not clear whether the decrease in floods or the prevention of low flows is the more important. There have been no long-term case-studies in Europe, but some changes are already evident on the Tees in northeast England below the Cow Green Reservoir which was completed in 1970. Immediately below the dam there have been increases in the growth of mosses and in the populations of various invertebrates. Much farther down, three species of submerged flowering plants have spread upstream into a stretch of river where previously only mosses and algae grew. Another species, the water-buttercup *Ranunculus penicillatus* var *calcareus*, is apparently new to the river. The serious fish-kills which used to occur in one lowland stretch of the Tees, when hot weather coincided with very low river flows, have not been recorded since the building of the dam.

The reason the engineer builds these regulatory reservoirs may sometimes have a little to do with keeping fish healthy in the river, but their main purpose is so that water can be taken out of the river at a downstream site. The farther downstream the water is removed, the shorter the stretch of river likely to suffer low flows during drought conditions. On the Wear, Co. Durham, water is removed at a site not far above the tidal limit of the river. The use of water from such lowland sites provides an important pressure on water management bodies to keep pollution in the river to a minimum. If the water is eventually to be used for drinking it has to be checked very carefully for possible pollutants, and water from the Wear is tested biologically by monitoring continuously its effect on fish in tanks.

In some regulation schemes there is a complication which may have long-term effects on river biology. This is the combination of upland regulatory reservoirs with the transfer of water from one particular river to one or more others, so that the water supply of a lowland city may come from a reservoir located on a quite different river, the two being connected by a large cross-country aqueduct. The Kielder Water scheme in northeast England is one such example: one of the largest man-made lakes in Britain, it controls the flow of water down the Tyne and, if the flow of water in the Wear or the Tees to the south is too low, water is pumped from the Tyne into these rivers. There is talk of an even grander scheme to come into operation at about the end of the century, in which upland reservoirs in Wales would supply water to the Severn; this water would pass down the Severn, be transferred to the Thames and then eventually reach southeast England. Thus, water which might once have flowed into the Bristol Channel may instead contribute to a London reservoir.

The entrances to the pipes are screened to prevent the intrusion of larger plants and animals, but there is nothing to stop the transfer of smaller species and the seeds or larvae of larger ones. As a result, some rivers receive a frequent inoculum of plants that did not grow there before. For instance, 26 species of larger plants growing in the Tyne are not present in the stretch of

Weed-collecting along the Erft in Germany.

the Tees immediately below the inflow pipe. As, however, there are plenty of other ways aquatic organisms can spread from one river to another, it is questionable whether these water transfer schemes will bring about major changes in the flora and fauna of the rivers. That will happen only if there is at the same time a big difference in the amounts of nutrients in the water. Large-scale water transfer will, however, permit the rapid spread of any fish disease, and nobody knows what will happen to migratory fish, such as sea trout *Salmo trutta*. These appear to recognize the waters of particular rivers, and it has been suggested that the mixing of waters may confuse the fish trying to reach their 'home' runs.

In mainland Europe, there are now more schemes for the construction of major canals than at any time since the early years of the industrial revolution. Some of the most important, such as the Europakanal linking the Main, and hence the Rhine, to the Danube are already well towards completion. An even larger project, the connection of the Oder to the Danube, has also been given serious consideration. Such schemes will make it more and more easy for aquatic organisms to spread from one part of Europe to another.

River banks and light
The greatest effect man has had on many streams and small rivers has been the destruction of the surrounding forest, with a consequent increase in the

amount of light reaching the stream bed. Many of the forests were cut down several thousand years ago, so people seldom stop to think what the streams would have been like before then. Some idea can, however, be obtained by looking at a stream in dense forest and then at a stretch in a clearing or, better still, at an adjacent stream away from the forest. Streams in dense forest often appear rather barren in summer, whereas otherwise similar streams in full sunlight may have an obvious cover of plants. The effect on animals is less clear: probably it is more one of changes in the groups of species present than in the total amounts. The removal of forests stops the addition to the stream of decaying leaves, the major food source for many animals.

When the forests were cleared, the trees in upland areas were often removed right down to the stream. In the lowlands, a fringe was frequently left along the bank. Sometimes this was done simply because the banks were difficult to reach, but elsewhere it was deliberate policy: the trees were useful shade for cattle, and were sometimes also pollarded. More recently, these fringes have frequently been destroyed, often when pasture has been changed to arable land. The effect of the resulting increase in light, combined with the widespread rise in plant nutrients, leads to a massive increase in the amount of submerged water-weeds in many streams. The effect on reed-swamp and bank-side species, such as the branched bur-reed *Sparganium erectum* and canary-grass, is equally pronounced.

Growths of water-weeds may hinder drainage so much that streams have to be cleaned, either mechanically or by the use of weed-killers. Both approaches are expensive, have obvious dangers to river life and may lead to erosion of the banks. This last is true especially if tall grasses like canary-grasses are treated by weed-killer, as their healthy roots have a powerful binding effect. The banks of new drainage schemes are frequently planted with short grasses to form a turf, but this is soon replaced by common (stinging) nettles *Urtica dioica*, creeping thistles *Cirsium arvense* or Indian balsam *Impatiens glandulifera* if the water is at all rich in nutrients or if manure from adjacent fields is allowed to drain on to the banks. One solution is to convert the stream into nothing more than a drainage channel by covering its banks, and perhaps also its bed, with cement. This solution is hardly likely, however, to appeal to the naturalist, and in any case brings with it other problems, such as a decreased ability of the stream to cope with pollution.

A quite different approach is becoming popular, especially in northwest Germany and the Netherlands. This is the deliberate planting of trees along the banks of streams and rivers to shade the bed. The most useful species for this purpose is the alder *Alnus glutinosa*: its roots penetrate into the soil below the ground-water level and so are especially effective in stabilizing the banks. Alders are much less likely to be blown down in a gale than willows *Salix* or poplars *Populus*. The trees also protect the banks against damage by musk rats *Ondatra zibethicus* where these are a serious nuisance. The leaves of alders decay especially quickly, and so cause less hindrance to stream flow than those of other species. The range of plant and animal life in such streams would certainly be favoured by the occasional deliberate planting of other trees and by leaving short, well-illuminated stretches. It is not clear whether any water management body has yet taken up such an enlightened policy as deliberate practice, but the planting of alders, combined with coppicing every ten years or so, seems certain to increase. One study in the Netherlands showed that the management of so-called 'green streams' requires only half the costs of conventional mowing, cutting and dredging.

Control of water-weeds

The planting of alders and other trees is only one way that plant growth can be controlled in places where it is not wanted. Along many rivers and streams, the vegetation at the sides and the submerged plants in the main current are cut at least annually; this takes a lot of labour, especially if the submerged plants have to be removed entirely from the river. On the Tweed, in Roxburghshire, the water-buttercups and other weeds cut in one stretch are simply allowed to float down to the next section, often leaving an unsightly deposit on someone else's part of the bank; this rather strange practice is only possible at all because weed growths are not a major nuisance there. Sometimes cut weed is left to float down river and then removed at a particular point: this arrangement is automated on the Erft, in Germany, weed floating downstream being trapped at a boom running diagonally across the river, removed continuously, and dumped on a large stack on the adjacent bank to form silage. Such an arrangement is, however, suitable only on a river where the flow does not vary too much during the cutting season.

An entirely different approach is to use weed-killers. At first employed mainly on ponds and ditches, their use has spread increasingly to the control of emergent vegetation along main rivers, and to a limited extent to that of the submerged species, though in their case only selected areas of weed are killed: otherwise, the levels of the chemical in the whole water body might rise to limits unsafe for any organisms, including man. Although some modern weed-killers can be employed in ways which have little directly harmful effect on animals, their widespread use may cause the destruction of so much of the plant community that many invertebrates may eventually also be lost. Selected sites should therefore be left unsprayed wherever weed-killers are used widely.

Drainage

The destruction of wetlands has accelerated in recent years, in part as a direct consequence of the demand for more agricultural land, and in part due to the excessive removal of subterranean water for the water supply of industry. The deliberate drainage of marshes and fens had been aided greatly by the widespread introduction of hydraulic excavators. It has already been mentioned that such schemes usually lead to the destruction of fringing vegetation, which may or may not be allowed to develop again. But the most serious effect of such schemes on wildlife is the general lowering of the water-table, even if small pockets of land are left undisturbed. As a result, such species as some of the wetland orchids (Orchidaceae) and sedges (Cyperaceae), which were once widespread, are becoming increasingly rare in many lowland parts of Europe. Even where the ground remains moist, there is a tendency for the water to be more nutrient-rich; the flora, and hence also the fauna, then become more restricted. The only way of keeping areas in anything like their original condition is to find some means of maintaining the local water-table at a higher level than in the surrounding fields.

The American mink was introduced from North America for its fur. It has escaped many times and may now be challenging the native otter.

INTRODUCTIONS AND OTHER INVADERS

A number of plants and animals have invaded the waters and wetlands of Europe during historical times. Some of these, such as the sweet-flag *Acorus calamus* and the common (brown) rat *Rattus norvegicus* have been here so long that it is hard to remember that they are not natives; others are much newer arrivals. Many of these plants and animals are from North America. Some European plants, such as the flowering-rush *Butomus umbellatus*, have not only made the journey the other way, but appear to be more of a nuisance as water-weeds there than in their original home. The invasion of some species can have obvious effects on the organisms originally present. Ponds and ditches in the warmer parts of western Europe may have such a dense cover of the water fern *Azolla filiculoides*, a native of subtropical America, that no other green plant can develop at the same site during summer months. On the other hand, native species may also sometimes do better as a result of introductions. The spread of the water fern has led in turn to the spread of the beetle *Stenopelmus rufinasus*, which feeds on it. Increases in the populations of tufted ducks *Aythya fuligula* in Britain are ascribed to the invasions of two animals valuable to them as food: these are the zebra mussel *Dreissena polymorpha*, which has spread from brackish to freshwater habitats, and a small mollusc, *Potamopyrgus jenkinsi*, which has probably come from Australasia.

Four wetland mammals have established themselves during the past 50 years in various parts of Europe. All can be considered reasonably successful, especially when compared with the native otter *Lutra lutra*, already mentioned, and also the European mink *Mustela lutreola* which is approaching extinction over most of the area covered by this book. The American mink *M. vison*, which was brought from North America to be bred for its fur, has escaped many times and is the most successful of the four. In Britain, Scandinavia, and probably elsewhere, it is still spreading and increasing in numbers, and has become locally common. As its habitat is rather similar to that of the otter, there has been speculation about the effect of the mink on that species. The mink certainly eats rather different foods: it is much less dependent on fish, but takes more birds and mammals, and has a bad reputation for raiding chicken-runs as well as for taking young birds nesting near water, as at Mývatn in Iceland. A detailed study, however, of the behaviour of the mink and the otter in a water system in southern Sweden has shown how complex the situation may be. During the warmer months there are clear differences between the habitats and foods of the two species: the mink lives in a wider range of places than the otter, being relatively more frequent in smaller lakes, streams and marshes; mammals and freshwater crayfish (Astacidae) are the main foods of the mink, whereas fish, especially perch *Perca fluviatilis*, are eaten more by otters. In winter the situation changes: freezing of the water reduces the number of suitable habitats and the amount of food available; as a result, especially in hard winters, the two mammals are in much closer competition. A further complication is that the otter may attack the mink, and the mink appears to be partially excluded from the shores of the larger lakes where the otter is most successful.

The other mammal introductions are the musk rat *Ondatra zibethicus* and the raccoon *Procyon lotor*, both from North America, and the coypu *Myocastor coypus*, from South America. The musk rat and coypu live in riverbanks and may cause considerable erosion, so there have been efforts to control them where they have become established. The musk rat had only a short existence in the wild in Britain, during 1930–37; but it is well established in many other parts of Europe, especially the Netherlands and lowland Germany. The coypu is rather more demanding in its habitat, needing large areas of reed-swamp, marsh or fen; it is established in the Norfolk Broads, the Netherlands and other areas, but nearly everywhere there have been determined efforts to reduce or even destroy the populations, and its future as a wild animal in Europe seems much more doubtful than that of the mink or the musk rat. Although the raccoon is at present found only in a few European countries, it seems likely that it will one day become as familiar here as it is in North America.

The zander *Stizostedion lucioperca* is a fish whose range in Europe has merely been increased from its original home in the slow-flowing reaches of rivers in catchments of the Rhine and Danube, but it has been remarkably successful where it has been introduced. It is not only good for eating, but also grows up to 12 kg in some areas, so it is popular with anglers. In France, it was deliberately spread into many ponds and rivers, especially from the 1950s onwards. In England, it was first established at Woburn, Bedfordshire, in 1878, but spread from there only in 1963 when some were introduced into the relief channel of the Great Ouse and bred very successfully. The species has since been introduced by anglers to many other places, and it is now common in lowland rivers in southern and eastern England.

The Canadian waterweed *Elodea canadensis* provides one of the most striking examples of a species expanding its range. It was recorded first in 1836 in Co. Down, Ireland. In 1842 it was found in small lakes in the grounds of Duns Castle in Berwickshire. By the end of the 19th century, it was an important component of the aquatic flora in most parts of Britain and Ireland. Once it had invaded, its expansion at a site could be very rapid: for instance, it had almost blocked the river at Burton-on-Trent only two years after the first record in 1849. Canadian waterweed reached France and Belgium by 1860, apparently by deliberate introduction; again it had spread by the end of the century to most parts of those two countries. One feature of its spread which has never been satisfactorily explained is that, at many sites, it produced vast crops within a few years of arrival, but then showed a decrease. A widely accepted theory is that some trace nutrient became used up, but there are as yet no satisfactory answers. Strangely enough, a related introduction, at present known as *E. nuttallii*, appears also to be spreading rapidly, and it will be interesting to see how the two species fare during the 1980s. A feature the Canadian waterweed shares with many other aquatic plants, and especially with those which have proved successful introductions, is that its spread has been entirely by means of pieces of the green plant and not by the seeds.

These examples of successful introductions are of species originally brought in by man, but smaller organisms and the seeds of flowering plants may go from site to site by quite different means. The smallest may simply be blown by wind, but most are probably transported by insects or birds. Charles Darwin first pointed out, in *The Origin of Species*, how readily wading birds, many of which migrate for long distances, might convey seeds in mud adhering to their feet. This is probably the explanation for the present distribution of some wetland plants: for instance, the white-fronted goose *Anser albifrons* may have been responsible for the spread of certain species on either side of the Atlantic, since part of the Greenland population winters on the mouth of the St Lawrence River and part in Europe. A plant whose distribution seems especially likely to have been influenced by birds is the marsh yellow-cress *Rorippa palustris*, which in Britain occurs only in the north and west, on bare ground subject to winter flooding. The various localities are all winter feeding grounds for geese, and it has been suggested that the marsh yellow-cress has been introduced from Iceland, where it is abundant in the Mývatn district; indeed, it seems quite likely that further inocula of its seeds are brought to the sites at frequent intervals.

Sometimes birds may play an even more important role: the seeds of some pondweeds *Potamogeton* are known to germinate better after passing through ducks. In an experiment on the broad-leaved pondweed *P. natans*, only 1 per cent of the seeds germinated, but after being eaten by ducks as many as 60 per cent did so.

WATERS AND WETLANDS OF EUROPE: SOME CASE-STUDIES

England: Norfolk Broads

The Norfolk Broads, a triangular region between Norwich and the sea, are now the most significant area of water and fen in Britain. They have had a complicated history, but two key processes have influenced their present character. During the post-glacial period, the valleys of the rivers draining the area became increasingly waterlogged as a result of a rise in the level of the sea, and were then covered with fen and peat, this process reaching its peak somewhere about 3000 BC. Much later, in early medieval times, vast amounts of this peat were removed by man, with the consequent formation of shallow lakes, many of which still exist today: these are the Broads. Most, but not all, are connected to the rivers.

The Broads form a complex of open water and wetland communities long recognized for the richness of its wildlife, especially plants and birds; however, many areas of open water have in recent years undergone marked changes far from favourable to wildlife. The loss of submerged plants has been documented fairly well. Most of the Broads are less than 2 m deep, and aquatic vegetation was at one time extensive. Many species started to disappear in the 1950s, and changes are still taking place fast. For instance, all submerged plants disappeared from Hickling Broad during 1973–74. The yellow water-lily *Nuphar lutea* and its white counterpart *Nymphaea alba* are often the last species to go.

There were no early studies of the small invertebrates of the Broads, so we cannot be quite sure whether losses among these have been equally serious. The present bottom-living fauna is, however, known to be much richer where submerged plants still occur, so it seems likely that these animals have suffered as much as the plants. Just as on Loch Leven, recent declines in overwintering populations of mute swans *Cygnus olor* and coots *Fulica atra* are probably a direct result of the decrease in submerged plants. The mute swan feeds on the storage structure of water plants rich in starch; if there is an adjacent fen community, then it can still get some food. The coot suffers especially, as it depends on green leaves and stems: many of the fen plants die back in autumn, and by late winter very few species are still useful to it as a source of food; among these, the reed sweet-grass *Glyceria maxima* is particularly well liked, but it is abundant only locally.

Each year more than a quarter of a million people take their holidays in this region, so anything which affects the general landscape or quality of the water is of considerable importance. What has caused the recent changes? The situation resembles the decline of the otter *Lutra lutra*, with a number of possible culprits, and various people blaming each other.

Coypus *Myocastor coypus* have a local impact on areas of bank vegetation, thus causing erosion, but they seem most unlikely to be a major problem here: in many cases, the loss of submerged plants did not coincide with their period of increase. Most people who have visited the Broads at long intervals have commented on the increased murkiness of the water: near boat channels, the bottom sediment is frequently stirred up and the banks are eroded. The propellers of launches also tend to cut up the submerged plants. Although no one has ever carried out experiments to measure how much damage boats may do, it seems unlikely that they are the only cause of change, since many private broads with no access for boats have also lost their vegetation. The chief cause is probably a heavy growth of algae, either in the plankton or smothering the leaves of larger plants. Increase of the algae has certainly come about because of great rises in the levels of nutrients in the waters, but the key argument centres on the source of these nutrients. Is it the end result of increased amounts of sewage, or is it due to run-off of agricultural fertilizers?

Three Broads – Upton, Calthorpe and Martham – still retain good growths of submerged plants; a few others also have small pockets. Of the three Broads with good growths, only Martham is in contact with a river, and even that contact is much less than for most of the other Broads. This might seem to favour the theory that stirring up bottom muds along the rivers is a key factor in reducing growths of submerged plants. Upton and Calthorpe Broads, however, both have large areas of woodland left in their catchments and so receive less run-off from agricultural fertilizers. We still do not know enough to argue convincingly for one cause rather than another in the loss of the plant growths. Possibly most of the causes suggested have made their contribution, although disturbance of sediments by boats and increased nutrients from agricultural run-off are the most likely at present.

Ireland: turloughs

'Turlough' is derived from two Irish words meaning a dry lake. This paradox is explained by the fact that these lakes, which occur in limestone regions, are subject to dramatic fluctuations in water-level. Such 'dry lakes' are especially characteristic of limestone in Clare and eastern Galway, but are found also in southeast Mayo and Roscommon. A few which once existed in Limerick have apparently all been destroyed by quarrying for a cement factory. Turloughs may be a few metres in diameter or may extend over many hectares. Recent drainage has, however, eliminated all but one of the really large examples.

After periods of low rainfall, a typical turlough appears as a shallow, grassy depression, with the occasional outcrop of limestone rock. Black patches of a dried moss, *Cinclidotus fontinaloides*, contrasting with the grey-white of the limestone, add to its distinctive appearance. Most of the turloughs are full during much of the winter, and summer flooding occurs after periods of heavy rainfall. Some hold water permanently in the lowest part of the depression, a shallow lake remaining even in the driest season. In others, a stream flows across the floor, appearing as a spring and disappearing in a swallow-hole. Many turloughs have no water at all in dry weather. The vegetation consists of a closely cropped turf, only a few centimetres high; this is because cattle, sheep, horses, rabbits *Oryctolagus cuniculus* and Irish hares *Lepus timidus* all move down in summer from the surrounding high ground to graze the new growth on the turlough slopes and floors. In addition to the effects of heavy grazing, plants and animals have to withstand alternate flooding and periods of drought, when the shallow soils may dry out completely. These soils may be derived from glacial drift, but are sometimes almost pure marl (fine limestone) and therefore drain especially quickly. The soils in the lower parts of some turloughs do, however, remain waterlogged for much of the year, even when the open water has receded, and there peat may develop.

One of the fascinations of a turlough for the naturalist is that it is easy, as one penetrates it, to recognize the changes that take place. The zonation of the vegetation is often immediately obvious, but sometimes it takes a little effort to work out the effects of differing periods of submergence, probably because of varying soil depth. Near the upper edge, there are usually a few small trees, mostly hawthorn *Crataegus monogyna*, blackthorn *Prunus spinosa*, ash *Fraxinus excelsior* and buckthorn *Rhamnus catharticus*. The first two usually extend farther down than the others. There is a complete absence of willows *Salix* and alder *Alnus glutinosa*. It seems likely that trees would have extended much deeper into the turloughs before the activities of man, so some of the species at present missing may well once have grown there. Below the tree zone, the carnation sedge *Carex panicea* and the autumn hawkbit *Leontodon autumnalis* are abundant; a violet, *Viola stagnina*, is sometimes common here. Silverweed *Potentilla anserina* is abundant in the next zone down and, if the turlough dries out, then this and the creeping bent *Agrostis stolonifera* may cover the entire bottom. If the soil remains wet or there is a small permanent lake, the more typically aquatic species may be present, such as amphibious bistort *Polygonum amphibium*, floating sweet-grass *Glyceria fluitans*, common club-rush *Scirpus lacustris* and water-plantain *Alisma plantago-aquatica*. At turloughs where peat develops, such as Carran in Co. Clare, sedges are especially abundant. At least one of the turloughs – near Turlough, Co. Clare – may be coloured white in late spring with a complete cover of dried and bleached filaments of a green alga, *Oedogonium*. This 'algal paper' is also known elsewhere in Europe. The 17th-century German naturalist I. J. Hartman explained it as having fallen from heaven and being of meteoric origin; such a cover has been known as *Meteorpapier* in Germany ever since.

Turloughs have long been famous as wintering grounds for waterfowl, especially wigeon *Anas penelope* and white-fronted geese *Anser albifrons*. The rest of their fauna is not known nearly as well, but clearly the regime of alternating flood and drying out causes as many problems for animals as plants. Neither aquatic nor dry-land species can complete their life-cycles unless these take only a few months. Consequently, water snails and many aquatic insects are absent unless there is permanent water. The speed with which turloughs flood gives a terrestrial animal like a spider little chance to escape the rising water. Apart from the large herbivores, the obvious dry-land animals of turloughs are mostly small, active carnivores, such as ground-beetles (Carabidae): these hibernate in winter while the turlough is flooded and, as the water recedes in spring, they become active at the edge, feeding on dying or dead invertebrates stranded there.

One of the largest of the invertebrates spending the whole of its life-cycle within the turloughs is a fairy shrimp, *Tanymastix*, which reaches about 2 cm in length. It survives dry weather as eggs which remain in the soil. These hatch as soon as the ground is flooded, and the fairy shrimps swim up into the water where they take about two months to become fully grown. They then produce large numbers of eggs which will not hatch until they have gone through a period of drying out.

Other small crustaceans are usually abundant in the water. There is also a variety of water-bugs (Hemiptera) and water-beetles (Coleoptera) which fly to the turlough from elsewhere; some of these feed on the small crustaceans and some on the tiny algal cells in the water. Sometimes the windward edge of a turlough lake has a striking fringe of froth; this is apparently always associated with the presence of a one-celled animal, *Ophrydium*, which forms gelatinous colonies visible to the naked eye.

Due to the recent programme of drainage, Rahasane in Co. Galway is the only large turlough remaining, and it is itself under threat. Over the total area of some 2000 km² where turloughs occur, perhaps half have been destroyed in recent years by arterial drainage, direct drainage or simply a lowering of the ground water-table. Arterial drainage in particular tends to destroy the large turloughs. Drainage has been mentioned often in this book as an ever-present hazard for wetlands, but the indiscriminate destruction of the turloughs of western Ireland for minimal agricultural gain seems so senseless that we put forward a special plea for them. They are of such interest to naturalists, research scientists and general tourists that no more should be destroyed without good reason.

Netherlands: canals and dykes

A large part of the Netherlands consisted of swamp up to about the year AD 1000, but then man started bringing about great changes. Huge areas were surrounded by dykes and reshaped into 'polders', with a carefully controlled water-table. About one-third of the country is at present below sea-level, and even more below peak river heights. An intricate network of canals was developed over the centuries to control the waters in the dykes, and nearly all those in the north and west are in some way connected. The ultimate source of much of the water is the Rhine, the similarly polluted Meuse playing a lesser role. Water is pumped from the rivers and from the IJsselmeer, the old Zuider Zee and now a huge reservoir, into the polders during the drier part of the year and in the reverse direction in the winter.

In view of the origins of their waters, it is not surprising that the flora and fauna of the dykes and the canals are those typical of eutrophic conditions. The waters of many of the larger dykes and the canals look like algal soups during the summer. No doubt some of them have long been rich enough in nutrients to lead to this effect, but in other instances the larger submerged plants have been replaced by algal blooms. The smaller dykes are often filled with submerged plants, such as water-milfoils *Myriophyllum* and various pondweeds *Potamogeton*, or have a floating cover of duckweeds *Lemna* or the shining green tubes of the alga *Enteromorpha*. In the past, the dykes were cleared by hand or mechanically of sufficient weed to permit the passage of water, but now many of them are sprayed annually with weed-killers. Different weed-killers influence different species, but in the end they all tend to favour the development of algal plankton or even the virtual absence of any green plants at all.

Germany and the Netherlands: the Rhine

A total length of 1326 km makes the Rhine the longest river discussed in this book. It is, however, already quite large by the time it reaches Germany from Switzerland. Both the main river and its tributaries receive many and diverse sorts of pollution, so the condition of the water is very poor by the time it arrives in the Netherlands. The minimum levels of oxygen there are extremely low; totally untreated sewage wastes still reach the river from many large towns. There are so many suspended particles in the water that the plankton algae can carry out photosynthesis only in the top few millimetres. There are also the effects of major nuclear and conventional power stations: those that use and return water for cooling purposes raise the temperature of the river and it is estimated that, if they all operated in this way, the water's summer temperature could rise to 35°C.

One of the worst problems of the Rhine results from the activities of the potash mines in Alsace, France, which are still increasing. As there is no sale for the salt (sodium chloride) which is extracted with the potash, this is put into the river: the salt content of the water at the Netherlands border has doubled in the last 30 years and the quality of the river is now approaching that of a brackish environment, although there is no influence of the sea there. This poses special problems for the Netherlands, which have an exceptionally high demand for freshwater, and the outflow of the river to the sea must

The Strokkur geyser east of Reykjavik, Iceland.

be sufficient to prevent the upstream penetration of salt water. That the usage of water in the Netherlands is as great as that of the whole of the USA is due mainly to the need to flush the polders. To cope with the demands for freshwater, large new reservoirs are planned. The IJsselmeer is already slightly less salty than the Rhine due to dilution by rainwater.

Iceland: hot springs

Hot springs provide a fascinating study area for biologists; they are often visually striking, coloured blues, greens and orange by algae and bacteria. As the temperature changes on passing downstream, biological changes are usually also very obvious. Hot springs are few in mainland northern Europe, but in southern Iceland there are many, especially in the Hengill-Olfusá district. There the water at source may be at temperatures of 70°C or more, but in Iceland as a whole the first signs of life are not obvious until the temperature drops rather lower. It is usually at about 63°C that growths of the blue-green alga *Mastigocladus* begin, though, in streams where there is hydrogen sulphide gas (indicated by a bad egg smell), the orange growths of a bacterium may occur at slightly higher temperatures. This bacterium can carry out photosynthesis when hydrogen sulphide is present, though it lacks chlorophyll.

Although *Mastigocladus* grows only at high temperatures, it is a hardy organism and can withstand freezing and desiccation for long periods. It was found growing on Surtsey in 1970, seven years after this volcanic island was first formed and at least 50 km from the nearest warm water site. Not all organisms from hot springs are so hardy, however, and another alga which grows at up to 73°C in the Yellowstone Park, USA, cannot survive freezing and desiccation like *Mastigocladus*. It would be of interest to know if this 73° alga could also grow in Iceland, but such an experiment might have harmful side-effects on the springs there.

CHANGE AND CONSERVATION

Few areas of water and wetland in Europe are free of man's influence. Much of this essay has been about change, of increases and decreases among species, of past engineering schemes and of those still to come. Many of the changes have had profound ecological consequences, but their frequency makes observation that much more interesting: there is always the chance of a surprise or something to muse over. This makes it all the more important that we should have an accurate record of the plants and animals of our lakes, rivers and marshes. Many people wish to do no more than enjoy watching, and perhaps photographing, the wildlife they encounter when walking, boating or scuba-diving. I hope, however, that some readers will be encouraged to make more detailed observations. The accounts of Victorian naturalists, whose knowledge of certain groups has still not been rivalled, and the old records of certain angling clubs are now often the most valuable clues to the changes that have already occurred. The more the naturalist understands what is happening to waters and wetlands, the better the chance of finding ways of conserving important habitats and species, and the better the chance of persuading organizations responsible for water management that such conservation matters.

Freshwaters and Wetlands of Northern Europe

Arctic circle

65°

ICELAND
Mývatn
Mt Hengill
Ólfusá

Norwegian

NE

60°

Sognefjord

WE

Hardangerfjord

Atlantic Ocean

55°

SCOTLAND
Loch Leven
Tweed
Tyne
Lough
Neagh
Derwent
Reservoir
Wear
Tees
The Burren
IRELAND
Windermere
Avoca
turloughs
Shropshire
Meres
WALES
ENGLAND
Gt Ouse
Bristol Channel
Thames
Itchen
English Channel

North Sea

BRITAIN

NETHERLANDS
IJsselmeer
Norfolk
Broads
Ouse
Washes
Naardermeer
Loosdrecht
broads

BELGIUM

LUXEMBOURG
Seine
Oise
Marne
Maas
Geul
Meuse

FRANCE

50°

| 0 | 50 | 100 | 150 | 200 | 250 | 300 Miles |

| 0 | 100 | 200 | 300 | 400 Kilometres |

20°   70°   10°   0°

10°

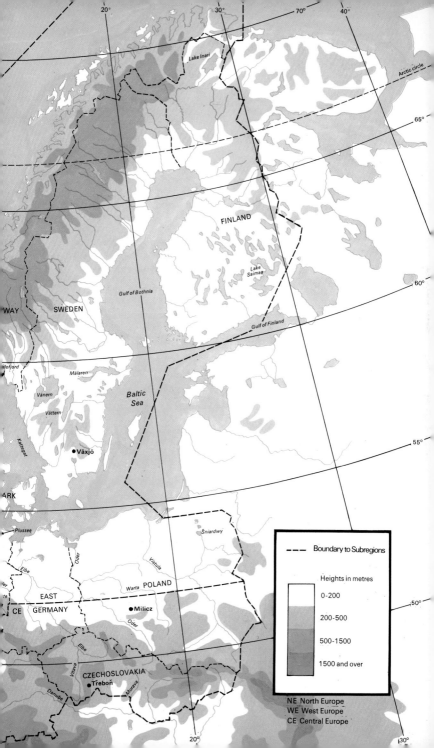

NE North Europe
WE West Europe
CE Central Europe

GLOSSARY

abdomen in insects, spiders, posterior section of body, lacking appendages

acid water highly acid waters produced in some mining areas by formation of sulphuric acid; slightly acid waters occur typically in peaty or moorland areas, but also widespread as result of rain polluted by industrial fumes

acute ending in a point

aerobic in presence of oxygen

alternate leaves placed singly at alternate positions along stem

amphibious adapted for both terrestrial and aquatic life

anaerobic in absence of oxygen

anal fin fin just behind anus

anther part of stamen producing pollen

aperture in snails, opening at base of shell

apex tip or summit; in insects, tip of wing; in bivalves, humped area in front of hinge; in snails, tip of spire (*qv*)

-ate describing 2-dimensional shape *eg* ovate

awn in grasses, long, stiff bristle projecting beyond grain

axil angle between leaf and stem

barbel in fish, 'whisker'

basal in plants, at base of stem; in animals, part nearest body

body whorl in snails, largest and most recently formed whorl of shell

bract modified leaf often at base of flower-stalk

calcareous containing or coated with lime (calcium or magnesium carbonate); *cf* acid

calyx, calyces (plural) all the sepals; term often used when the sepals are joined together to form a tube

carapace in crustaceans, spiders, shield covering head and thorax; in tortoises, dorsal bony shield

cerci projections from rear of abdomen

chitin horny, protective material found in invertebrate cuticle (*qv*)

chrysalis pupa (*qv*) of butterfly

ciliate edged with hairs

clitellum in annelid worms, saddle-like region which secretes mucus (see cocoon)

cocoon in insects, protective covering, often silk, for the pupa; in spiders, protective covering of silk for the eggs; in worms, mucous covering round eggs and sperm, secreted by clitellum (*qv*)

cuticle in invertebrates, hard outer covering of body

dextral in snails, shell with right-handed spiral; *cf* sinistral

dorsal in animals, of the back or upper side

dorsal fin in fish, fin in mid-line of back

dorsum in arthropods, dorsal surface

elytra in beetles, hardened forewings covering abdomen

ephippium in cladocerans, thickened cuticle (*qv*) of carapace (*qv*) which is cast off as the egg case

eutrophic fens, lakes and rivers rich in plant nutrients; the last two often with dense algal growths

femur, femora (plural) in insects, basal part of leg

fleshy fin in bony fish, fin between dorsal and tail fins lacking bony support

furca in crustaceans, paired projections borne by telson (*qv*)

gills in aquatic animals, membranous structures which extract oxygen from water

gill arch in fish, one of several paired cartilaginous structures beneath the gill covers which bear gills on the outer side and usually gill rakers (*qv*) on the inner side

hard water water rich in lime (calcium or magnesium carbonate); *cf* soft water

hemelytra in bugs, half hardened, half membranous forewings

hermaphrodite in animals, having male and female organs in the same individual; in plants, having male and female organs in the same flower

inflorescence flower branch, including bracts, flower-stalk and flowers

lanceolate spear-shaped

larva free-living, immature stage differing in structure and habits from the adult (see metamorphosis, nymph)

lateral line line running along side of body of fish. A row of sensory cells which detect vibrations lie beneath this line

linear long and narrow

metamorphosis change of form found in insects and amphibians. In insects, complete metamorphosis: young (larva) radically different from adult, involves a pupal stage (*qv*), *eg* caterpillar to butterfly; incomplete metamorphosis: young (nymph) broadly similar to adult, no pupal stage, *eg* dragonfly

nauplius in crustaceans, typical first larval form bearing 3 pairs of appendages: 1st and 2nd antennae and jaws

nerve strand of strengthening or conducting tissue running through leaf

nymph insect young which hatches out in state closely resembling the adult, but has undeveloped wings and reproductive organs; *cf* larva (see metamorphosis)

ob- inverted, with broadest part of structure near apex, *eg* obovate

-oid describing 3-dimensional shape, *eg* ovoid

oligotrophic fens, lakes and rivers with very low levels of nutrients; such lakes typically deep, upland and clear

operculum in snails, hard plate which fits across shell aperture (*qv*); in bony fish, largest of several flat bones forming gill cover

opposite leaves paired on opposite side of stem; *cf* alternate

ovate, ovoid egg-shaped (see -ate, -oid)

ovipositor egg-laying apparatus of female insects; in worker bees and wasps, modified into sting

palps in insects, paired sensory appendages close to mouth

palmate arrangement of lobes, segments or leaflets spreading from the same point, like fingers from palm of hand

pannicle branched inflorescence

parthenogenesis reproduction without fertilization by male

pectoral fins fins on sides of body immediately behind head

pelvic fins fins on belly; their bony support is situated in front of the anus

perianth segment one floral leaf, used when petals and sepals are indistinguishable

peristome in snails, outer lip of shell aperture

pinnate regular arrangement of leaflets in 2 rows on either side of stalk (simply

p.); each leaflet divided again (twice p.)

placenta in animals, flattened structure forming connection between mother and young through which food and oxygen reach developing young

plumose hairy, feathered

primaries outermost flight feathers of bird's wing, usually 10; *cf* secondaries

proboscis in insects, tubular mouthparts for sucking; in worms, trunk-like process of the head

pronotum in insects, dorsal front of thorax

prothorax in insects, 1st segment of thorax bearing 1st pair of legs but not wings

pupa in life history of insects which undergo complete metamorphosis (*qv*), immobile, 'resting' stage during which insect changes from larva to adult (see chrysalis)

raker in fish, stiff structures on the inner surface of the gill arch, best developed in fishes which sieve planktonic organisms from water

ray-florets in Compositae, elongated florets which form outer ring of petals

rhizome creeping, underground stem

rostrum in crustaceans, insects, pointed 'snout' or beak

scutellum in bugs, triangular section in centre of thorax

secondaries inner flight feathers of bird's wing; *cf* primaries

sepals outer ring of floral leaves, usually green and less conspicuous than petals

simple leaf or flower not divided into segments

sinistral in snails, shell with left-handed spiral; *cf* dextral

soft water water poor in lime (calcium carbonate)

species group of similar individuals which can interbreed; cannot usually interbreed with other species to produce fertile offspring

spikelet in grasses, one or more florets enclosed by a pair of stiff bracts

spinneret in spiders, spinning organs on abdomen through which silk is extruded

spire in snails, shell above most recently formed whorl (*qv*)

spore in plants, minute reproductive body, produced asexually and of simpler structure than seed

stamen male organ of flower

stigma part of female organ of flower which receives pollen

stipule modified leaf at base of leaf-stalk

style part of female organ of flower below stigma (*qv*)

subimago in mayflies, stage before the imago or adult ('dun' of fishermen); closely resembles adult but has a thin dull skin covering body and wings

subspecies group of individuals within a species (*qv*) having distinctive features

superciliary in birds, stripe above the eye

suture in snails, groove between successive shell whorls

tarsus in insects, outermost part of leg next to tibia (*qv*) usually divided into segments and bearing claws at tip

telson in crustaceans, the terminal segment of the abdomen

thallus plant body undifferentiated into leaf, stem

thorax in insects, spiders, region between head and abdomen, bearing legs, wings

tibia in insects, middle section of leg

umbel cluster of flowers whose stalks (rays) radiate from top of stem

umbilicus in snails, hollow base of coiling axis of spiral shells

variety group of individuals within a species (*qv*) having one or more distinctive characteristics; less differentiated from other members of species than a subspecies

ventral of the underside

vestigial small or reduced and non-functional structure

viviparous giving birth to live young

whorls leaves or flowers arising in circles around stem; in snails, sections of shell (see body whorl)

ABBREVIATIONS

The ranges in the order of their listing in the field guide

W	widespread
T	throughout
Br	Britain (England, Scotland, Wales)
Ir	Ireland
Ic	Iceland
Fr	France, north of the Loire
Lu	Luxembourg
Be	Belgium
Ne	Netherlands
De	Denmark
Ge	Germany
Cz	Czechoslovakia
Po	Poland
Fi	Finland
Sw	Sweden
No	Norway
FS	Fenno–Scandia (Norway, Sweden, Finland)
SC	Scandinavia (Norway, Sweden)
NE	Fenno–Scandia, Denmark, north Germany, north Poland
CE	Czechoslovakia, south Germany, south Poland
WE	Britain, Ireland, France, Luxembourg, Belgium, Netherlands

n, s, e, w, c north, south, east, west, central
When the species is not native but introduced and naturalized, the countries are put in brackets, *eg* Fr, Ge, (Br, Ir)

c	about
av	average
esp	especially
fld	flowered
fl(s)	flower(s)
fl-head	flowerhead
fr(s)	fruit(s)
imm	immature
inflor	inflorescence
juv	juvenile
lf(lvs)	leaf (leaves)
lflet	leaflet
lfy	leafy
microsp(p)	microspecies
sp	species (singular)
spp	species (plural)
ssp	subspecies
var	variety

MEASUREMENTS

Scale in the plates: the relative sizes of the plants and animals are preserved whenever possible, but the measurements in the entries themselves should be noted.

BL	body length (excludes tail in mammals, includes antennae in insects)
FA	forearm length
H	height
L	total length (includes beak, tail)
SB	shell breadth: in snails, diameter of body whorl; in bivalves, width of cross-section across the 2 valves when closed
SH	shell height: in snails, from tip of spire to base of shell; in bivalves, from apex of valves at the hinge to ventral surface where the 2 valves meet
SL	shell length: in bivalves, length from anterior to posterior
TL	tail length
W	number of whorls
WS	wingspan

SYMBOLS

♀	female
♂	male
<	up to
>	more than
?	doubtful

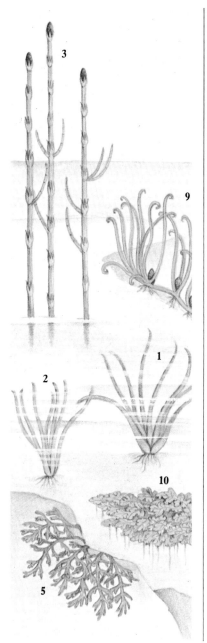

Quillwort *Isoetes lacustris* ISOETACEAE
H 8–25 cm. Submerged, rosette-forming,
aquatic plant. Lvs stiff, cylindrical,
<5 mm wide, of 4 longitudinal tubes,
dark green. Swollen lf-bases surround
sporangia which contain large, rough-
surfaced ♀ spores, or small, yellowish-
brown ♂ spores; spores ripe May–Jul.
Stony lakes. T, ex Lu, Be. [1]

Spring Quillwort *Isoetes echinospora*
ISOETACEAE H 5–15 cm. Similar to *I.
lacustris*, but smaller. Lvs <2 mm wide,
rather flaccid, paler green. ♀ spores covered
in long, sharp spines; spores ripe May–
Jul. Peaty lakes. T. [2]

Water Horsetail *Equisetum fluviatile*
EQUISETACEAE H 50–140 cm. Erect,
hairless perennial, with creeping
rhizomes. Aerial stems green, with central
hollow; unbranched, or with irregular
whorls in middle. Fertile and sterile stems
alike. Spores in terminal ovoid cones,
<2 cm; spores ripe Jun–Jul. Still,
shallow water. T. [3]

Marsh Horsetail *Equisetum palustre*
EQUISETACEAE H 10–60 cm. Erect,
branching, hairless perennial, with
creeping rhizomes. Aerial stems green,
hollow, outermost cavities same size as
central one. Fertile and sterile stems alike.
Spores in terminal cones, <3 cm; spores
ripe May–Jul. Marshes, bogs, wet woods.
T. [4]

Wilson's Filmy-fern *Hymenophyllum
wilsonii* HYMENOPHYLLACEAE H 2–8 cm.
Moss-like, with cotton-thin rhizomes;
trailing, forms dense mats. Lvs <8 cm,
translucent, olive green, divided into
oblong, toothed lobes, veined to apex.
Sporangia in sori near tips of lobes; spores
ripe Jun–Jul. Damp, shady rocks. Br, Ir,
Fr, No. [5]

Marsh Fern *Thelypteris palustris*
THELYPTERIDACEAE H 25–75 cm. Perennial
with slender, creeping rhizomes. Lvs
solitary, hairy, once-divided into deeply-
cut, oblong-triangular segments; blade of
lf as long as stalk. Sporangia in row near

dge of segments with inrolled margins; pores ripe Jul–Aug. Marshy woods. T, x Ic. [6]

Crested Buckler-fern *Dryopteris cristata* ASPIDIACEAE H 30–100 cm. Perennial with stout, creeping rhizomes. Lvs <1 m, twice-divided into stalkless, ovate-lanceolate, toothed segments, largest <25 mm, nearest main stem. Sporangia in rows on margins of segments of inner lvs, outer lvs sterile; spores ripe Jul–Aug. Wet heaths, marshes. T, ex Ir, Ic, Lu. [7]

Narrow Buckler-fern *Dryopteris carthusiana* ASPIDIACEAE H 30–100 cm. Yellowish-green perennial with short, creeping rhizomes. Lvs <1 m, 3-times divided into oblong segments with long, incurved teeth; base of lf-stalk covered in uniformly pale-brown scales. Sporangia in rows on margins of segments; spores ripe Jul–Sep. Wet woods, marshes, bogs. T, ex Ic. [8]

Pillwort *Pilularia globulifera* MARSILIACEAE H 3–15 cm. Aquatic fern with long, creeping, hairy, branched rhizomes. Lvs thread-like, <15 cm, incurling from tip. Sporangia in 4-chambered, hairy, spherical capsule, <3 mm across, at base of lvs; large ♀ sporangia above smaller ♂ sporangia; spores ripe June–Sep. Slightly acid ponds, lake-margins. T, ex Ic, Lu. [9]

Water Fern *Azolla filiculoides* AZOLLACEAE Large, bluish-green, floating masses, red in autumn; plants <5 cm across, branched. Lvs <2·5 mm, in 2 rows, overlapping, 2-lobed; upper lobe blunt with clear margin, hairy above. Lower lobe of first lf of each branch bearing large ♀ and small ♂ sporangia; spores ripe Jun–Sep. Stagnant water. (Br, Ir, Fr, Be, Ne, Ge, Cz, from N America.) [10]

Fungus *Russula claroflava* RUSSULINEAE H 6–10 cm. Cap <12 cm, bright chrome-or lemon-yellow; slightly ridged at margin; gills becoming pale-yellow with age; stalk veined longitudinally, white at first becoming greyish; Sep–Nov. Wet birch woods. T, ex Ir. [11]

moss *Aulacomnium palustre* MEESIACEAE
H 3–12 cm. Conspicuous, yellowish-green
moss, with stems matted together by
brown hairs. Lvs <6 mm, oblong-
lanceolate, margins toothed above, nerved
almost to tip. Spore capsules curved,
stalks furrowed, <5 cm; spores ripe early
summer. Bogs. T. [1]

Willow Moss *Fontinalis antipyretica*
FONTINALACEAE H 50–70 cm. Robust, dark
green, aquatic moss; stems long,
irregularly branched, bare below. Lvs
<7 mm, folded, sharply keeled, nerveless,
in 3 rows. Spore capsules cylindrical,
almost hidden by lvs; spores ripe summer.
Lakes, rivers. T. [2]

moss *Drepanocladus aduncus* HYPNACEAE
H 25–30 cm. Green or golden-yellow,
aquatic moss, very variable in size and
branching. Lvs lanceolate, often strongly
curved, tapering to fine tip, nerved to
$\frac{1}{2}$-way. Spore capsules oblong, curved,
on stalks <5 cm, rare; spores ripe
summer. Marshes, pools, springs. T. [3]

moss *Scorpidium scorpioides* HYPNACEAE
H 10–15 cm. Robust, little-branched moss,
yellowish-green at tips, dark brown to
blackish below. Lvs <4 mm, all curved to
one side, broad with short, acute points,
nerve short, forked. Spore capsules large,
curved, long-stalked, rare; spores ripe
summer. Fens. T. [4]

moss *Brachythecium rivulare* HYPNACEAE
Creeping, bright golden-green moss, with
numerous, crowded, glossy, upright
shoots. Lvs <3 mm, ovate-triangular,
abruptly-pointed, nerved to slightly above
middle, margins finely-toothed. Spore
capsules oval-oblong, on rough stalks
<3 cm, rare; spores ripe autumn.
Springs, streams, marshy woods. T. [5]

moss *Rhynchostegium riparioides* HYPNACEAE
H 8–15 cm. Robust, bright green, aquatic
moss; sparingly branched above, bare
below. Lvs <25 mm, broadly ovate, nerve
thick, to $\frac{2}{3}$ length of lf, margins strongly

oothed. Spore capsules oval, with long
peak, on stalks <2 cm; spores ripe
autumn. Fast-flowing water. T, ex Ic. [6]

iverwort *Calypogeia fissa* JUNGERMANNI-
CEAE Delicate, creeping stems, forming
bluish-green patches. Lvs <1·5 mm, in
two rows, notched at tip, nerveless.
Spore capsules cylindrical, brownish,
ong-stalked; spores ripe Apr–Jun. Also
reproduces asexually by granular buds
(gemmae) at shoot-tips. Wet, sandy banks,
peat bogs. T, ex Ic. [7]

iverwort *Marchantia polymorpha*
MARCHANTIACEAE Creeping, dark green
thallus, 2–10 cm long, <2 cm wide, with
conspicuous midrib; grows in large
patches. Spores produced in umbrella-
like structures, ♂ disc-shaped, ♀ 9-rayed;
spores ripe Jul. Also reproduces by
kidney-shaped buds (gemmae) in flask-
like cups on surface of thallus. Marshes,
stream-banks. T. [8]

iverwort *Conocephalum conicum*
MARCHANTIACEAE Creeping thallus,
<20 cm long, <1 cm wide, branched,
ribbon-like, shiny, dark green, with pores
on surface and conspicuous midrib. Spores
produced in mushroom-shaped structures,
on stalks <6 cm long; spores ripe Feb–
Apr. Wet banks and rocks. T, ex Ic. [9]

iverwort *Riccia fluitans* SPHAEROCARPACEAE
2 forms; floating: delicate, narrow,
regularly branched thallus, <5 cm long,
<1 mm wide; on mud: thicker, broader
thallus, <2 mm wide. Spore capsules in
spherical swelling on underside of thallus,
rare. Ponds, ditches. T, ex Ic. [10]

Stonewort *Chara hispida* CHARACEAE
Robust, prickly-looking, aquatic alga,
heavily encrusted with lime. Spirally
twisted stems with whorls of 9–11
branches. Separate ♂ and ♀ reproductive
branches, ♂ organs pale orange spheres,
♀ pineapple-like; spores ripe Jun. Still
water. T, ex Ic. [11] *C. vulgaris* similar
but smaller. W.

Bay Willow *Salix pentandra* SALICACEAE
H <7 m. Shrub or small tree; twigs
hairless, shining; bark fissured. Lvs
<12 cm, elliptical, glossy above, paler
beneath. Catkins after lvs; ♂ fls with
(usually) 5 stamens; May–Jun. Marshes,
wet woods. T, ex Ic, (but Be). [1]

Crack Willow *Salix fragilis* SALICACEAE
H <25 m. Dome-shaped tree; bark deeply
fissured; twigs break easily at junctions,
hence name. Lvs <15 cm, lanceolate,
asymmetrical at base, toothed. Catkins
appear with lvs, Apr. River-banks, wet
woods. T, ex Ic, (but Ir, De, FS). [2]

Osier *Salix viminalis* SALICACEAE H 3–
10 m. Shrub with long, straight, flexible
stems, hairy when young. Lvs <25 cm,
drooping, lanceolate, dark green above,
silky beneath. Catkins before lvs, Apr–
May. By water, in hedgerows. T, ex Ic,
(but De, FS). [3]

Purple Willow *Salix purpurea* SALICACEAE
H 1·5–3 m. Slender, very variable shrub;
twigs straight, shining, purplish when
young. Lvs <10 cm, oblong, finely
toothed, often opposite, bluish-green
above, paler beneath. Catkins before lvs,
Mar–Apr. By water, in marshes, wet
meadows. T, ex Ic, De, Fi, (but SC). [4]

Grey Willow *Salix cinerea* SALICACEAE
H 2–10 m. Shrub or small tree; twigs
hairy, with raised lines in wood under
bark. Lvs <7 cm, ovate, hairy above when
young, with grey or rust-coloured hairs
beneath. Catkins before lvs, Mar–Apr.
Water-sides, marshes, wet woods. T, ex
Ic. [5]

Alder *Alnus glutinosa* BETULACEAE
H <20 m. Tree with oblong crown;
young twigs sticky; bark dark brown,
fissured. Lvs <10 cm, ovate, blunt,
double-toothed, bright green, hairless
except for tufts of yellowish hairs in axils
of veins beneath. ♂ and ♀ catkins often
before lvs, Feb–Mar. Fruiting catkins
ovoid, woody, cone-like, <3 cm, stalked,
persistent for a year. By water, wet woods.
T, ex Ic. [6]

Grey Alder *Alnus incana* BETULACEAE
H <10 m. Tree or shrub; young twigs
hairy, pale grey; bark smooth. Lvs
<10 cm, ovate, pointed, double-toothed,
dull green above, grey-green and
somewhat hairy beneath. Catkins before
lvs, Feb–Mar. Fruiting catkins woody,
cone-like, <2 cm, stalkless, persistent.
By water, wet woods. T, ex Ic, (but Br,
Ir, Fr, Lu, Be, Ne). [7]

Water-pepper *Polygonum hydropiper*
POLYGONACEAE H 25–75 cm. Shining
green annual with burning, peppery taste.
Lvs <10 cm, lanceolate, almost stalkless,
with scattered, marginal hairs. Fls of 5
greenish perianth segments covered with
glandular, yellowish dots; in slender,
nodding spike; Jul–Sep. Frs dull
blackish, <3 mm. T, ex Ic. [8]

Small Water-pepper *Polygonum minus*
POLYGONACEAE H 10–30 cm. Dull green
annual, not peppery to taste. Lvs
lanceolate, <5 cm, blunt, almost stalkless.
Fls pink (rarely white), of 5 perianth
segments; in slender, erect spikes; Aug–
Sep. Frs black, shiny, <2·5 mm. Water-
sides, marshes. T, ex Ic. [9] Tasteless
water-pepper *P. mite* similar, but lvs
abruptly narrowed at base; inflor slightly
nodding; frs <4·5 mm. Water-sides,
marshes. T, ex Ic, De, FS. [10]

Amphibious Bistort *Polygonum
amphibium* POLYGONACEAE H 30–75 cm.
Perennial with two distinct forms;
aquatic: floating lvs <15 cm, ovate-
oblong, abruptly narrowed at base,
hairless; terrestrial: lvs <12 cm,
lanceolate, gradually narrowed at base,
hairy. Fls deep pink; in dense, terminal
spikes, <25 mm long; Jul–Sep. Lakes,
slow-moving water; terrestrial form in
marshes. T. [11]

Common Bistort *Polygonum bistorta*
POLYGONACEAE H 25–50 cm. Perennial.
Basal lvs <15 cm, ovate, with long,
winged stalks; upper lvs triangular-
lanceolate. Fls bright pink (rarely white),
of 5 segments; in stout, terminal spikes,
<7 cm long; Jun–Aug. Meadows,
roadsides. T, ex Ic, (but Ir, De, FS). [12]

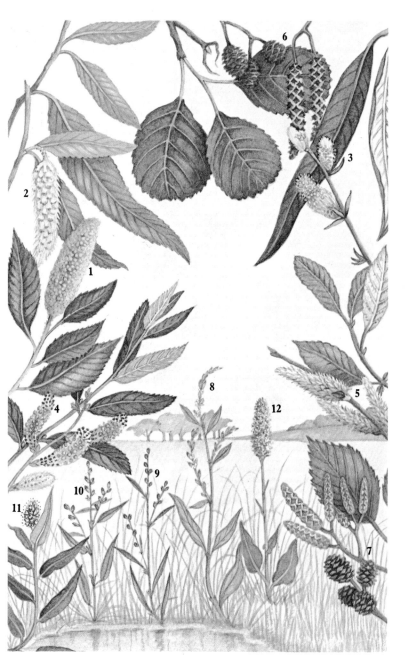

Water Dock *Rumex hydrolapathum*
POLYGONACEAE H 50–200 cm. Stout
perennial. Lvs <1 m, ovate, lanceolate,
tapering at both ends; lateral veins at
right-angles to mid-rib. Inflor dense, of
many erect branches, lfy below; Jul–Sep.
Fruiting perianth segments triangular,
each with prominent, elongated swelling.
Water-sides. T, ex Ic. [1]

Clustered Dock *Rumex conglomeratus*
POLYGONACEAE H 30–100 cm. Erect
perennial with branches at angles of 30–
90°. Lvs <20 cm, oblong, rounded at
base. Inflor lax, lfy almost to top; Jul–
Aug. Fruiting perianth segments ovate-
oblong, each with prominent, oblong
swelling on surface. Damp grassland,
woods. T, ex Ic, SC. [2]

Wood Dock *Rumex sanguineus* POLYGON-
ACEAE H 30–100 cm. Erect perennial with
branches at angles of *c*20°. Lvs <20 cm,
ovate-lanceolate, rounded at base. Inflor
much-branched, lfy only near base; Jun–
Aug. Fruiting perianth segments oblong,
only central one with globular swelling,
others very small. Damp woods, water-
sides, marshes. T, ex Ic. [3]

Golden Dock *Rumex maritimus* POLY-
GONACEAE H 30–60 cm. Erect or ascending,
much-branched annual or biennial;
golden-yellow in fr. Lvs <20 cm,
narrowly elliptical. Fl-stalks very slender,
longer than fls; inflor crowded, lfy to top;
Jun–Sep. Fruiting perianth segments
triangular, each with swelling on surface
and fine teeth larger than segments.
Muddy places. T, ex Ic, (but Fi). [4]
Marsh dock *R. palustris* similar, but fl-
stalks thick, rigid, as long as fls; fruiting
perianth segments tongue-shaped, with
rigid teeth shorter than segments. T, ex
Ir, Ic, Fi, No. [5]

Red Goosefoot *Chenopodium rubrum*
CHENOPODIACEAE H 10–90 cm. Procumbent
to erect, much-branched, hairless, usually
reddish annual. Lvs <5 cm, variable,
rhomboid-lanceolate, usually coarsely
toothed. Fls greenish, with perianth
segments of lateral fls joined to ½-way; in

dense, often pyramidal and lfy inflor;
Jul–Sep. Pond-margins, waste places,
often near sea. T, ex Ic. [6]

Oak-leaved Goosefoot *Chenopodium
glaucum* CHENOPODIACEAE H 5–50 cm.
Procumbent to erect, much-branched,
almost hairless annual. Lvs <5 cm,
rhomboid-lanceolate, coarsely toothed,
green above, mealy beneath. Fls in little-
branched, axillary and terminal spikes,
<3 cm; Jun–Sep. Waste ground by
water, rarely near sea. T, ex Ir, Ic. [7]

Blinks *Montia fontana* PORTULACEAE H 2–
50 cm. Annual or perennial; weak and
straggling in water; short, tufted and
erect on land. Lvs <2 cm, opposite,
roundish, narrowed into stalk-like base.
Fls <3 mm, greenish, of 5 petals; in
small clusters, often hidden by branches;
May–Oct. Muddy or marshy places by
water. T. [8]

Marsh Stitchwort *Stellaria palustris*
CARYOPHYLLACEAE H 20–60 cm. Erect,
straggling, hairless perennial, with slender,
4-angled stems. Lvs <5 cm, opposite,
linear-lanceolate, stalkless, ascending,
bluish-green. Fls <18 mm, of 5 white
petals divided almost to base, twice as
long as sepals; solitary or in few-fld
terminal clusters; May-Jul. Marshes,
lime-rich fens. T, ex Ir, Ic, Lu. [9]

Bog Stitchwort *Stellaria alsine* CARYOPH-
YLLACEAE H 5–10 cm. Creeping perennial
with slender, hairless, 4-angled stems. Lvs
<1 cm, opposite, elliptical-lanceolate,
stalkless. Fls <6 mm, of 5 white petals
divided almost to base, shorter than
sepals; in few-fld, terminal clusters; May-
Jun. Stream-sides, marshes. T, ex Ic. [10]

Water Chickweed *Myosoton aquaticum*
CARYOPHYLLACEAE H 20–100 cm. Prostrate
or ascending perennial, glandular-hairy
above. Lvs <5 cm, ovate, short-stalked.
Fls <15 mm, petals divided almost to
base, <1½ times as long as sepals; in
regularly branched clusters; Jul–Aug. Frs
capsules, longer than sepals, drooping at
first, later horizontal. T, ex Ir, Ic. [11]

Strapwort *Corrigiola litoralis* CARYOPHYLL-ACEAE H <25 cm. Creeping annual. Lvs <3 cm, linear, widest near tip. Fls tiny, <1 mm, of 5 white petals, equalling white-margined sepals; in crowded terminal or axillary clusters; Jul–Aug. Wet sand or gravel. T, ex Ir, Ic, FS. [1]

Coral-necklace *Illecebrum verticillatum* CARYOPHYLLACEAE H <20 cm. Hairless, creeping annual with slender tap-root and spreading, often reddish branches. Lvs <6 mm, linear, blunt. Fls <5 mm, of 5 white petals, shorter than thick, spongy, shining, white sepals; in whorls; Jul–Sep. Wet, sandy places. T, ex Ir, Ic, De, FS. [2]

Ragged Robin *Lychnis flos-cuculi* CARYOPHYLLACEAE H 20–90 cm. Erect, branching perennial, stems rough above, with few, downward-pointing hairs. Lvs <10 cm, opposite, oblong-lanceolate; lower narrowed into short stalks. Fls <4 cm, of 5 petals, deeply divided into 4 linear segments; inflor loose, regularly branching; May–Jun. Marshes, damp woods. T. [3]

White Water-lily *Nymphaea alba* NYMPHAEACEAE Submerged perennial, with stout, creeping rhizome. Lvs floating, <30 cm, circular, dark green above, paler beneath. Fls floating, <20 cm, of 20–25 spreading, white petals; Jul–Aug. Frs flat-topped, spongy, berry-like capsules, <4 cm across, with 14–20 radiating lines. Lakes, ponds. T, ex Ic. [4]

Small Water-lily *Nymphaea candida* NYMPHAEACEAE Like *N. alba*, but rhizome erect or ascending. Lvs floating, with overlapping basal lobes. Fls of 15–18 petals, only ½ open; Jul–Aug. Frs concave at top with 6–14 radiating lines. Lakes, ponds, rivers. Fr, Ge, Cz, Po, FS.

Yellow Water-lily *Nuphar lutea* NYMPH-AEACEAE Submerged perennial, with very stout rhizome, <8 cm thick. Lvs floating, <40 cm, ovate, leathery, with basal lobes overlapping. Fls above water, <6 cm across, of many petals, ⅓ length of the 5–6 yellowish sepals; Jun–Aug. Frs flask-shaped, with 15–20 radiating lines. Smells of alcohol, hence other name 'brandy-bottle'. Still and slow-moving water. T, ex Ic. [5]

Least Water-lily *Nuphar pumila* NYMPH-AEACEAE Like *N. lutea* but rhizome more slender, <3 cm thick. Lvs floating, <14 cm, with divergent basal lobes. Fls <35 mm across; Jul–Aug. Frs pear-shaped, with 7–14 radiating lines; less fragrant than *N. lutea*. Lakes. T, ex Ir, Ic, Lu, Ne.

Rigid Hornwort *Ceratophyllum demersum* CERATOPHYLLACEAE Densely lfy, stiff, dark green, submerged plant. Lvs <2 cm, of linear segments, once or twice forked, in whorls of 4–5. Fls of 8–12 narrow perianth segments; ♂ and ♀ separate, solitary in axils of different whorls; Jul–Sep. Frs ovoid, warty, long-spined nuts, <4 mm. Still and slow-moving water. T, ex Ic. [6]

Marsh-marigold *Caltha palustris* RANUNCULACEAE H 15–30 cm. Perennial with hollow stems. Lvs <15 cm, rounded, bluntly toothed; basal lvs long-stalked. Fls <5 cm, of 5–8 segments; Mar–Jul. Frs beaked capsules, in groups of 5–13, <18 mm. Marshes, wet woods. T. [7]

Celery-leaved Buttercup *Ranunculus sceleratus* RANUNCULACEAE H 20–60 cm. Shining green, fleshy, much-branched annual, with hollow, grooved stem. Lvs variable; lower long-stalked, kidney-shaped, 3-lobed, with toothed margins; upper short-stalked, more deeply divided into narrower segments. Fls <1 cm, yellow, of 5 narrow petals; in many-fld, terminal spikes; May–Sep. Marshes, water-sides. T, ex Ic. [8]

Greater Spearwort *Ranunculus lingua* RANUNCULACEAE H 50–120 cm. Perennial with hollow stem, creeping at first, then erect. Lvs <20 cm; lower ovate, long-stalked, soon withering; upper short-stalked, oblong-lanceolate, toothed. Fls <5 cm, of 5 yellow petals; in loose, few-fld clusters; Jun–Sep. Marshes, fens. T, ex Ic. [9] Lesser spearwort *R. flammula* very similar but much smaller. T.

Ivy-leaved Crowfoot *Ranunculus hederaceus* RANUNCULACEAE Creeping annual or biennial with branching stems. Lvs <3 cm wide, stalked, kidney-shaped or roundish, 3–5 lobed, lobes widest at base. Fls <6 mm, of 5 white petals as long as sepals; solitary, each opposite a lf; Jun–Sep. Frs 1-seeded, hairless, <1·5 mm. Mud, shallow water. T, ex Ic, Cz, Po, Fi, (but No). [1]

Three-lobed Crowfoot *Ranunculus tripartitus* RANUNCULACEAE Creeping annual or perennial. Lvs of 2 types; floating: <20 mm, kidney-shaped to circular in outline, deeply divided into 3–5 lobes; submerged: finely divided into thread-like segments. Fls <1 cm across, of 5 white petals, not overlapping, twice as long as sepals; solitary, each opposite a lf; Apr–Jun. Ditches, shallow, muddy pools. Br, Ir, Fr, Ne, Ge. [2]

Pond Water-crowfoot *Ranunculus peltatus* RANUNCULACEAE Creeping annual or perennial, with branched, submerged stems. Lvs of 2 types; floating: <4 cm, kidney-shaped to circular, divided into 3–5, bluntly-toothed lobes; submerged: finely divided. Fls <35 mm, of 5 or more white, almost overlapping petals, solitary on stout stalk <15 cm, May–Aug. Fr-stalks tapering above. Ponds, ditches, shallow streams. T, ex Ic. [3]

Common Water-crowfoot *Ranunculus aquatilis* RANUNCULACEAE Similar to *R. peltatus*, but floating lvs sharply toothed. Fls <25 mm; May–Jun. Fr-stalks <5 cm, shorter than stalk of lf opposite, scarcely tapering above. Ponds, ditches, streams. T, ex Ic. [4]

Fan-leaved Water-crowfoot *Ranunculus circinatus* RANUNCULACEAE Slender, submerged perennial with few branches. Lvs all submerged, <2 cm, circular in outline, divided into short, rigid, linear segments, which lie in one plane forming fan-like shape. Fls <18 mm, of 5 white, scarcely-overlapping petals; solitary; Jun–Aug. Fr-stalks <8 cm, longer than stalk of lf opposite. Still and slow-moving, mineral-rich water. T, ex Ic, Lu, No. [5]

water-buttercup *Ranunculus fluitans* RANUNCULACEAE Robust, creeping perennial with strong rhizome and submerged, lfy stems, <6 m. Lvs submerged, <30 cm, much-divided into slender, linear, greenish-black segments. Fls <30 mm, of 5–10, white, overlapping petals; on short stalks; Jun–Sep. Fr-stalks project water. Fast-flowing streams. T, ex Ir, Ic, De, Fi, No. [6]

water-buttercup *Ranunculus penicillatus* RANUNCULACEAE Robust, creeping perennial with submerged, lfy stems. Lvs mostly submerged, <8 cm, much-divided into long, stiff, almost parallel segments, of irregular length. Fls <3 cm, of 5 or more, white, almost overlapping petals; on stout stalks; May–Aug. Fr-stalks <15 cm, tapering at top. Fast-flowing streams. T, ex Ic, Lu, Be, Fi, No. [var *calcareus* 7]

Thread-leaved Water-crowfoot *Ranunculus trichophyllus* RANUNCULACEAE Creeping annual or perennial. Lvs all submerged, < 4 cm, divided into short, dark green, linear segments, not lying in one plane. Fls <1 cm, of 5 white petals, not overlapping, soon falling; on short, down-turned stalks; May–Jun. Fr-stalks <4 cm. Ponds, ditches, slow-moving water. T. [8]

Mousetail *Myosurus minimus* RANUNCULACEAE H 5–12 cm. Hairless, rosette-forming annual. Lvs <8 mm, linear, somewhat fleshy. Fls <4 mm; of 5 or more, linear, greenish-yellow sepals, with spur at base, surrounding 5 greenish, tubular petals; in dense spike <5 cm, on erect, lfless stem ('mouse tail'); Jun–Jul. Cultivated fields, wet in winter. T, ex Ir, Ic. [9]

Common Meadow-rue *Thalictrum flavum* RANUNCULACEAE H 50–100 cm. Perennial with furrowed stems. Lvs divided into 3- or 4-lobed lflets. Fls of 4–5 yellow segments, soon falling, and numerous, erect stamens; in dense clusters; Jul–Aug. Damp meadows, fens, stream-sides. T, ex Ic. [10]

Great Yellow-cress *Rorippa amphibia*
CRUCIFERAE H 40–120 cm. Erect perennial.
Lower lvs elliptical, short-stalked;
upper lanceolate. Fls <6 mm, of 4 yellow
petals, twice as long as sepals; in many-
fld, terminal spikes; Jun–Aug. Frs ovoid
pods, <6 mm, less than ½ as long as
stalks. Water-sides. T, ex Ic. [1]

Marsh Yellow-cress *Rorippa palustris*
CRUCIFERAE H 10–60 cm. Erect annual
or biennial, with hollow, angled stem.
Lvs <6 cm; lower deeply divided into
3–6 irregularly toothed segments; upper
less divided. Fls <3 mm, of 4 pale yellow
petals, almost equalling sepals; in loose
clusters; Jun–Sep. Frs sausage-shaped,
<9 mm. Bare, damp areas. T. [2]

Water-cress *Nasturtium officinale*
CRUCIFERAE H 10–60 cm. Creeping
perennial with hollow, angular, ascending
stems. Lvs <10 cm, once-divided into
3–4 pairs of rounded-elliptical, toothed
lflets. Fls <6 mm, of 4 white petals,
c twice as long as sepals; May–Oct. Frs
sausage-shaped, <18 mm, longer than
stalks. Streams, ditches. T, ex Ic. [3]

Cuckooflower *Cardamine pratensis*
CRUCIFERAE H 15–60 cm. Rosette-forming
perennial. Lvs <8 cm, once-divided into
3–7 pairs of toothed lflets. Fls <18 mm,
of 4 lilac petals (rarely white), 3 times as
long as sepals, anthers yellow; Apr–Jun.
Frs narrow pods, <4 cm, longer than
stalks. Wet meadows, stream-banks. T,
ex Ic, Fi. [4]

Larger Bitter-cress *Cardamine amara*
CRUCIFERAE H 10–60 cm. Like *C. pratensis*
but lacking rosette of basal lvs. Fls
smaller, <12 mm, of 4 usually white
petals, twice as long as sepals, anthers
purple; Apr–Jun. Wet woods, stream-
sides. T, ex Ic. [5]

Marsh Saxifrage *Saxifraga hirculus*
SAXIFRAGACEAE H 10–20 cm. Erect
perennial; stems with reddish hairs. Lower
lvs <25 mm, lanceolate, obtuse, long-
stalked; upper shorter, narrower. Fls
<15 mm, of 5 bright yellow petals, often
with red spots near base; Aug. Frs ovoid

capsules, <1 cm. Springs in bogs. T, ex
Lu, Be, Ne. [6]

Opposite-leaved Golden-saxifrage
Chrysosplenium oppositifolium SAXIFRAG-
ACEAE H 5–15 cm. Creeping, somewhat
hairy perennial. Lvs <2 cm, opposite,
roundish, with shallow teeth; stalks as
long as lvs. Fls <4 mm, lacking petals,
but with 4–5 bright yellowish-green sepals
in lfy, regularly-branching, terminal
clusters; Apr–Jul. Stream-sides, flushes,
often in woods. T, ex Ic, Fi, Sw. [7]
Alternate-leaved golden-saxifrage *C.
alternifolium* like *C. oppositifolium* but lvs
alternate, kidney-shaped; stalks several
times as long as lvs. T, ex Ir, Ic. [8]

Grass-of-Parnassus *Parnassia palustris*
PARNASSIACEAE H 5–40 cm. Erect, tufted
perennial. Lvs <5 cm, long-stalked, ovate
roundish, base heart-shaped. Fls <3 cm,
of 5 white petals with conspicuous veins,
over twice as long as sepals; solitary on
1-lvd stems; honey-scented; Jul–Oct. Frs
ovoid capsules, <2 cm. Marshes, bogs,
wet sand dunes. T. [9]

Meadowsweet *Filipendula ulmaria*
ROSACEAE H 60–120 cm. Erect perennial.
Lvs divided into 2–5 pairs of ovate, double
toothed lflets, <8 cm. Fls <5 mm, of 5–
creamy-white petals; in dense, terminal
clusters; strongly scented; Jun–Sep. Frs
spirally twisted clusters. Marshes, damp
woods. T. [10]

Great Burnet *Sanguisorba officinalis*
ROSACEAE H 20–100 cm. Erect perennial,
branched above. Lvs <15 cm, divided
into 3–7 pairs of ovate, stalked, toothed
lflets, <4 cm. Fls <5 mm, lacking petals
of 4 crimson sepals; in dense heads,
<2 cm; Jun–Sep. Frs with 4 narrow
wings. Damp meadows. T, (but Fi). [11]

Water Avens *Geum rivale* ROSACEAE H 20–
60 cm. Erect perennial. Lvs divided into
3–6 pairs of unequal leaflets. Fls <15 mm
nodding, bell-shaped, of 5 dull reddish-
pink, notched petals, as long as sepals;
in small clusters; May–Sep. Frs hairy, in
stalked heads. Marshes, stream-sides, wet
mountain ledges. T. [12]

Marsh Cinquefoil *Potentilla palustris*
ROSACEAE H 15–45 cm. Erect, somewhat
hairy perennial with black, woody
rhizome. Lvs <15 cm, divided into 5–7
oblong, coarsely toothed lflets, <6 cm.
Fls <3 cm, of 5 conspicuous, purplish
sepals and 5 small, purple petals; May–
Jul. Marshes, fens, bogs. T. [1]

Silverweed *Potentilla anserina* ROSACEAE
H 2–10 cm. Creeping, silky-haired, rosette-
forming perennial. Lvs silvery on both
sides or beneath only, <25 cm, divided
into 7–12 pairs of oval, toothed lflets,
<6 cm, alternating with smaller ones. Fls
<25 mm, of 5 yellow petals, *c* twice as
long as sepals; Jun–Aug. Meadows,
ditches, waste places. T. [2]

Marsh Pea *Lathyrus palustris* LEGUMIN-
OSAE H 60–120 cm. Scrambling perennial
with winged stems. Lvs divided into 2–5
pairs of linear lflets, <8 cm; lf-stalks
with basal stipules. Fls <2 cm, pale
purplish-blue; in spikes of 2–8; May–Jul.
Frs flattened, hairless pods, <5 cm. Fens,
damp grassland. T. [3]

Narrow-leaved Bird's-foot-trefoil *Lotus
tenuis* LEGUMINOSAE H 20–90 cm. Creeping,
slender, sparsely hairy perennial. Lvs of 5
linear-lanceolate lflets, <15 mm. Fls
<12 mm long; in 1–4 fld heads, on long
stalks; Jun–Aug. Frs pods, <3 cm,
twisting after opening. Damp grassland.
T, ex Ir, Ic, (but Fi, No). [4]

Greater Bird's-foot-trefoil *Lotus
uliginosus* LEGUMINOSAE H 30–100 cm.
Erect or ascending, hairy, hollow-stemmed
perennial. Lvs of 5 ovate, blunt lflets,
<25 mm. Fls <18 mm, orange-yellow,
with long calyx teeth; in 5–12 fld heads,
on long, slender stalks; Jun–Aug. Frs
pods, <35 mm. Marshes, damp grassland.
T, ex Ic, (but Fi, No). [5]

Marsh Crane's-bill *Geranium palustre*
GERANIACEAE H 20–60 cm. Erect, hairy
perennial. Lvs <10 cm, round, deeply
divided into 5–7 toothed lobes. Fls <3 cm,
of 5 petals; in few-fld clusters, on stalks
turned down in fr; Jun–Aug. Frs beaked,

<25 mm. Wet meadows. Fr, Lu, Be, De,
Ge, Cz, Po, Fi, Sw. [6]

Touch-me-not Balsam *Impatiens
nolitangere* BALSAMINACEAE H 20–100 cm.
Erect annual. Lvs <12 cm, ovate-oblong,
with 20–30 coarse teeth, stalked. Fls
<35 mm, of 5 petals, yellow with brown
spots, upper one large, others united in
pairs, lower sepal tapering into spur;
Jun–Sep. Frs explosive capsules, <15 mm.
Wet woods. T, ex Ir, Ic. [7]

Indian Balsam *Impatiens glandulifera*
BALSAMINACEAE H 1–2 m. Erect annual.
Lvs <15 cm, opposite or in 3's,
lanceolate-elliptical, sharply toothed,
stalked. Fls <4 cm, helmet-shaped,
purplish-pink (rarely white); Jul–Oct. Frs
explosive capsules, <3 cm, opening when
touched. River-banks, waste places. (T,
ex Ic, from Himalayas.) [8]

Alder Buckthorn *Frangula alnus*
RHAMNACEAE H <5 m. Thornless,
deciduous shrub with branches at acute
angles to main stem, and buds without
scales. Lvs <7 cm, obovate, hairy below,
with *c*7 pairs of veins when young. Fls
<3 mm, greenish; in axillary clusters;
May–Jun. Frs red berries, violet-black
when ripe, <1 cm. Wet, slightly acid
woodland, bogs. T, ex Ic. [9]

Marsh St John's-Wort *Hypericum elodes*
HYPERICACEAE H 10–30 cm. Softly hairy,
creeping perennial with erect stems. Lvs
<3 cm, opposite, half-clasping stem. Fls
<15 mm, petals spirally twisted in bud,
3 times as long as sepals; Jun–Sep. Bogs,
slightly acid streams, wet heaths. Br, Ir,
Fr, Be, Ne, Ge. [10]

Square-stalked St John's-Wort
Hypericum tetrapterum HYPERICACEAE
H 30–100 cm. Erect, creeping perennial
with ascending, 4-angled, winged stems.
Lvs <3 cm, opposite, broadly elliptical,
half-clasping stem, covered with
translucent dots. Fls <1 cm, petals 1½
times as long as sepals; Jun–Sep. Marshes,
wet meadows, water-sides. T, ex Ic, No.
[11]

Marsh Violet *Viola palustris* VIOLACEAE
H 5–10 cm. Hairless, rosette-forming
perennial with creeping rhizome. Lvs
<6 cm, wider than long, kidney-shaped,
on slender stalk, <6 cm. Fls <15 mm,
scentless, of 5 pale lilac petals with dark
veins and blunt spur; solitary, on long
stalks with pair of lfy bracts at or below
middle; Apr–Jul. Frs hairless capsules,
<5 mm. Bogs, marshes, wet heaths. T. [1]

Heath Dog-violet *Viola canina* VIOLACEAE
H 10–40 cm. Prostrate to erect perennial.
Lvs <8 cm, ovate-lanceolate, heart-
shaped at base, shallowly toothed, hairy
above, lf-stalk with 2 distantly toothed
basal stipules. Fls <25 mm, of 5 blue or
white petals, with long, thick, blunt,
yellowish spur; Apr–Jun. Frs hairless
capsules, <9 mm. Heaths, dunes, fens.
T. [2]

Fen Violet *Viola persicifolia* VIOLACEAE
H 10–25 cm. Creeping perennial. Lvs
<4 cm, triangular-lanceolate, shallowly
toothed, lf-stalk with 2 basal stipules ½ as
long as stalk. Fls <15 mm, of 5 white or
bluish-white petals, circular, with short
greenish spur; solitary on long stalks;
May–Jun. Frs hairless capsules, <7 mm.
Marshes, fens. T, ex Ic. [3]

German Tamarisk *Myricaria germanica*
TAMARICACEAE H <2·5 m. Shrub with erect
branches. Lvs <5 mm, linear-lanceolate,
blunt, stalkless, flat on stem, overlapping.
Fls <1 cm, of 5 pink petals longer than
sepals; in long, slender spikes; May–Aug.
Frs capsules, <1 mm, splitting vertically
to release plumed seeds. River gravels,
waste places. Fr, Ge, Cz, Po, FS. [4]

Water-purslane *Lythrum portula*
LYTHRACEAE H 5–10 cm. Creeping annual.
Lvs <15 mm, opposite, spoon-shaped,
narrowing into short stalk. Fls <1 mm,
of 6 purple petals soon falling; solitary in
lf axils; Jun–Aug. Frs almost spherical
capsules, <1·5 mm. Open, wet, lime-
free places. T, ex Ic. [5]

Purple Loosestrife *Lythrum salicaria*
LYTHRACEAE H 50–150 cm. Erect, hairy

perennial. Lvs <7 cm, opposite or in 3's,
upper sometimes alternate, lanceolate,
stalkless, half-clasping stem. Fls <15 mm,
of 6 magenta petals; in whorls in axils of
bracts, forming dense, terminal spikes;
Jun–Aug. Frs oblong capsules, <4 mm,
enclosed in calyx. Water-sides, marshes.
T, ex Ic. [6]

Great Willowherb *Epilobium hirsutum*
ONAGRACEAE H 80–150 cm. Erect, very
hairy perennial with fleshy, white
rhizomes. Lvs <12 cm, mostly opposite,
oblong-lanceolate, toothed, stalkless, half-
clasping stem. Fls <23 mm, of 4 bright
purplish-pink, notched petals, with
prominent, cross-shaped, white stigmas;
in lfy terminal clusters; Jul–Aug. Frs
downy capsules, <8 cm. Water-sides,
ditches, marshes. T, ex Ic, (but Fi, No).
[7]

Hoary Willowherb *Epilobium parviflorum*
ONAGRACEAE H 30–90 cm. Erect, softly
hairy perennial. Lvs <7 cm, lower
opposite, oblong-lanceolate, distantly
toothed, stalkless, not clasping stem. Fls
<9 mm, of 4 deeply notched petals,
stigmas cross-shaped; in lfy terminal
spikes; Jul–Aug. Frs somewhat hairy
capsules, <6 cm. Water-sides, ditches,
marshes. T, ex Ic. [8]

Marsh Willowherb *Epilobium palustre*
ONAGRACEAE H 15–60 cm. Erect, somewhat
hairy perennial, with thread-like runners in
autumn. Lvs <6 cm, opposite, lanceolate,
stalkless. Fls <6 mm, drooping in bud, of
4 notched petals, stigma club-shaped;
in loose, branched clusters; Jul–Aug.
Frs downy capsules, <8 cm. Ditches,
marshes, on lime-free soils. T. [9]

Short-fruited Willowherb *Epilobium
obscurum* ONAGRACEAE H 20–90 cm. Erect,
downy perennial with thread-like stolons
in autumn. Lvs <7 cm; lower opposite,
ovate-lanceolate, stalkless. Fls <9 mm,
of 4, 2-lobed petals, erect in bud, with
glandular hairs on calyx, stigma club-
shaped; in much-branched clusters;
Jul–Aug. Frs downy capsules, <6 cm.
Water-sides, damp woods. T, ex Ic. [10]

Alternate Water-milfoil *Myriophyllum alterniflorum* HALORAGACEAE H 20–120 cm. Submerged aquatic with branching shoots. Lvs <25 mm, in whorls of 4, divided into 6–18 thread-like segments. Fls <3 mm, ♂ above, ♀ below; in spike above water; May–Aug. Frs cylindrical, <2 mm. Lime-deficient streams, lakes. T. [1] Spiked water-milfoil *M. spicatum* similar but larger. Lvs of 13–38 segments. Fls <4 mm, of 4 large petals, soon falling; Jun–Jul. Frs almost spherical, <3 mm. Slow-flowing rivers, lakes. T. [2]

Mare's-tail *Hippuris vulgaris* HALORAG-ACEAE H 30–60 cm. Perennial with erect, partially submerged shoots. Lvs <75 mm, linear, in whorls of 6–12. Fls tiny, <1 mm, green; solitary in axils of lvs; Jun–Jul. Still and slow-moving water. T. [3]

Marsh Pennywort *Hydrocotyle vulgaris* UMBELLIFERAE H <25 cm. Creeping perennial. Lvs <5 cm, circular, shallowly lobed, shining green. Fls <2 mm, of 5 pinkish-green petals; in few-fld whorls hidden by lvs; Jun–Aug. Marshes, bogs, damp meadows. T, ex Ic, Fi. [4]

Greater Water-parsnip *Sium latifolium* UMBELLIFERAE H 1–2 m. Erect perennial with hollow, grooved stems. Lvs <30 cm, divided into 4–6 pairs of stalkless, ovate, toothed segments, <15 cm. Fls <4 mm, of 5 white petals; in umbels of 20–30 rays; Jul–Aug. Frs longer than broad, <3 mm, with thick ridges. Fens, marshes. T, ex Ic, (but No). [5]

Lesser Water-parsnip *Berula erecta* UMBELLIFERAE H 30–100 cm. Erect perennial with hollow, grooved stems. Lvs <30 cm, divided into 7–10 pairs of stalkless, ovate, sharply toothed segments, <5 cm. Fls <2 mm, of 5 white petals; in umbels of 10–15 rays; Jul–Sep. Frs broader than long, <2 mm. Marshes, shallow water. T, ex Ic, Fi. [6]

Tubular Water-dropwort *Oenanthe fistulosa* UMBELLIFERAE H 30–60 cm. Erect, hollow-stemmed perennial. Basal lvs <20 cm, twice divided into ovate, lobed

segments; upper divided into linear segments. Fls <3 mm, of 5 white petals; in umbels of 2–5 flat-topped clusters; Jul–Sep. Frs cylindrical, <4 mm. Marshes, shallow water. T, ex Ic, Fi, No. [7]

Fine-leaved Water-dropwort *Oenanthe aquatica* UMBELLIFERAE H 30–150 cm. Erect, hollow-stemmed perennial. Lvs <30 cm, 3-times divided into ovate, acute segments; segments linear if submerged. Fls <2 mm, of 5 white petals; in umbels of 4–10 rays; Jun–Sep. Frs elliptical, <5 mm. Shallow, stagnant water. T, ex Ic. [8]

Fool's Water-cress *Apium nodiflorum* UMBELLIFERAE H 30–100 cm. Creeping or ascending, hollow-stemmed perennial. Lvs <30 cm, divided into 4–6 pairs of stalkless, lanceolate-ovate, toothed segments, <35 mm. Fls <2 mm, of 5 white petals; in umbels of 3–12 rays; Jul–Aug. Frs ovoid, <2 mm. Shallow water. Br, Ir, Fr, Lu, Be, Ne, Ge. [9]

Lesser Marshwort *Apium inundatum* UMBELLIFERAE Usually submerged or floating perennial. Lvs pinnate; lower divided into linear lobes; upper into ovate, often 3-lobed segments. Fls <1 mm, of 5 white petals; in umbels of 2–3 rays; Jun–Aug. Frs elliptical, <2 mm. Shallow water. T, ex Ic, Cz, Fi, No. [10]

Whorled Caraway *Carum verticillatum* UMBELLIFERAE H 30–60 cm. Erect perennial. Lvs <25 cm, much-divided into hair-like segments, <1 cm. Fls <1 mm, of 5 white or pinkish, deeply notched petals; in umbels of 8–12 rays; Jul–Aug. Frs elliptical, <4 mm. Damp, slightly acid grassland. Br, Ir, Fr, Be, Ne. [11]

Cambridge Milk-parsley *Selinum carvifolia* UMBELLIFERAE H 30–100 cm. Erect perennial with narrowly winged stems. Lvs <30 cm, 2–3 times divided into minutely toothed lobes, <1 cm. Fls <2 mm, of 5 white, notched petals; in umbels of 10–20 rays; Jul–Oct. Frs ovoid, <4 mm. Fens, damp meadows, open woodland. T, ex Ir, Ic. [12]

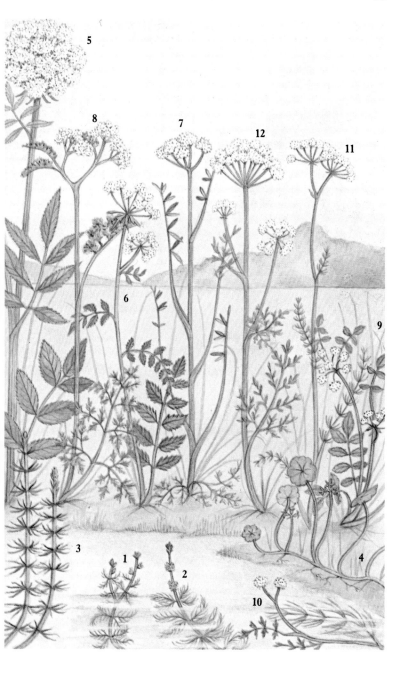

Wild Angelica *Angelica sylvestris*
UMBELLIFERAE H 30–200 cm. Erect
perennial with hollow, usually purple
stems. Lvs <60 cm, 2–3 times divided
into oblong, lobed, toothed, stalked
segments. Fls <2 mm, of 5 white or pink
petals; in umbels of 20–30 rays; Jul–Sep.
Frs ovate with papery wings, <5 mm.
Damp, shady places. T. [1]

Garden Angelica *Angelica archangelica*
UMBELLIFERAE H 30–200 cm. Like *A.
sylvestris* but stems green; lvs more
irregular in outline, teeth more jagged,
segments stalkless, lf-stems aromatic. Fls
greenish-white or cream; Jul–Aug. Frs
with thick, corky wings. Damp meadows,
river-sides. T, ex Ir, Ic, Po, (but Br, Fr,
Lu, Be). [2]

Milk Parsley *Peucedanum palustre*
UMBELLIFERAE H 50–150 cm. Erect,
hollow-stemmed biennial. Lvs <40 cm,
much-divided into pinnately lobed
segments with blunt tips. Fls <2 mm, of
5 greenish-white petals; in umbels of 20–40
hairy rays; Jul–Sep. Frs ovoid, <5 mm.
Fens, marshes. T, ex Ir, Ic, Lu. [3]

Labrador-tea *Ledum palustre* ERICACEAE
H <1 m. Evergreen shrub, stems with
rust-coloured hairs. Lvs <45 mm,
leathery, with inrolled margins, rusty-
haired below. Fls <15 mm, of 5 creamy
petals; in umbel-like terminal clusters;
Jun–Jul. Frs oblong capsules, <5 mm.
Bogs. Ge, Cz, Po, FS, (Br). [4]

Bog Rosemary *Andromeda polifolia*
ERICACEAE H 15–35 cm. Creeping,
evergreen shrub. Lvs <35 mm, linear-
elliptical, with down-turned margins,
short-stalked. Fls <7 mm, pink, globular,
long-stalked; in clusters of 2–8; May–
Sep. Frs spherical capsules, <5 mm.
Bogs, wet heaths. T, ex Ic. [5]

Water-violet *Hottonia palustris*
PRIMULACEAE H 30–90 cm. Floating
perennial with erect stems. Lvs <10 cm,
1–2 times divided into numerous, comb-
like segments. Fls <25 mm; in whorls of
3–8; May–Jun. Frs spherical capsules,

<5 mm, longer than glandular calyx.
Ponds, ditches. T, ex Ic, Lu, Fi, No. [6]

Creeping Jenny *Lysimachia nummularia*
PRIMULACEAE H <60 cm. Creeping
perennial. Lvs <3 cm, rounded, opposite,
on short stalks. Fls <25 mm, petals
twice as long as ovate sepals; solitary on
stout stalks in axils of lvs; Jun–Aug. Frs
spherical capsules, <3 mm, rare. Marshes,
damp, shady places. T, ex Ic, Fi. [7]
Yellow pimpernel *L. nemorum* similar
but lvs ovate, acute, rounded at base. Fls
<12 mm, with petals almost equalling
linear-lanceolate sepals; on fine stalks
longer than lvs; May–Sep. [8]

Yellow Loosestrife *Lysimachia vulgaris*
PRIMULACEAE H 60–150 cm. Erect, hairy
perennial. Lvs <12 cm, ovate-lanceolate,
dotted with orange or black glands, almost
stalkless, opposite or in whorls of 3–4.
Fls <15 mm, of 5 joined, yellow petals,
twice as long as orange-edged sepals;
Jul–Aug. Frs spherical capsules,
<5·5 mm. T, ex Ic, Fi. [9]

Tufted Loosestrife *Lysimachia thyrsiflora*
PRIMULACEAE H 30–60 cm. Erect perennial.
Lvs <10 cm, opposite, lanceolate, dotted
with black glands, stalkless; basal lvs
smaller. Fls <5 mm, of 5 joined, yellow
petals equalling calyx; on slender stalks, in
dense axillary clusters; Jun–Jul. Frs ovoid
capsules, <2·5 mm. Marshes, shallow
water. T, ex Ir, Ic. [10]

Bog Pimpernel *Anagallis tenella*
PRIMULACEAE Creeping perennial. Lvs
<5 mm, opposite, roundish, short-
stalked. Fls <14 mm, pink, petals 2–3
times as long as lanceolate sepals; on long
stalks, solitary in lf-axils; Jun–Aug. Frs
spherical capsules, <3 mm. Damp
grassland, bogs, ditches. Br, Ir, Fr, Lu,
Be, Ne, Ge. [11]

Marsh Gentian *Gentiana pneumonanthe*
GENTIANACEAE H 10–40 cm. Erect or
ascending perennial. Lvs <4 cm,
opposite, linear, blunt. Fls <4 cm,
tubular, 5-lobed; in dense terminal clusters
of <7 fls; Aug–Sep. Frs capsules,
<12 mm. Wet heaths. T, ex Ir, Ic, Fi. [12]

Yellow Centaury *Cicendia filiformis*
GENTIANACEAE H 3–12 cm. Slender, erect
annual. Lvs <6 mm, opposite, united at
base, soon withering. Fls <5 mm, of 4
joined petals; Jun–Aug. Frs ovoid
capsules, <5 mm. Damp sand, peat,
often near sea. Br, Ir, Fr, Be, Ne, Ge. [1]

Bogbean *Menyanthes trifoliata* GENTIAN-
ACEAE H <30 cm. Aquatic perennial with
lvs and fls above water. Lvs of 3 elliptical
lflets, <7 cm. Fls <15 mm, of 5 joined,
whitish-pink petals, covered in white hairs
above; in 10–20 fld spikes, on stalks <30
cm; May–Jun. Frs spherical capsules,
<3 mm. Ponds, lakes, marshes. T. [2]

Fringed Water-lily *Nymphoides peltata*
GENTIANACEAE Aquatic perennial. Lvs
floating, <10 cm, round, heart-shaped at
base. Fls <3 cm, of 5 joined, yellow
petals with fringed margins; on stalks
<10 cm, in 2–5 fld clusters in axils; Jul–
Aug. Frs ovoid, beaked capsules,
<15 mm. Still and slow-moving water.
T, ex Ir, Ic, Fi, No, (but De, Sw). [3]

Fen Bedstraw *Galium uliginosum*
RUBIACEAE H 10–60 cm. Slender,
scrambling perennial with prickly, 4-
angled stems. Lvs <1 cm, linear, in
whorls of 6–8, narrowed to sharp-pointed
tip. Fls <3 mm, of 4 joined, white petals;
in narrow panicle; Jul–Aug. Frs hairless
capsules <1 mm. Fens, marshes. T. [4]

Common Marsh-bedstraw *Galium
palustre* RUBIACEAE H 15–120 cm. Slender
perennial with smooth or slightly prickly,
4-angled stems. Lvs <35 mm, in whorls
of 4–6. Fls <5 mm, of 4 joined, white
petals; in pyramidal panicle; Jun–Jul.
Frs hairless, <2 mm. Wet places. T. [5]

Greater Dodder *Cuscuta europaea*
CONVOLVULACEAE Parasite, usually of
nettle or hop, with fine, reddish stems.
Lvs tiny, scale-like. Fls bell-like, of 5
blunt, pinkish petals; in dense heads;
Jul–Sep. Frs spherical capsules. T, ex Ir,
Ic. [6]

Common Comfrey *Symphytum
officinale* BORAGINACEAE H 30–120 cm.
Erect, hairy perennial. Lvs <25 cm;

lf-stalks with wings continuing down stem.
Fls of 5 yellowish-white or carmine
lobes; May–Jul. Frs shining black
nutlets. Fens, ditches, river-banks. T, ex
Ic, (but Ir, De, FS). [7]

Water Forget-me-not *Myosotis
scorpioides* BORAGINACEAE H 15–45 cm.
Hairy perennial. Lvs <7 cm, oblong-
lanceolate, blunt, stalkless. Fls <1 cm,
of 5 joined, notched, sky-blue petals,
calyx tube with teeth $\frac{1}{4}$–$\frac{1}{3}$ its length, style
equalling or exceeding tube; on stalks 1–2
times calyx length; May–Sep. By water.
T, ex Po, Sw. [8]

Creeping Forget-me-not *Myosotis
secunda* BORAGINACEAE H 20–40 cm.
Slender, very hairy perennial. Lvs
<4 mm, elliptical, obtuse, stalkless. Fls
<6 mm, of 5 joined, slightly notched,
blue petals, calyx tube with teeth $\frac{1}{2}$ its
length, style equalling or exceeding tube;
on stalks 3–5 times calyx length; May–
Aug. Wet, slightly acid places. Br, Ir, Fr.
[9]

Tufted Forget-me-not *Myosotis
caespitosa* BORAGINACEAE H 20–40 cm.
Erect annual or biennial, covered in
appressed hairs. Lvs <8 cm, lanceolate,
blunt, stalkless. Fls <4 mm, of 5 joined,
rounded, sky-blue petals, calyx tube with
teeth $\frac{1}{3}$–$\frac{3}{4}$ its length, style $\frac{1}{2}$ length of tube;
on stalks 2–3 times calyx length; May–
Aug. Marshes. T. [10]

Common Water-starwort *Callitriche
stagnalis* CALLITRICHACEAE H <60 cm.
Submerged or terrestrial. Submerged:
lvs narrowly elliptical; terrestrial: lvs
broader, with notched tips. Fls tiny, green;
solitary in axils of upper lvs; May–Sep.
Frs round, keeled, <2 mm. Still or slow-
moving water, mud. T. [11]

Intermediate Water-starwort *Callitriche
hamulata* CALLITRICHACEAE H <80 cm.
Submerged or floating. Submerged: lvs
linear with tip expanded, deeply notched;
floating: lvs narrowly tongue-shaped.
Fls tiny, green; solitary in axils of lvs;
Apr–Sep. Frs smaller than *C. stagnalis*.
Lime-deficient streams, lakes. T. [12]

Water Germander *Teucrium scordium*
LABIATAE H 10–60 cm. Erect, hairy
perennial. Lvs <5 cm, opposite, oblong,
coarsely toothed, stalkless. Fls <12 mm,
with single, 5-lobed, purple lip; in whorls
in axils of bracts; Jul–Oct. Fens and wet,
calcareous dunes. T, ex Ic, Fi, No. [1]

Skullcap *Scutellaria galericulata* LABIATAE
H 7–70 cm. Erect, hairy perennial. Lvs
<5 cm, opposite, heart-shaped at base,
bluntly toothed, short-stalked. Fls <2 cm,
2-lipped, with slightly curved tube; in
pairs in axils of lvs; Jun–Sep. Marshes,
water-sides. T, ex Ic. [2]

Spear-leaved Skullcap *Scutellaria
hastifolia* LABIATAE H 20–40 cm. Erect,
sparsely hairy perennial. Lvs <25 mm,
opposite, spear-shaped at base, short-
stalked. Fls <25 mm, 2-lipped, with
strongly curved tube; in terminal clusters;
Jun–Sep. Damp grassland, woodland. Fr,
De, Ge, Cz, Po, Fi, Sw, (Br). [3]

Lesser Skullcap *Scutellaria minor*
LABIATAE H 10–20 cm. Ascending,
sparsely hairy perennial. Lvs <2 cm,
opposite, with 1–2 blunt teeth, short-
stalked. Fls <1 cm, 2-lipped, with dark
spots, tube straight; in pairs in lf-axils;
Jul–Oct. Wet heaths, woods. Br, Ir, Fr,
Lu, Be, Ne, Ge, Sw. [4]

Marsh Woundwort *Stachys palustris*
LABIATAE H 40–100 cm. Erect, somewhat
hairy perennial. Lvs <12 cm, opposite,
linear-lanceolate, bluntly toothed, short-
stalked. Fls <15 mm, 2-lipped; in 6-fld
whorls in lf-axils; Jul–Sep. Water-sides,
marshes, damp arable fields. T, ex Ic. [5]

Gipsywort *Lycopus europaeus* LABIATAE
H 30–100 cm. Erect, somewhat hairy
perennial. Lvs <10 cm, opposite, ovate-
lanceolate, coarsely toothed at apex. Fls
<4 mm, of 4 joined petals, one purple-
spotted; in whorls in lf-axils; Jun–Sep.
Marshes, water-sides. T, ex Ic. [6]

Pennyroyal *Mentha pulegium* LABIATAE
H 10–30 cm. Creeping, somewhat hairy
perennial with pungent scent. Lvs
<3 cm, opposite, elliptical, hairy beneath,
toothed, short-stalked. Fls <6 mm, of 4
joined petals; in many-fld whorls in lf-
axils; Aug–Oct. Pond margins, damp
meadows. T, ex Ic, De, FS. [7]

Water Mint *Mentha aquatica* LABIATAE
H 15–90 cm. Erect, somewhat hairy, often
purplish, strongly scented perennial. Lvs
<6 cm, ovate, toothed, stalked. Fls
<8 mm, weakly 2-lipped; in terminal
head with 1–3 whorls below; Jul–Oct.
Marshes, wet woods. T, (but Ic). [8]

Peppermint *Mentha × piperita* LABIATAE
H 30–80 cm. Erect, thinly hairy, purplish
perennial smelling of peppermint. Lvs
<8 cm, lanceolate, acute, sharply toothed,
stalked. Fls <8 mm, 4-lobed; in oblong,
terminal spike of whorls, clustered above,
separate below; Jul–Oct. Ditches, stream-
banks; escape from cultivation. (T, ex Ic,
FS.) [9]

Water Figwort *Scrophularia auriculata*
SCROPHULARIACEAE H 50–100 cm. Erect
perennial with square, winged stems. Lvs
<12 cm, opposite, ovate, often lobed at
base, bluntly toothed, with winged stalks.
Fls <1 cm, 2-lipped, brownish-purple
above, green below; in much-branched
panicle; Jun–Sep. Frs spherical capsules,
<6 mm. Wet woods, ditches, water-sides.
Br, Ir, Fr, Lu, Be, Ne, Ge. [10]

Monkey-flower *Mimulus guttatus*
SCROPHULARIACEAE H 20–50 cm. Erect or
ascending perennial, glandular-hairy
above, with hollow stems. Lvs <7 cm,
opposite. Fls <4 cm, 2-lipped, lower lip
2-lobed, yellow with small red spots on
throat; solitary in lf-axils; Jul–Sep. Frs
oblong capsules, <2 cm. Stream-banks.
(T, ex Ic, from N America.) [11]

Gratiola *Gratiola officinalis* SCROPHULARI-
ACEAE H 10–50 cm. Erect, hairless
perennial with hollow, 4-angled stems.
Lvs <5 cm, opposite, linear-lanceolate,
toothed, stalkless, half-clasping stem. Fls
<18 mm, white, veined and tinged
purple, 2-lipped, upper lip 2-lobed, lower
3-lobed; solitary in lf-axils; May–Oct.
Wet meadows, water-sides. Fr, Be, Ne,
Ge, Cz, Po. [12]

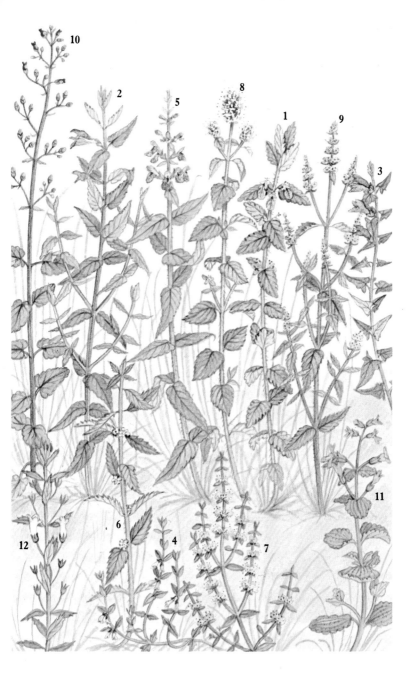

Mudwort *Limosella aquatica* SCROPH-
ULARIACEAE H 5–15 mm. Rosette-forming
annual. Lvs <15 mm, elliptical, long-
stalked; lower lvs very narrow. Fls
<5 mm, white, of 5 joined petals;
solitary in lf-axils; Jun–Oct. Frs oval
capsules, <5 mm. Bare mud. T. [1]

Brooklime *Veronica beccabunga* SCROPH-
ULARIACEAE H 20–60 cm. Creeping and
ascending perennial. Lvs <6 cm, opposite,
toothed, short-stalked. Fls <8 mm, blue,
of 4 joined petals; in lf-axils; May–Sep.
Frs rounded capsules, <3 mm. Streams,
ponds, marshes. T, ex Ic. [2]

Blue Water-speedwell *Veronica
anagallis-aquatica* SCROPHULARIACEAE
H 30–60 cm. Ascending perennial. Lvs
<12 cm, opposite, ovate-lanceolate,
sparsely toothed, half-clasping stem. Fls
<6 mm, blue, of 4 joined petals; in lf-
axils; Jun–Aug. Frs rounded capsules,
<4 mm, on stalks at acute angle to stem.
Ponds, stream-sides, muddy marshes. T.
[3] Pink water-speedwell *V. catenata*
similar but with pink fls and stems tinged
purple. Frs on stalks at right angle to
stem. T, ex Ic, Fi, No. [4]

Marsh Speedwell *Veronica scutellata*
SCROPHULARIACEAE H 10–50 cm.
Ascending perennial. Lvs <4 cm,
opposite, linear-lanceolate, sparsely
toothed, half-clasping stem. Fls <7 mm,
of 4 joined petals, white or pale blue;
Jun–Aug. Frs flattened, kidney-shaped
capsules, <5 mm. Bogs, marshes, water-
sides. T. [5]

Moor King *Pedicularis sceptum-
carolinum* SCROPHULARIACEAE H 15–80 cm.
Reddish, rosette-forming perennial. Basal
lvs <20 cm, lanceolate, deeply divided
into ovate, blunt-toothed segments; stem
lvs few. Fls <32 mm, pale yellow, 2-
lipped, lower lip 3-lobed with red margin;
in loose spike; Jul–Aug. Damp meadows,
wet woods. De, Ge, Cz, Po, FS. [6]

Marsh Lousewort *Pedicularis palustris*
SCROPHULARIACEAE H 5–70 cm. Perennial
or biennial, branching from below. Lvs
<4 cm, opposite or alternate, divided into

toothed, oblong segments. Fls <25 mm,
purplish-pink, 2-lipped, upper lip with 4
teeth; calyx hairy, inflated in fr; May–
Sep. Frs ovoid capsules, <15 mm.
Marshes, wet heaths. T, ex Ic. [7]

Alpine Butterwort *Pinguicula alpina*
LENTIBULARIACEAE H 5–11 cm.
Insectivorous, rosette-forming perennial.
Lvs <4 cm, elliptical, pale yellowish-
green, with margins inrolled and digestive
glands above. Fls <16 mm, 2-lipped,
white spotted yellow, with curved spur
<3 mm; Jun–Aug. Frs ovoid capsules.
Damp mountain meadows. Fr, Ge, Cz,
Po, FS. [8]

Common Butterwort *Pinguicula
vulgaris* LENTIBULARIACEAE H 5–18 cm.
Similar to *P. alpina*, but lvs <8 cm, ovate,
bright yellowish-green. Fls violet with
white patch on throat, and with straight
spur <7 mm; May–Jul. Bogs, wet
heaths, wet rocks. T, ex Lu. [9]

Greater Bladderwort *Utricularia
vulgaris* LENTIBULARIACEAE H <1 m.
Submerged, carnivorous perennial,
lacking roots. Lvs <25 mm, of toothed,
thread-like segments bearing green air-
bladders <3 mm, which trap small
aquatic animals. Fls <18 mm, bright
yellow, 2-lipped, with conical spur
<7 mm; Jul–Aug. Frs spherical capsules,
<5 mm. Still water. T, ex Ic. [10]

Intermediate Bladderwort *Utricularia
intermedia* LENTIBULARIACEAE H <25 cm.
Submerged, carnivorous perennial. Lvs
<15 mm, palmately lobed into linear,
toothed segments, with 1–2 bristles on
teeth, bladders <4 mm. Fls <15 mm,
yellow, with conical spur <6 mm; in
small clusters above water; Jul–Sep. Fls
and frs rare. Shallow, peaty water. T, ex
Lu. [11]

Lesser Bladderwort *Utricularia minor*
LENTIBULARIACEAE H <25 cm. Similar to
U. intermedia but very slender. Lvs
<6 mm, lacking teeth and bristles,
bladders <2 mm. Fls <8 mm, yellow,
spur very short, blunt; Jun–Sep. Shallow,
peaty water. T. [12]

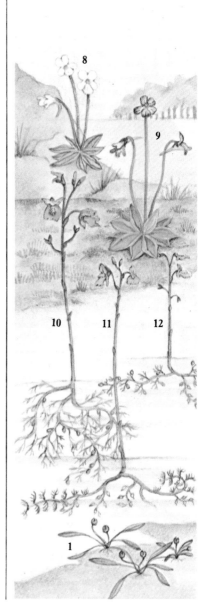

Shoreweed *Littorella uniflora* PLANTAGIN-ACEAE H <10 cm. Creeping, aquatic perennial. Lvs <10 cm, cylindrical, pointed, all in basal rosettes. Fls <5 mm, usually of 4 perianth segments; ♂ and ♀ fls separate, on stalks shorter than lvs; Jun–Aug, but only flowers if plant exposed. Sandy or gravelly shores of non-calcareous lakes. T, ex Lu. [1]

Common Valerian *Valeriana officinalis* VALERIANACEAE H 20–150 cm. Perennial. Lvs <20 cm, opposite, divided into lanceolate, sparsely toothed segments. Fls <5 mm, funnel-shaped, of 5 joined petals; in compact, terminal clusters; Jun–Aug. Frs one seeded, <4 mm, with feathery extension. Damp, grassy places. T. [2]

Marsh Valerian *Valeriana dioica* VALERIANACEAE H 15–30 cm. Bright green perennial with long runners. Lvs <10 cm; basal lvs long-stalked; upper lvs once-divided, stalkless. Fls funnel-shaped, of 5 joined petals, ♂ and ♀ fls on separate plants, ♂ <5 mm, ♀ <2 mm; May–Jun. Frs one-seeded, <3 mm. Marshy meadows, fens, bogs. T, ex Ir, Ic, Fr. [3]

Small Teasel *Dipsacus pilosus* DIPSAC-ACEAE H 30–120 cm. Prickly, rosette-forming biennial with furrowed stems. Lvs <30 cm; basal lvs ovate, narrow, long-stalked, bluntly toothed, with weak spines on midrib below; upper lvs opposite, short-stalked. Fls <9 mm, of 4 joined, unequal petals; in spherical heads; Aug–Sep. Damp ditches, margins of wet woods. T, ex Ir, Ic, FS. [4]

Devil's-bit Scabious *Succisa pratensis* DIPSACACEAE H 15–100 cm. Rosette-forming perennial. Lvs <30 cm; basal lvs ovate-elliptical, short-stalked; upper lvs opposite, narrow, sparsely toothed. Fls <7 mm, of 4 joined, equal petals; in hemispherical heads <25 mm, of either ♂ or ♀ fls, rarely mixed; Jun–Oct. Marshes, woods. T. [5]

Water Lobelia *Lobelia dortmanna* CAMPANULACEAE H 20–60 cm. Rosette-forming perennial with slender, smooth, hollow stems. Lvs <4 cm, linear, blunt,

usually submerged. Fls <2 cm, 2-lipped, upper lip 2-lobed, lower lip 3-lobed; nodding, in loose, terminal clusters; Jul–Aug. Frs nodding capsules. Still, slightly acid water. T, ex Ic, Lu, Cz. [6]

Hemp-agrimony *Eupatorium cannabinum* COMPOSITAE H 30–150 cm. Hairy perennial. Most lvs opposite, divided into 3–5 ovate-lanceolate, toothed, short-stalked segments, <10 cm. Fl-heads <5 mm, reddish-purple or whitish; in dense, terminal clusters; Jun–Sep. Marshes, water-sides, damp sea-cliffs. T, ex Ic. [7]

Marsh Cudweed *Gnaphalium uliginosum* COMPOSITAE H 5–20 cm. Hairy annual with trailing or ascending stems, much branched from base. Lvs <5 cm, narrowly oblong, woolly on both sides. Fl-heads brownish, <4 mm; in dense, terminal clusters of 3–10; Jul–Aug. Open, often animal-trodden places, soils with alternate wetting and drying. T. [8]

Willow-leaved Fleabane *Inula salicina* COMPOSITAE H 25–75 cm. Almost hairless, lfy perennial, with slender rhizomes. Lvs <7 cm; upper elliptical, half-clasping stem. Fl-heads <3 cm, golden-yellow, with numerous ray-florets; solitary or in small clusters; Jul–Aug. Marshes, damp rocks, woods. T, ex Br, Ic. [9]

Meadow Fleabane *Inula britannica* COMPOSITAE H 20–75 cm. Usually densely hairy biennial. Lvs <15 cm, elliptical; upper stalkless, slightly clasping stem. Fl-heads <4 cm, golden-yellow, with numerous ray-florets; usually solitary, rarely 2–3 together; Jul–Aug. Wet meadows, woods, water-sides. T, ex Br, Ir, Ic, (but Fi).

Common Fleabane *Pulicaria dysenterica* COMPOSITAE H 20–60 cm. Hairy perennial. Lvs <8 cm, oblong-lanceolate; upper stalkless, clasping stem, distantly toothed, densely hairy beneath. Fl-heads <3 cm, golden-yellow, with numerous ray-florets; in almost flat-topped clusters; Aug–Sep. Marshes, wet meadows, water-sides. T, ex Ic, FS.

Nodding Bur-marigold *Bidens cernua*
COMPOSITAE H 10–90 cm. Annual,
branched above. Lvs <15 cm, opposite,
lanceolate, coarsely toothed, stalkless. Fl-
heads <25 mm, yellow, usually lacking
ray-florets; solitary, drooping; Jul–Sep.
Marshes, water-sides. T, ex Ic. [1]

Trifid Bur-marigold *Bidens tripartita*
COMPOSITAE H 15–60 cm. Much-branched
annual. Lvs <15 cm, opposite, usually
divided into 3 coarsely toothed segments,
stalks winged. Fl-heads <25 mm, yellow,
usually without ray-florets; solitary,
almost erect; Jul–Sep. Frs develop 2
barbed bristles. Ditches, ponds, lake-
margins. T, ex Ic. [2]

Sneezewort *Achillea ptarmica* COMPOSITAE
H 50–150 cm. Perennial with irregular,
branched stems, hairy above. Lvs <8 cm,
linear-lanceolate, finely toothed, stalkless.
Fl-heads <18 mm, with 8–13 white ray-
florets; Jul–Aug. Marshes, damp
meadows, water-sides. T, (but Ic). [3]

Butterbur *Petasites hybridus* COMPOSITAE
H 10–150 cm. Perennial with stout
rhizomes. Lvs <90 cm across, roundish,
greyish-woolly beneath at maturity. Fls in
separate ♂ and ♀ spikes, of pale reddish
or yellowish fl-heads; stalks of ♂ with *c*
20 scale lvs, of ♀ with <40; before lvs,
Mar–May. Water-sides, wet meadows,
woods. T, ex Ic, (but De, FS). [4]

Marsh Ragwort *Senecio aquaticus*
COMPOSITAE H 25–80 cm. Biennial with
ascending branches. Basal lvs elliptical,
often undivided, long-stalked; upper lvs
divided, half-clasping stem. Fl-heads
<3 cm, with 12–15 golden-yellow ray-
florets; Jul–Aug. Marshes, wet meadows,
water-sides. T, ex Ic, Fi. [5]

Fen Ragwort *Senecio paludosus*
COMPOSITAE H 80–200 cm. Cottony
perennial, branching above. Lvs <20 cm,
linear-lanceolate, short-stalked; upper
smaller, half-clasping stem. Fl-heads
<4 cm, with 10–14 yellow ray-florets;
in flat-topped clusters; May–Sep.
Marshes, fens, water-sides. Br, Fr, Be,
Ne, Ge, Cz, Po, Sw. [6]

Marsh Fleawort *Senecio palustris*
COMPOSITAE 30–100 cm. Stout, woolly
biennial or perennial; stems furrowed,
very lfy. Lvs <12 cm, broadly lanceolate;
stem lvs pale yellowish-green, half-
clasping stem. Fl-heads <3 cm, with
<20 sulphur-yellow ray-florets; in dense
clusters; Jun–Jul. Marshes, damp
meadows, water-sides. Fr, Be, Ne, De,
Ge, Cz, Po, SC. [7]

Greater Burdock *Arctium lappa*
COMPOSITAE H 90–150 cm. Hairy biennial
with much-branched stems. Lvs <50 cm,
broadly ovate, heart-shaped at base, with
solid stalks. Fl-heads ovoid, <4 cm, of
reddish-purple florets surrounded by
shiny, golden-green, hooked bracts; Jul–
Sep. Open places, river-banks. T, ex Ic.
[8]

Cabbage Thistle *Cirsium oleraceum*
COMPOSITAE H 50–120 cm. Sparsely hairy
perennial; stems furrowed, unwinged.
Lvs <30 cm, elliptical-lanceolate; lower
stalked, divided into triangular lobes. Fl-
heads <4 cm, of pale yellow florets; in
terminal clusters surrounded by 2–10
pale yellow, bract-like upper lvs; Jul–
Sep. Damp meadows, woods. T, ex Ic,
(but Br, Ir, Fi). [9]

Marsh Thistle *Cirsium palustre*
COMPOSITAE H 50–120 cm. Hairy biennial
with short, erect branches; stems furrowed,
spiny-winged. Lvs <30 cm, oblanceolate
in outline, divided into shallow, spined
lobes. Fl-heads <2 cm, dark red-purple,
rarely white; in crowded, lfy clusters at
branch ends; Jul–Sep. Marshes, damp
meadows, woods. T, ex Ic. [10]

Meadow Thistle *Cirsium dissectum*
COMPOSITAE H 18–50 cm. Cottony
perennial; stems ascending, unbranched,
unwinged. Lvs <25 cm, whitish below,
margins prickly; lower elliptical in outline,
lobed, stalked; upper hardly lobed,
stalkless. Fl-heads <3 cm, dark red-
purple; solitary; Jun–Aug. Wet, peaty
meadows. Br, Ir, Fr, Be, Ne, Ge, (No).
[11]

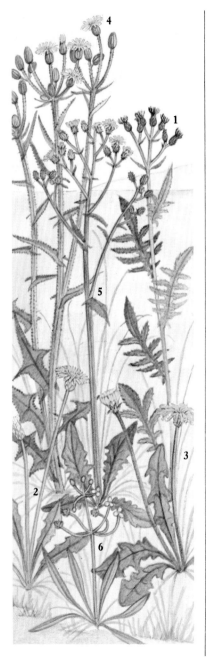

Saw-wort *Serratula tinctoria* COMPOSITAE H 30–90 cm. Perennial with branched, wiry, grooved stems. Lvs <25 cm, ovate-lanceolate, from undivided to pinnate, margins with bristly teeth. Fl-heads <2 cm, reddish-purple, ♀ heads larger than ♂; in loose, terminal clusters; Jul–Sep. Damp woods, calcareous grassland. T, ex Ic, Fi. [1]

Narrow-leaved Marsh-dandelion *Taraxacum palustre* COMPOSITAE H 5–20 cm. Rosette-forming perennial. Lvs <20 cm, linear-lanceolate, undivided or lobed, with long, often purplish stalks. Fl heads <4 cm across, pale yellow, with appressed bracts; solitary, terminal on hairless, lflless stalks; Apr–Jun. Marshes, meadows, stream-sides. T, ex Ic. [2] Broad-leaved marsh-dandelion *T. spectabr* similar but with larger, broader lvs; stalks almost always reddish-purple. Fl-heads bright yellow, with spreading bracts; Apr–Aug. Br, Ir, Ic, De, SC. [3]

Marsh Sow-thistle *Sonchus palustris* COMPOSITAE H 100–250 cm. Perennial with hollow, angled stem, glandular-hairy above. Lvs deeply divided into segments with spine-tipped teeth; upper stalkless, clasping stem. Fl-heads <4 cm, pale yellow, covered in blackish-green, glandular hairs; Jul–Sep. Marshes, water-sides. T, ex Ir, Ic, Lu, Fi. [4]

Marsh Hawk's-beard *Crepis paludosa* COMPOSITAE H 25–100 cm. Hairless perennial; stem furrowed, branched abov Lvs <28 cm, toothed; lower oblanceolate narrowed into winged stalks; upper linear clasping stem. Fl-heads <25 mm, yellow, covered with black, glandular hairs; Jul–Sep. Wet meadows, damp woods, stream-sides. T. [5]

Lesser Water-plantain *Baldellia ranunculoides* ALISMATACEAE H 5–20 cm. Rosette-forming perennial. Lvs <4 cm, linear-lanceolate, narrowed into long stalks. Fls <15 mm, petals pale pink with basal yellow blotch; long-stalked, in terminal whorls of 6–10 fls; May–Aug. Frs in spherical heads. Wet ditches, marshes. T, ex Ic, Lu, Cz. [6]

Floating Water-plantain *Luronium natans* ALISMATACEAE H <50 cm. Slender perennial with floating stems rooted at base. Lvs <10 cm, long-stalked; lower linear, submerged; upper ovate-elliptical, floating. Fls <15 mm, petals white with yellow spot; usually solitary in axils, long-stalked; Jul–Aug. Frs in hemispherical heads. Slow-moving, slightly acid water. Br, Fr, Be, Ne, De, Ge, Po, SC. [7]

Water-plantain *Alisma plantago-aquatica* ALISMATACEAE H 20–100 cm. Perennial; stem stout, branched above. Lvs <20 cm, ovate, heart-shaped at base, long-stalked. Fls <1 cm, open in afternoon; in much-branched whorls; Jun–Aug. Frs with style arising below middle; *c*20 in flat head. On mud, in or beside still water. T, ex Ic. [8] Narrow-leaved water-plantain *A. lanceolatum* similar but lvs lanceolate, narrowed gradually into stalk. Fls open in morning. Frs with style arising near top. T, ex Ic, No. [9]

Arrowhead *Sagittaria sagittifolia* ALISMATACEAE H 30–90 cm. Perennial. Lvs <20 cm; submerged lvs linear, translucent; floating lvs lanceolate-ovate; aerial lvs arrow-shaped, long-stalked. Fls <3 cm, petals white, crimson at base; in much-branched whorl, upper fls ♂, lower, short-stalked, ♀; Jul–Aug. Frs hemispherical heads, <15 mm. Still and slow-moving water. T, ex Ic. [10]

Flowering-rush *Butomus umbellatus* BUTOMACEAE H 50–150 cm. Rosette-forming perennial. Lvs rush-like, with thick midrib; as long as stem and sheathing it at base. Fls <3 cm, of 6 pink petals with darker veins; in irregular umbel; Jul–Sep. Frs clusters of 6–9 capsules. Water-sides. T, ex Ic. [11]

Water-soldier *Stratiotes aloides* HYDRO-CHARITACEAE H 15–50 cm. Submerged aquatic rising to surface at flowering. Lvs < 50 cm, rigid, brittle, sharply-toothed, in pineapple-like rosettes. Fls <4 cm, white; ♂ fls in clusters, ♀ solitary; Jun–Aug. Still, lime-rich waters. Br, Fr, Be, Ne, Ge, Cz, Po, (Ir, De, Fi, Sw). [12]

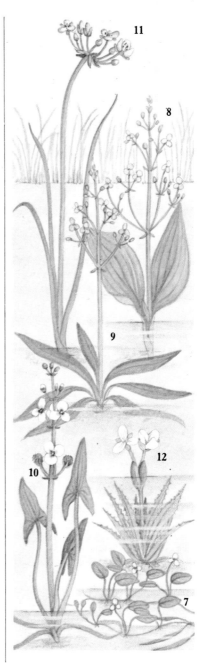

Frog-bit *Hydrocharis morsus-ranae*
HYDROCHARITACEAE Floating perennial.
Lvs <3 cm across, kidney-shaped, long-
stalked. Fls <2 cm, petals white with
yellow spot near base; ♂ fls in clusters,
♀ solitary; Jul–Aug. Frs fleshy capsules,
rare in north. Still, lime-rich water. T,
ex Ic, Lu, (but Be). [1]

Canadian Waterweed *Elodea canadensis*
HYDROCHARITACEAE H <3 m. Submerged
perennial spreading vegetatively. Lvs
<1 cm, oblong-lanceolate, blunt, finely
toothed, in whorls of 3–4. Fls <5 mm;
floating, on long, slender stalks, <30 cm,
♂ and ♀ fls separate, ♂ fls rare; May–
Oct. Still and flowing waters. (T, ex Ic,
from N America.) [2]

Marsh Arrowgrass *Triglochin palustris*
JUNCAGINACEAE H 15–30 cm. Perennial.
Lvs semi-cylindrical, furrowed near base
on upper surface. Fls <4 mm, of 6 purple-
edged, greenish segments; in slender
spikes; Jun–Aug. Frs oblong, flattened to
stem. Marshes. T. [3]

Broad-leaved Pondweed *Potamogeton*
natans POTAMOGETONACEAE H 50–500 cm.
Aquatic perennial. Submerged lvs
<30 cm, linear, channelled; floating lvs
<12·5 cm, elliptical, shining, leathery.
Fls green, in dense spikes <8 cm; above
water on stalks little longer than spikes;
May–Sep. Still and slow-moving water.
T. [4] Bog pondweed *P. polygonifolius*
similar but smaller and all lvs distinctly
stalked. Fls in spikes <4 cm; on stalks
much longer than spike. Bogs, slightly
acid streams. T, ex Ic. [5]

Red Pondweed *Potamogeton alpinus*
POTAMOGETONACEAE H 15–200 cm.
Aquatic perennial. Submerged lvs
<15 cm, reddish, narrowly elliptical,
blunt, translucent; floating lvs <8 cm,
oblanceolate, blunt, transverse veins
visible against light. Fls in spikes <4 cm;
on stalks not thickened in fr; Jun–Sep.
Still and slow-moving water. T. [6]

Shining Pondweed *Potamogeton lucens*
POTAMOGETONACEAE H 1–3 m. Aquatic
perennial. Lvs all submerged, <20 cm,

oblong-lanceolate, margins minutely
toothed, short-stalked. Fls in spikes
<6 cm; on stalks <25 cm, thickening
upwards in fr; Jun–Sep. Still and slow-
moving water. T, ex Ic. [7]

Perfoliate Pondweed *Potamogeton*
perfoliatus POTAMOGETONACEAE H 50–
200 cm. Aquatic perennial. Lvs all
submerged, <6 cm, usually ovate, with
heart-shaped base, blunt, translucent,
margins minutely toothed, clasping stem.
Fls in spikes <3 cm; on stalks, <10 cm,
not thickened upwards in fr; Jun–Sep.
Still and flowing waters. T. [8]

Curled Pondweed *Potamogeton crispus*
POTAMOGETONACEAE H 30–120 cm.
Aquatic perennial with 4-angled stems.
Lvs all submerged, <9 cm, linear-
lanceolate, blunt, toothed, with wavy
margins, stalkless. Fls in spikes, <2 cm;
on slender, curved stalks <7 cm,
narrowing upwards in fr; May–Oct. Still
and flowing waters. T, ex Ic. [9]

Various-leaved Pondweed *Potamogeton*
gramineus POTAMOGETONACEAE H 50–
100 cm. Aquatic perennial. Submerged
lvs <8 cm, linear-lanceolate, margins
minutely toothed; floating lvs few, <7 cm,
elliptical, long-stalked. Fls in spikes
<5 cm; on stout stalks <8 cm, thickened
upwards in fr; Jun–Sep. Still and slow-
moving water. T, ex Lu. [10]

Grass-wrack Pondweed *Potamogeton*
compressus POTAMOGETONACEAE H 50–
200 cm. Aquatic perennial with flattened,
winged stems. Lvs all submerged,
<20 cm, linear, rounded at tip, with 5
longitudinal veins. Fls in spikes, <3 cm;
on stout, flattened stalks, <6 cm, not
thickened upwards in fr; Jun–Sep. Still
and slow-moving water. T, ex Ic, Lu. [11]

Opposite-leaved Pondweed *Groenlandia*
densa POTAMOGETONACEAE H 10–30 cm.
Aquatic perennial. Lvs all submerged,
<25 mm, opposite, overlapping, minutely
toothed, clasping stem. Fls in spikes of
4 fls; on slender stalks, shorter than lvs,
<15 mm, curved in fr; May–Sep. Clear
water. T, ex Ic, Lu, FS. [12]

Bog Asphodel *Narthecium ossifragum*
LILIACEAE H 5–40 cm. Perennial with
extensive, creeping rhizomes. Basal lvs
<30 cm, spear-shaped, curved, with blade
vertical; stem lvs few, smaller. Fls <2 cm,
petals yellow, green on back; in dense,
terminal spike; Jul–Sep. Frs narrow, 6-
grooved capsules, <12 mm. Bogs, wet
heaths. Br, Ir, Fr, Be, Ne, De, Ge, SC.
[1]

Yellow Iris *Iris pseudacorus* IRIDACEAE
H 40–150 cm. Perennial with rhizome
< 4 cm across. Lvs <150 cm long, narrow,
pale green; all lvs in one plane. Fls
<10 cm, pale yellow-orange; 2–3 fls at
top of flattened, lfless stalk; May–Jul.
Frs elliptical capsules, <7 cm. Marshes,
wet woods, water-sides. T, ex Ic. [2]

Toad Rush *Juncus bufonius* JUNCACEAE
H 3–25 cm. Slender annual, very variable
in size, usually much-branched from base.
Lvs <5 cm, narrow, finely pointed,
deeply channelled. Fls <12 mm, of 6
narrow, pale green, finely pointed
segments; solitary, usually stalkless, in
much-branched, lfy panicle; May–Sep.
Frs blunt, oblong capsules, <6 mm.
Damp, open habitats. T, ex Lu. [3]

Hard Rush *Juncus inflexus* JUNCACEAE
H 50–90 cm. Densely tufted perennial;
stems slender, stiffly erect, with 12–18
prominent ridges, lfless, hairless, grey-
green, shining dark brown or blackish at
base. Fls <4 mm, of 6 greenish perianth
segments; in loose clusters on side of
stem below top; Jun–Aug. Damp, usually
calcareous, pastures. T, ex Ic, No. [4]

Soft Rush *Juncus effusus* JUNCACEAE
H 30–150 cm. Densely tufted perennial;
stems stiffly erect, lfless, hairless, smooth,
glossy, bright green, dark brown or
reddish, but not shining, at base. Fls
<5 mm, of 6 greenish perianth segments;
in loose or compact clusters, on sides of
stems below top; Jun–Aug. Damp,
frequently acid, pastures, marshes, woods.
T, ex Ic. [5]

Compact Rush *Juncus conglomeratus*
JUNCACEAE H 30–120 cm. Similar to
J. effusus, but less robust; stems greyish-
green, not glossy, with numerous ridges
below inflor, slightly blunt above. Fls
usually in compact clusters, with stem
broadened out behind (narrower in
J. effusus). Damp, acid pastures, marshes,
bogs. T, ex Ic. [6]

Thread Rush *Juncus filiformis* JUNCACEAE
H 15–30 cm. Slender, wiry perennial, not
forming tufts; stems green, stiffly erect,
faintly ridged, brownish at base. Fls
<6 mm, becoming straw-coloured; in
compact, few-fld heads, ½-way down stem
Jun–Sep. Frs almost spherical capsules.
Shores of stony lakes, reservoirs. T, ex
Ir, Lu. [7]

Sharp-flowered Rush *Juncus acutiflorus*
JUNCACEAE H 30–100 cm. Stiffly erect
perennial with stout, far-creeping
rhizomes. Lvs deep green, narrow,
roundish, hollow, with 18–25 conspicuous,
transverse partitions inside. Fls <6 mm,
of 6 chestnut-brown segments, with awn-
like points; in much-branched inflor; Jul–
Sep. Marshes, wet meadows, woods. T,
ex Ic, Fi, Sw. [8]

Bulbous Rush *Juncus bulbosus* JUNCACEAE
H 3–15 cm. Slender perennial with stems
slightly swollen at base; erect and tufted,
procumbent and rooting at nodes, or
floating with much-branched stems. Lvs
<10 cm, thread-like, finely pointed. Fls
<4 mm, of 6 brownish-red segments;
in 2–6 fld heads; Jun–Sep. Wet heaths,
bogs. T. [9]

Jointed Rush *Juncus articulatus* JUNCACEAE
H 20–80 cm. Prostrate or ascending
perennial with slender, knotted rhizome.
Lvs deep green, narrow, laterally
compressed, hollow, with 18–25
inconspicuous, transverse partitions inside.
Fls <3 mm, of 6 dark chestnut-brown
segments, with acute points; in much-
branched inflor; Jun–Sep. Marshes, wet
meadows. T. [10]

Heath Wood-rush *Luzula multiflora*
JUNCACEAE H 20–50 cm. Densely tufted
perennial. Lvs <15 cm, bright green,
with sparse, long, white hairs. Fls
<6 mm, of 6 chestnut-brown segments
with transparent margins; in 8–16 fld
clusters, in much-branched panicle; Apr–
Jun. Frs spherical capsules with oblong
seeds. Wet heaths, bogs. T. [1]

Common Reed *Phragmites australis*
GRAMINEAE H 1·5–3 m. Stout, erect,
perennial grass with extensive, creeping
rhizomes, growing in dense clumps. Lvs
<60 cm long, <2 cm wide, tapering to
fine point, greyish-green, with ring of
hairs at base. Fls awnless, in 2–6 fld
spikelets, <16 mm; in loose, silkily
hairy panicles, <40 cm; Aug–Sep.
Swamps, shallow water. T, ex Ic. [2]

Whorl-grass *Catabrosa aquatica*
GRAMINEAE H 10–60 cm. Creeping
perennial grass, rooting at nodes, with
hairless, ascending stems. Lvs <14 cm
long, <1 cm wide, tapering to hooded
point, bright green. Fls <4 mm, awnless,
in 1–3 fld spikelets, <5 mm; in loose
panicles, ovate in outline, <30 cm; May–
Jul. In or beside shallow water. T. [3]

Floating Sweet-grass *Glyceria fluitans*
GRAMINEAE H 25–100 cm. Creeping
perennial grass, rooting at nodes, with
ascending stems. Lvs <25 cm long, <1 cm
wide, tapering to pointed tip. Fls
<8 mm, awnless, in 8–16 fld spikelets,
<35 mm; in loose, nodding, little-branched
panicles, <50 cm; May–Aug. Marshes,
in or beside shallow water. T. [4]

Reed Sweet-grass *Glyceria maxima*
GRAMINEAE H 60–200 cm. Stout, erect,
hairless, perennial grass, spreading by
rhizomes to form large patches. Lvs
<60 cm long, <2 cm wide, bright green,
abruptly pointed. Fls <4 mm, awnless, in
4–10 fld spikelets, <12 mm; in many-
branched, clustered panicles, <45 cm;
Jun–Aug. Margins of still and slow-
moving water. T, ex Ic. [5]

Tufted Hair-grass *Deschampsia cespitosa*
GRAMINEAE H 20–200 cm. Tussock-
forming, perennial grass. Lvs <60 cm
long, <5 mm wide, extremely rough
above, tapering to point. Fls <4 mm,
awned, in 2-fld spikelets, <6 mm; in
much-branched, silvery, erect or nodding
panicles, <5 cm; Jun–Aug. Wet meadows,
marshes. T. [6]

Wood Small-reed *Calamagrostis epigejos*
GRAMINEAE H 60–200 cm. Erect, perennial
grass. Lvs <70 cm long, <1 cm wide,
rough, tapering to fine point. Fls <2 mm,
shortly-awned, surrounded by fine, white
hairs, in 1-fld spikelets, <7 mm; in much-
branched, erect panicles, <30 cm; Jun–
Jul. Damp woods, ditches, marshes. T,
ex Ic. [7]

Marsh Foxtail *Alopecurus geniculatus*
GRAMINEAE H 15–45 cm. Creeping
perennial grass with ascending stems. Lvs
<12 cm long, <7 mm wide, tapering to
tip. Fls awned, <3 mm, with purple
anthers, in flattened, 1-fld spikelets,
<4 mm; in dense, narrow, cylindrical
panicles, <7 cm long; Jun–Aug. Wet
meadows, ditches. T. [8]

Reed Canary-grass *Phalaris arundinacea*
GRAMINEAE H 60–200 cm. Stout, erect,
perennial grass with far-creeping
rhizomes. Lvs <35 cm long, <4 cm wide,
tapering to fine point. Fls <4 mm, awnless,
in flattened, 1-fld spikelets, <7 mm; in
dense, oblong panicles, <25 cm long;
Jun–Aug. Marshes, water-sides. T, ex Ic,
Lu. [9]

Cut-grass *Leersia oryzoides* GRAMINEAE
H 30–120 cm. Erect or ascending,
perennial grass with slender rhizomes
and stems hairy on nodes. Lvs <30 cm
long, <1 cm wide, tapering to point,
yellowish-green. Fls awnless, <4 mm, in
flattened, 1-fld spikelets, <5 mm; in
loose panicle, <22 cm long, with
spreading branches; Aug–Oct. Wet
meadows, ditches. T, ex Ir, Ic, No. [10]

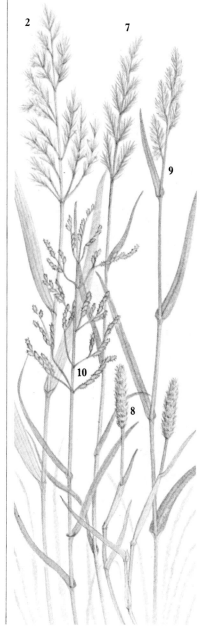

Brown Galingale *Cyperus fuscus*
CYPERACEAE H 5–20 cm. Annual with
triangular stems. Lvs <3 mm wide,
shorter than stems. Fls <1 mm, dark
brown; in dense umbel of 3–7 rays, with
long, lf-like bracts; Jul–Sep. Drying-up
ponds. T, ex Ir, Ic, Fi, No. [1]

Common Cottongrass *Eriophorum
angustifolium* CYPERACEAE H 20–60 cm.
Erect perennial with stems rounded at
top. Lvs <6 mm wide, channelled,
tapering to long, triangular point. Fls in
2–7 nodding heads; producing tufts of
white, silky hairs in fr; Apr–Jul. Bogs,
marshes. T. [2]

Slender Cottongrass *Eriophorum gracile*
CYPERACEAE H 20–50 cm. Similar to *E.
angustifolium*, but more slender and with
stems triangular at top. Lvs <2 mm wide.
Fls in 3–5 heads; Jun–Jul. Wet, acid bogs.
T, ex Ic, Lu. [3]

Floating Club-rush *Scirpus fluitans*
CYPERACEAE Slender, floating, yellowish-
green perennial with flattened, much-
branched stems. Lvs <5 cm long,
<1 mm wide. Fls in solitary, 3–5 fld
spikes, <3 mm; Jun–Sep. Peaty ditches,
ponds, streams. Br, Fr, Be, Ne, De, Ge,
Cz, Po, SC.

Bristle Club-rush *Scirpus setaceus*
CYPERACEAE H 3–15 cm. Slender,
densely-tufted, bright green annual.
Lvs shorter than stems. Fls in 2–4 dark
brown, ovoid spikelets, <5 mm; on
thread-like stems with lf-like bract; Jun–
Sep. Bare, damp sand or mud. T, ex Fi.
[4]

Common Club-rush *Scirpus lacustris*
CYPERACEAE H 1–3 m. Stout perennial
forming large clumps; stems rounded,
<15 mm across. Fls in clusters of reddish-
brown spikelets, <1 cm long, on one side
of stem near top; Jun–Jul. In stagnant and
slow-moving water. T, ex Ic. [5]

Flat-sedge *Blysmus compressus* CYPERACEAE
H 10–35 cm. Perennial with far-creeping

rhizomes. Lvs flat, <2 mm wide, tapering,
with rough margins. Fls in 10–12 reddish-
brown spikelets, <7 mm, in 2 ranks;
Jun–Aug. Wet meadows, marshes. T,
ex Ir, Ic, Lu. [6]

Common Spike-rush *Eleocharis palustris*
CYPERACEAE H 10–60 cm. Perennial with
far-creeping rhizomes. Stems cylindrical,
lfless, <4 mm thick, reddish at base.
Fls in terminal spikelet, <2 cm long;
May–Jul. Marshes, water-sides. T. [7]
Few-flowered spike-rush *E. quinqueflora*
similar, but smaller, H 5–30 cm, and
tufted, with short rhizome. Damp, peaty
places. T.

Black Bog-rush *Schoenus nigricans*
CYPERACEAE H 15–75 cm. Tufted, wiry-
stemmed perennial. Lvs <½ as long as
stem, almost cylindrical, with red-brown,
basal sheaths. Fls in 1–4 fld spikelets; in
black, terminal heads, with basal, lf-like
bract; May–Jun. Fens, bogs. T, ex Ic,
Lu, No. [8]

White Beak-sedge *Rhynchospora alba*
CYPERACEAE H 10–50 cm. Slender, tufted
perennial; stems cylindrical below,
triangular above. Lvs as long as stems,
narrow, channelled. Fls in 1–2 fld
spikelets; in whitish, terminal heads,
hardly exceeded by basal, lf-like bracts;
Jul–Aug. Wet peat. T, ex Ic. [9]

Brown Beak-sedge *Rhynchospora fusca*
CYPERACEAE H 10–30 cm. Similar to *R.
alba*, but with far-creeping rhizomes. Lvs
much shorter than stems. Fls in dark
reddish-brown spikelets; basal bracts 2–4
times as long as heads; May–Jun. Wetter
peat than *R. alba*. T, ex Ic, Lu. [10]

Great Fen-sedge *Cladium mariscus*
CYPERACEAE H 1–3 m. Tough, erect
perennial with creeping rhizomes. Lvs
<2 cm wide, with sharp, saw-edged
margins, ending in long, triangular point.
Inflor much-branched, with terminal
clusters of 1–3 fld, reddish-brown
spikelets, <4 mm; Jul–Aug. Fens.
T, ex Ic, Lu. [11]

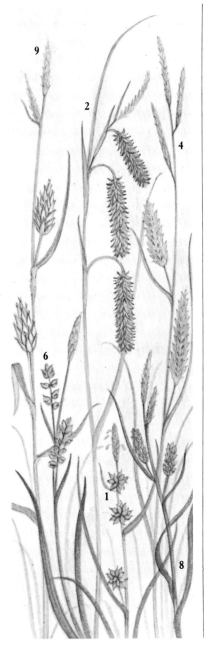

Common Yellow-sedge *Carex demissa*
CYPERACEAE H 5–30 cm. Tufted perennial.
Lvs yellowish-green, <5 mm wide. ♂ and
♀ fls separate; ♂ in one terminal spike,
♀ in 2–4 spikes with prominent bract,
upper spikes close together, lower distant;
Jun–Jul. Damp, slightly acid grassland,
bogs. T. [1]

Cyperus Sedge *Carex pseudocyperus*
CYPERACEAE H 40–90 cm. Tufted perennial;
stem sharply 3-angled. Lvs bright
yellowish-green, <12 mm wide. ♂ and ♀
fls separate; ♂ in one spike, ♀ in 3–5,
clustered, cylindrical, nodding spikes;
May–Jun. Still water-sides. T, ex Ic. [2]

Bladder Sedge *Carex vesicaria* CYPERACEAE
H 30–60 cm. Perennial; stems 3-angled,
rough above. Lvs yellowish-green,
<6 mm wide, longer than stems. ♂ and ♀
fls separate; ♂ in 2–3 spikes, ♀ in 2–3
lower, distant, nodding spikes; Jun–Jul.
Wet peat, water-sides. T, ex Ic. [3]

Bottle Sedge *Carex rostrata* CYPERACEAE
H 20–100 cm. Creeping perennial; stems
erect, 3-angled, rough above. Lvs
<7 mm wide, grey-green. ♂ and ♀ fls
separate; ♂ in 2–4 spikes above, ♀ in 2–5
overlapping spikes below, or lowest
spikes may be distant; June–Jul. Peaty
water-sides. T. [4]

Greater Pond-sedge *Carex riparia*
CYPERACEAE H 60–130 cm. Tufted
perennial; stems rough, sharply 3-angled.
Lvs <2 cm wide, keeled. ♂ and ♀ fls
separate; ♂ in 3–6 clustered spikes, ♀ in
1–5 distant spikes, lower nodding; May–
Jun. Beside still and slow-moving water.
T, ex Ic. [5]

Carnation Sedge *Carex panicea*
CYPERACEAE H 10–60 cm. Perennial;
stems 3-angled. Lvs grey-green, flat,

<5 mm wide, 3-angled at tip. Fls in 2–4 erect spikes, single ♂ spike above; May–Jun. Frs inflated. Wet meadows. T. [6]

Bog Sedge *Carex limosa* CYPERACEAE H 10–40 cm. Creeping perennial; stems slender, rough. Lvs <1·5 mm wide, channelled, with finely toothed margins. ♂ and ♀ fls separate; ♂ in 1 spike, ♀ in 1–3 nodding spikes; May–Jun. Very wet bogs. T, ex Lu. [7]

Glaucous Sedge *Carex flacca* CYPERACEAE H 10–40 cm. Creeping perennial. Lvs flat, <4 mm wide, tapering to fine point, grey-green below, dull green above. ♂ and ♀ fls separate; ♂ in 1–3 spikes above, ♀ in 2 distant spikes, lower often nodding; May–Jun. Marshes, bogs, also dry grassland. T. [8]

Hairy Sedge *Carex hirta* CYPERACEAE H 15–70 cm. Creeping perennial; stems smooth, 3-angled. Lvs <5 mm wide, hairy on both sides. ♂ and ♀ fls separate; ♂ in 2–3 spikes above, ♀ in 2–3 spikes, lowest often near base of stem; May–Jun. Damp meadows, woods. T, ex Ic. [9]

Common Sedge *Carex nigra* CYPERACEAE H 10–70 cm. Far-creeping perennial; stems slender, 3-angled, rough above. Lvs <3 mm wide, longer than stems. ♂ and ♀ fls separate; ♂ in 1–2 spikes above, lower ♂ spike smaller, ♀ in 1–4 erect spikes, often overlapping; May–Jul. Damp grassland. T. [10]

Greater Tussock-sedge *Carex paniculata* CYPERACEAE H 60–150 cm. Forms tussocks <1·5 m high, <1 m across; stems 3-angled, rough. Lvs <7 mm wide, stiff, channelled. Inflor branched, of many, few-fld spikes, ♂ at top; May–Jun. Wet fens, river-sides. T, ex Ic. [11]

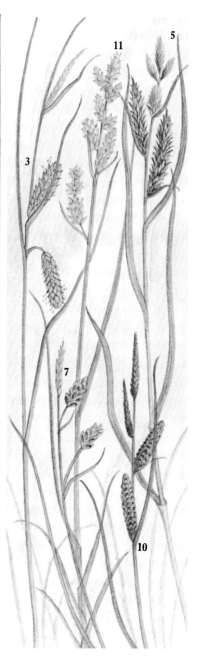

False Fox-sedge *Carex otrubae*
CYPERACEAE H 30–100 cm. Perennial;
stems sharply 3-angled. Fls in clustered,
light brown spikes, ♂ at top; Jun–Jul.
Damp grassland. T, ex Ic. [1]

Star Sedge *Carex echinata* CYPERACEAE
H 10–40 cm. Perennial; stems 3-angled.
Fls in clustered, star-shaped spikes; May–
Jun. Marshes, bogs. T. [2]

Oval Sedge *Carex ovalis* CYPERACEAE
H 20–90 cm. Perennial; stems stiff, curved,
3-angled. Fls in 3–9 clustered, oval spikes;
upper spike ♀ at top, ♂ at base, lower
spikes all ♀; Jun–Jul. Wet meadows, woods.
T, ex Ic. [3]

Flea Sedge *Carex pulicaris* CYPERACEAE
H 10–30 cm. Perennial, forming dense
patches; stems smooth, stiff, slender. Fls
in single, terminal spike, ♂ at top, ♀
below, drooping when frs ripe; May–Jun.
Lime-rich fens, flushes. T. [4]

Sweet-flag *Acorus calamus* ARACEAE
H 50–100 cm. Perennial. Lvs with wavy
margins, sweet-smelling when crushed.
Fls yellowish, in spike-like branch, at 45°
to stem; May–Jul. Water-sides. (T, ex
Ic, from S Asia.) [5]

Bog Arum *Calla paulstris* ARACEAE
H 15–30 cm. Aquatic perennial. Lvs
<10 cm across, heart-shaped, long-
stalked. ♂ and ♀ fls separate, on fleshy
spike (spadix), not enclosed by enlarged
bract (spathe); Jun–Aug. Swamps, lakes.
T, ex Ir, Ic, Lu, (but Br). [6]

Common Duckweed *Lemna minor*
LEMNACEAE Aquatic herb having rounded,
lf-like structures with root below. Fls rare,
tiny, in pocket at margin of 'lvs'; Jun–
Jul. Still water. T, ex Ic. [7] Ivy-leaved
duckweed *L. trisulca* similar but 'lvs'
lanceolate, attached to each other by
short stalks, translucent; root often hooked.
Fls rare; May–Jun. Still water. T, ex
Ic. [8]

Branched Bur-reed *Sparganium erectum*
SPARGANIACEAE H 50–150 cm. Erect,
aquatic perennial. Lvs erect, <15 mm

wide, keeled, triangular in section. ♂ and
♀ fls in separate, spherical heads; in
branched inflor, ♂ above, ♀ below; Jun–
Aug. Water-sides, marshes. T, ex Ic. [9]

Bulrush *Typha latifolia* TYPHACEAE
H 150–250 cm. Stout perennial. Lvs
linear, leathery, <18 mm wide. Fls in
single terminal spike, ♂ above, ♀ below;
Jun–Jul. Margins of ponds, lakes, slow-
moving water. T, ex Ic. [10] Lesser bulrush
T. angustifolia similar but with lvs <5 mm
wide, often twisted. T, ex Ic, Lu. [11]

Early Marsh-orchid *Dactylorhiza
incarnata* ORCHIDACEAE H 5–50 cm.
Yellowish-green perennial. Lower lvs
<20 cm, with hooded tip; upper lvs
bract-like. Fls <1 cm across, flesh-pink,
lower lip with sides turned back, spur
conical, <9 mm; May–Jul. Marshes; also
sand when has magenta fls. T, ex Ic. [12]

Southern Marsh-orchid *Dactylorhiza
praetermissa* ORCHIDACEAE H 15–60 cm.
Dark-green perennial. Lower lvs <20 cm,
with slightly hooded tip. Fls <2 cm
across, reddish-purple, sides of lower lip
not turned back, spur conical, stout, <1
mm; Jun–Aug. Marshes, fens. T. [13]

Common Spotted-orchid *Dactylorhiza
fuchsii* ORCHIDACEAE H 15–50 cm. Perennial
Lower lvs <20 cm, keeled, upper
narrower; all blotched. Fls <15 mm
across, pale pink, lower lip with red lines,
central lobe longest; May–Jul. Wet woods,
meadows. T. [14]

Frog Orchid *Coeloglossum viride*
ORCHIDACEAE H 6–25 cm. Perennial. Lower
lvs <5 cm, upper lvs smaller, acute. Fls
<5 mm across, greenish, spur <2 mm,
translucent; Jun–Aug. Damp grassland.
T. [15]

Fragrant Orchid *Gymnadenia conopsea*
ORCHIDACEAE H 15–40 cm. Perennial.
Lower lvs <15 cm, with blunt, hooded
tip; upper clasping stem. Fls <4 mm
across, reddish-pink, fragrant, spur
<13 mm, very slender, curved below;
Jun–Aug. Fens, marshes; also calcareous
grassland. T, ex Ic. [16]

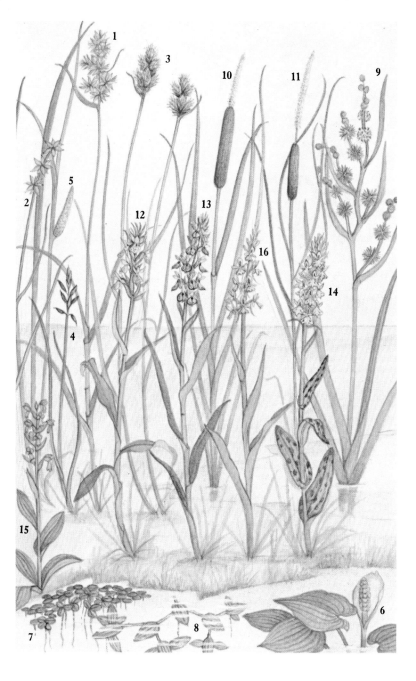

Freshwater snails are mostly herbivorous, rasping vegetation with tongue; mussels filter water for small particles. Some spp hermaphrodite, mating to exchange sperm; in other spp sexes are separate. Most spp lay eggs in batches on stones, vegetation; mussels and river snail brood young within shell. Snail young are miniature adults; mussels have larval stage.

River Snail *Viviparus viviparus*
VIVIPARIDAE SH 30–40 mm, SB 25–30 mm, W 6–7. Shell dextral, with rounded whorls, deep sutures, blunt apex; umbilicus small; operculum oval, rather thick, very glossy. Shell greenish-brown, usually with 3 darker bands; animal mottled. Favours slow-flowing rivers with hard water. T, ex nBr, Ir, Ic, nFS. [1]

Jenkins' Spire Shell *Potamopyrgus jenkinsi* HYDROBIIDAE SH 4·5–5·5 mm, SB 3 mm, W 5–5½. Shell dextral, with tall, pointed spire, sutures fairly deep; aperture pear-shaped; has operculum; umbilicus tiny. Shell brownish but often appears darker; animal pale grey, tentacles paler. Running water, rarely ponds. Has spread rapidly through NW Europe in recent years. (T, ex Ic, nFS.) [2]

snail *Bithynia tentaculata* BITHYNIIDAE SH 10–15 mm, SB 6–7 mm, W 5–6. Shell dextral, conical, rounded below, with pointed spire, whorls rounded, sutures fairly deep; aperture pear-shaped; operculum concentrically grooved. Shell yellowish, surface glossy; animal grey. Rivers, lakes; prefers hard water. T, ex Ic, nFS. [3]

Bladder Snail *Physa fontinalis* PHYSIDAE SH 10–12 mm, SB 6–8 mm, W 4–5. Shell sinistral, rather inflated, with short, blunt spire; aperture large; umbilicus absent. Shell pale horn-coloured, thin, transparent, surface very shiny; animal pale to dark grey; mantle overlaps side of shell. Fast-flowing rivers with rich vegetation, rarely lakes. T, ex Ic, nFS. [4]

Dwarf Pond Snail *Lymnaea truncatula*
LYMNAEIDAE SH 8–12 mm, SB 4–6 mm, W 5–6. Shell dextral, with short, blunt spire, sutures deep, whorls rather flattened, umbilicus open, medium-sized. Shell brown to horn-coloured, thin, with fine transverse striations; animal grey. Marshy grassland, around ponds, lakes and rivers. Intermediate host of sheep liver-fluke *Fasciola hepatica*. T. [5]

Great Pond Snail *Lymnaea stagnalis*
LYMNAEIDAE SH 35–50 mm, SB 20–30 mm, W 7–8. Shell dextral, with large body whorl and much narrower, pointed spire, rather irregular outline; aperture long, narrow; umbilicus absent. Shell thin-walled, with fine striations, horn-brown but often covered with coloured encrustation; animal dark grey. Ponds, more rarely slow-flowing rivers; prefers hard water. Feeds on vegetation, carrion. T, ex nBr, Ic. [6]

Wandering Snail *Lymnaea peregra*
LYMNAEIDAE SH 15–25 mm, SB 12–15 mm, W 4–5. Shell dextral, rarely sinistral, very variable in shape, body whorl large, spire very short, pointed or blunt; aperture may be very expanded; umbilicus partly or completely covered. Shell pale to dark horn-brown, surface matt or slightly glossy; animal greyish. Still and slow-flowing waters. T. [7]

Ram's-horn Snail *Planorbis planorbis*
PLANORBIDAE SH 3–3·5 mm, SB 14–18 mm, W 5–6. Shell sinistral, spiral almost flat; whorls rounded with marginal keel; umbilicus very wide and shallow. Shell pale to dark horn-brown, surface matt; animal blackish. Marshes, ponds, lakes, rivers, esp shallow, weedy areas; prefers hard water. T, ex nBr, Ic, nFS. [8]

Great Ram's-horn Snail *Planorbarius corneus* PLANORBIDAE SH 10–12 mm, SB 30–35 mm, W 5–6. Shell very large, sinistral, surface glossy with battered appearance; no marginal keel; aperture rounded with sharp, slightly inflated lip; shell wall thick and solid; umbilicus broad, rather deep. Shell greyish-green to olive; animal deep reddish-brown. Larger ponds, lakes, rivers; prefers hard water. T, ex nBr, Ic, nFS. [9]

River Limpet *Ancylus fluviatilis*
ANCYLIDAE SH 2–5 mm, SL 4–9 mm,
SB 3–7 mm. Shell conical, barely coiled,
with low spire curved to the right; thin-
walled. Shell and animal grey-black.
Fast-flowing streams, wave-washed shores
of large lakes, attached to stones and
vegetation. T, ex Ic, nFS. [1]

Amber Snail *Succinea putris*
SUCCINEIDAE SH 15–25 mm, SB 10–14 mm,
W 5. Shell dextral, with short, blunt
spire, tall body whorl; aperture oval,
pointed above; shell lip sharp; umbilicus
absent. Shell pale yellow to horn-brown,
thin, transparent, glossy, with fine striations; animal yellow-grey. Damp grassland, marshes. T, ex nBr, Ic, nFS. [2]

Pearl Mussel *Margaritifera margaritifera*
MARGARITIFERIDAE SH 55–57 mm, SL 120–
150 mm, SB 30–45 mm. Shell outline
oval, apex of valves low, 1 tooth inside
right valve, 2 inside left. Young shell
yellow-brown, older shell dark brown to
black with matt surface, often eroded
exposing mother-of-pearl layer beneath.
Soft water, on sandy bottoms of rivers.
Occasionally forms small pearls. Once
fished commercially, now less widespread.
T, ex Ic. [3]

Painter's Mussel *Unio pictorum*
UNIONIDAE SH 30–60 mm, SL 60–150 mm,
SB 25–30 mm. Shell outline elongated, oval,
with pointed posterior; apex of valves
project well above line of hinge; teeth
inside valves well-developed, prominent.
Shell yellowish-green to brown, young
shell with diverging rays. Rivers, lakes,
large ponds; prefers hard water. T, ex
nBr, Ir, Ic, nFs. [4]

Swan Mussel *Anodonta cygnea* UNIONIDAE
SH 60–120 mm, SL 100–200 mm, SB 30–60.
Shell outline elongated, oval, angled
posteriorly; apex of valves low, barely
projecting above line of hinge; no
prominent teeth inside valves, only
elongated ridges. Shell yellowish-green to
olive-brown. Slow-flowing rivers, lakes,
large ponds; prefers hard water. T, ex
nBr, Ic, nFS. [5]

Oligochaete worms have segmented bodies
with bristles on each segment. Most
are hermaphrodite but mate to exchange
sperm. Eggs and sperm are deposited in a
cocoon secreted by the clitellum.
Fertilization occurs in the cocoon; small
worms emerge. Clitellum is indistinct
except in earthworms. Naididae and
Aeolosomatidae may also bud, forming
chains of individuals which then separate.
Aeolosomatidae, Naididae and Tubificidae
are aquatic (in freshwater); they ingest
organic matter in bottom mud or browse
on micro-organisms on water-plants. Only
a few earthworms (Lumbricidae) are truly
aquatic; they ingest organic matter in soil
or browse on vegetation.

Square-tailed Worm *Eiseniella tetraedra*
LUMBRICIDAE BL 30–60 mm. Body
cylindrical in front of clitellum,
quadrangular behind. Clitellum begins on
22nd or 23rd segment, ends on 26th or
27th. Colour dark red-brown to bright
golden-yellow or greenish. Amphibious, in
moist soil, beside or in water. T. [6]

earthworm *Helodrilus oculatus*
LUMBRICIDAE BL 35–70 mm. Body
cylindrical. Clitellum begins on 21st or
22nd segment, ends on 32nd. Flesh-
coloured. In wet clay on river-banks, in
mud of ditches. Br, Fr, Be, Ne, Ge. [7]

worms *Aeolosoma* AEOLOSOMATIDAE
BL < 10 mm. Transparent, usually with
green, orange or red spots; no eyes.
Usually on water-plants. T. [8]

worms *Nais* NAIDIDAE BL 5–20 mm. More
or less transparent, often pink or brown
anteriorly; eyes present. In mud. T. [9]

worm *Stylaria lacustris* NAIDIDAE
BL 5–18 mm. More or less transparent;
eyes present; long, slim proboscis. On
water-plants. T. [10]

worms *Tubifex* TUBIFICIDAE BL 20–80 mm.
Slimmer than earthworms, usually red;
no eyes. Coils tightly when disturbed.
Burrows in mud with tail exposed. T. [11]

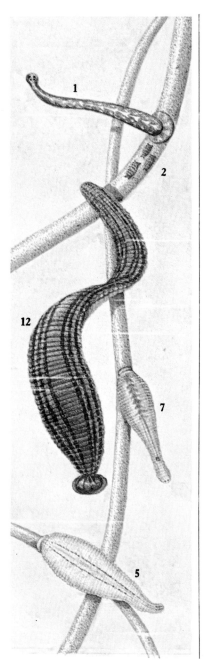

Leeches (Hirudinea) are mainly aquatic.
Reproduce as earthworms, but clitellum
distinct only during breeding season.

fish leech *Piscicola geometra* PISCICOLIDAE
BL 20–50 mm. Body cylindrical; anterior
sucker large. Greenish, yellowish or brown
with 8 rows of white spots. Feeds on
blood of freshwater fish. In cool, well
aerated waters, fast-flowing streams and
wave-washed lakes. Cocoons (L *c*2 mm)
spherical, covered with spongy outer layer,
cemented to solid objects under water. T,
ex Ic. [1] [cocoon 2] *Cystobranchus* similar,
but body with distinct neck and abdomen.
Fr, Be, Ne, Ge

fish leech *Hemiclepsis marginata*
GLOSSIPHONIIDAE BL 16–30 mm. Body
flattened, leaf-shaped; anterior sucker
slightly wider than segments just behind.
Translucent, pale yellow with green or
brown pattern. Feeds on blood of fish,
amphibians. Usually in small bodies of
standing water. Cocoons gelatinous,
carried on underside of parent's body
until young have hatched and used up
yolk reserves. T, ex Ic. [3] [cocoon 4]

leech *Glossiphonia complanata*
GLOSSIPHONIIDAE BL 15–35 mm. Body
flattened, leaf-shaped; anterior sucker no
wider than segments behind. Translucent,
green or brown, with 2 interrupted lines
along back. Feeds mainly by sucking body
fluids of gastropods. In running water,
often under stones. Carries cocoon and
young as *H. marginata*. T. [5] *G. heteroclita*
similar, but amber coloured, common in
still and slow-moving soft waters. T.

leech *Theromyzon tessulatum*
GLOSSIPHONIIDAE BL 10–30 mm. Body
slightly flattened, very soft; anterior
sucker no wider than segments behind.
Amber or olive-grey with 6 rows of yellow
spots along back, underside pale grey.
Invades nasal passages and mouths of
ducks, other waterfowl, and feeds on
blood. Widespread, except in fast-flowing
rivers. Carries young and cocoon as *H.
marginata*. T. [6]

leech *Helobdella stagnalis* GLOSSIPHONIIDAE
BL 8–26 mm. Body flattened, leaf-shaped;
anterior sucker no wider than segments
behind; chitinous plate on front part of
back. Translucent, pale grey, often with
green, yellow or brownish hue. Feeds by
sucking body fluids of aquatic
invertebrates. Abundant in sluggish rivers
and lakes, esp where hard water. Carries
cocoon and young as *H. marginata*. T. [7]

leech *Erpobdella octoculata*
ERPOBDELLIDAE BL 50–70 mm. Body
elongated, slightly flattened. Deep
reddish-brown or yellowish, usually with
black spots on back, underside paler.
Feeds on insect larvae, oligochaetes,
cladocerans. Widespread, often under
stones. Cocoons (L *c*4 mm) flattened,
oval, translucent, brown; attached to
undersides of stones. T. [8] [cocoon 9]
E. testacea similar, but smaller, with or
without median black stripe on back.
Adapted to anaerobic conditions *eg* dense
weed-swamps in eutrophic ponds. T.

Horse Leech *Haemopis sanguisuga*
HIRUDIDAE BL 40–147 mm. Body
elongated, slightly flattened. Blackish- or
yellowish-green on back, underside paler.
Feeds on earthworms, other animal
tissue; does not suck blood. In winter
under stones in up to 1 m of water; in
summer usually under stones just above
water-level. Cocoons (L *c*10 mm) ovoid,
with spongy outer layer, under stones or
among grass roots just above water-level.
T. [10] [cocoon 11] *Trocheta subviridis*
similar, but grey-green or reddish, usually
with 2 brown lines along back. Terrestrial,
but breeds in water. T, ex Ic, FS.

Medicinal Leech *Hirudo medicinalis*
HIRUDIDAE BL 30–125 mm. Body
elongated, slightly flattened. Olive or
blackish-green with 6 red-brown or
yellow stripes along back, underside
yellow-green with pair of black marginal
stripes. Sucks blood of fish and
amphibians when young, of mammals
when adult. Rare, but locally common in
ponds and streams frequented by large
mammals. Cocoons similar to those of *H.
sanguisuga*. T, ex Ic, SC. [12]

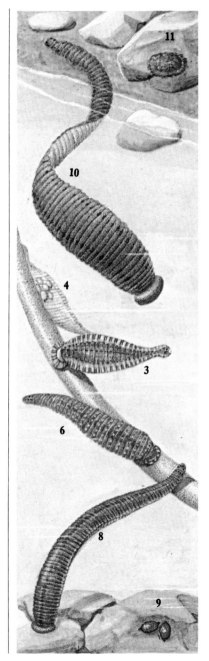

Crustaceans are well represented in fresh-water. A few spp are large and conspicuous, but many are microscopic. A small pond may contain millions of individuals.

fairy shrimp *Chirocephalus diaphanus* CHIROCEPHALIDAE BL <35 mm. Paired, stalked compound eyes; 11 pairs of similar, thoracic limbs ventrally; no carapace; ♀ with egg pouch; ♂ with antennae modified for grasping ♀. Usually swims upside down using abdomen and telson as rudder. Thoracic limbs filter out fine food particles from water. Temporary ponds; esp early in year. Eggs drought-resistant; hatch as nauplius larvae. W, ex Ir, Ic, nFS. [♂ 1]

conchostracan *Cyzicus tetracerus* CYZICIDAE BL ♀ <13 mm, ♂ larger. Carapace robust, encloses body like mussel shell, can close completely; growth lines prominent. Pink-brown. Feeds using thoracic limbs to filter out fine food particles. Apr–Jun; temporary ponds; usually swims near bottom. Eggs drought-resistant; hatch into larvae. CE. [♀ 2]

notostracan *Triops cancriformis* TRIOPSIDAE BL <100 mm (including furca), but usually smaller. Carapace large, stout, dorsal; 2 eyes; abdomen and furca long; many ventral, thoracic limbs. Pinkish-brown. Omnivorous. May–Oct; temporary ponds; usually swims near bottom. Eggs drought-resistant; hatch into larvae. W, ex Ir, Ic, FS, rare Br. [3]

water-flea *Sida crystallina* SIDIDAE BL ♂ <2 mm, ♀ <4 mm. Carapace thin. Sucker on back of head. Feeds using thoracic limbs to filter out food particles. Summer; pond- and lake-margins; swims, but often attached to plants by sucker. Life cycle as *Daphnia* but resting eggs not enclosed in ephippium. T. [♀ 4]

water-flea *Daphnia magna* DAPHNIIDAE BL ♂ <2 mm, ♀ <5 mm. Carapace thin, internal organs visible; becomes red by producing haemoglobin when oxygen is scarce; single compound eye. Feeds using thoracic limbs to filter out particles. Esp summer; richer ponds, lake-margins, sometimes further offshore in large bodies

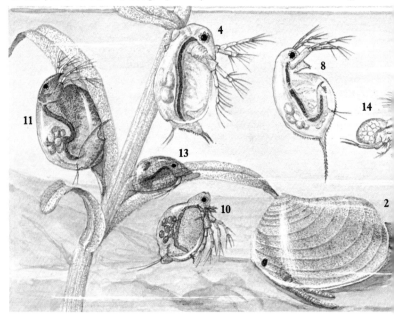

of water; swims in jerks (hence 'flea') using antennae. ♀ usually parthenogenetic; eggs hatch into miniature adults within brood pouch. In adverse conditions, ♂s are produced which fertilize ♀s; ♀ then produces ephippium containing 2 drought-resistant eggs which hatch when conditions become favourable. T, ex n and wBr, Ir, Ic. [parthenogenetic ♀ **5**] [♀ with ephippium **6**] [ephippium **7**]. *Daphnia hyalina* (BL ♀ <2·5 mm, ♂ smaller) similar, but transparent; in open water of lakes. Br, NE ex extreme n. [♀ **8**]

water-flea *Scapholeberis mucronata* DAPHNIIDAE BL ♀ <1 mm, ♂ smaller. Ventral edges of carapace dark, straight, with modifications for swimming suspended from surface film; also swims freely. Ponds; bays of lakes where quiet. T. [♀ **9**]

water-flea *Moina brachiata* MOINIDAE BL ♂ <1·1 mm, ♀ <1·5 mm. Life cycle and structure similar to *Daphnia* but has 'placenta' to nourish parthenogenetic eggs in brood pouch; robust ephippium. Pinkish-brown. Summer; temporary ponds. W, ex Ir, Ic, FS, rare Br. [♀ **10**]

water-flea *Eurycercus lamellatus* CHYDORIDAE BL ♂ <1·3 mm, ♀ <4 mm. Carapace robust, with broad head shield. Brownish. Feeds by scraping plant surfaces. Ponds and lake-margins; crawls among plants; can swim. Life cycle as *Daphnia*. T. [♀ **11**] 2 related spp: *Alona affinis* (BL ♂ <0·7 mm, ♀ <1 mm) on bottom of ponds, lakes. Carries only 2 young. T. [**12**] *Graptoleberis testudinaria* (BL ♂ <0·5 mm, ♀ <0·7 mm) glides over plant surfaces on ventral edges of carapace. T. [♀ **13**]

water-flea *Polyphemus pediculus* POLYPHEMIDAE BL ♂ <1 mm, ♀ <2 mm. Body and limbs not enclosed in carapace; long spine at rear; single enormous eye. Blue, pink and brown. Seizes animals and plants with thoracic limbs. Near lake-margins; often in shoals; swims rapidly using antennae. In summer partheno-genetic ♀ carries eggs in dorsal brood pouch. Sexes mate in autumn; resting eggs lie on bottom until spring. T. [♀ **14**]

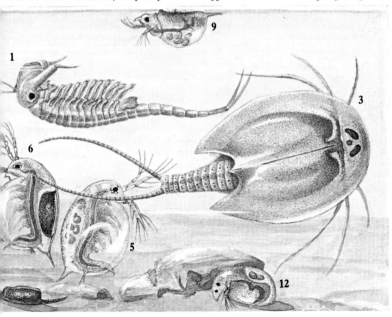

ostracod *Herpetocypris reptans* CYPRIDAE
BL <2·6 mm. Carapace of 2 calcified
valves; when closed, entire body contained
and resembles tiny mussel. Green. Feeds
on relatively large food particles. Ponds
and lakes, also other waters; crawls along
bottom, over vegetation; cannot swim. ♀s
only; orange eggs attached in clusters to
plants. T, ex Ic, ?Ir. [1]

ostracod *Notodromas monacha* CYPRIDAE
BL ♂ <1·2 mm, ♀ <1·1 mm. As
Herpetocypris reptans, but almost black
ventrally, lighter, sometimes green
dorsally. Usually suspended from surface
film; swims beneath surface film, also in
open water. Feeds on fine particles.
Ponds, lakes esp where rich and
undisturbed. T, ex Ir, Ic. [♀ 2]

ostracod *Cypridopsis vidua* CYPRIDAE
BL ♀ <0·7 mm. Yellowish-white with
dark bands. 1st pair of antennae with
long, whiplash-like bristles, used for
swimming. Ponds and lakes, esp among
submerged vegetation; not in acidic

waters. ♂ unknown. T, ex ?Ic. [♀ 3]

copepod *Eudiaptomus gracilis* DIAPTOMIDAE
BL ♂ <1·5 mm, ♀ <1·65 mm. Colour
variable. ♀ carries single egg sac. Elongate
1st pair of antennae act as balancers while
2nd pair of antennae propel animal
through water and create feeding currents.
Darts using 4 pairs of thoracic swimming
legs. Ponds, inshore waters of lakes;
member of plankton in open water. Eggs
hatch as larvae, moulting by stages into
adult. T, ex Ic. [♀ 4] [nauplius larva 5]

copepod *Macrocyclops fuscus* CYCLOPIDAE
BL ♂ <1·2 mm, ♀ <2·5 mm. Forepart of
body broader, 1st pair of antennae shorter
than *Eudiaptomus gracilis*; purple-green.
♀ with 2 egg-sacs. Seizes and kills larger
animals. In clear, weedy waters; swims
usually near bottom using legs. T, ex Ic.
[♀ 6] 2 similar spp: *Microcyclops minutus*
(BL ♂ <0·9 mm, ♀ <1 mm) colourless;
in temporary ponds. Larval stages able to
withstand desiccation. W, ex Ir, Ic, FS,
rare Br. [7] *Eucyclops agilis* (BL ♂ <0·8 mm,

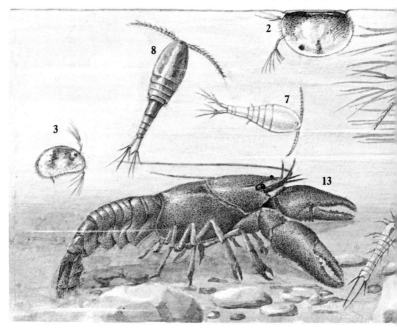

♀ <1·5 mm) brownish with orange on abdomen. Feeds on algae. In flowing and standing water; swims actively on bottom. Commonest cyclopoid. T. [8]

copepod *Bryocamptus pygmaeus* CANTHOCAMPTIDAE BL ♀ <0·5 mm, ♂ smaller. 1st pair of antennae short. Colourless. ♀ carries single egg sac. Throughout year; crawls, in ponds, lakes, wet moss or moist leaf-litter. ♂ sometimes attached to furca of ♀ and towed by her. T. [♀ 9] *Canthocamptus staphylinus* (BL <1 mm) similar, but pinkish. Throughout year, common in winter, spring; in rivers, streams, ponds, ditches; crawls actively over bottom; can swim. T, ex Ic. [♀ 10]

water-louse *Asellus aquaticus* ASELLIDAE BL <15 mm. Body flattened from above downwards; 2 compound eyes not on stalks. Grey-brown. Scavenges on decaying organic matter. In rivers, streams and standing water; crawls over mud, stones, in vegetation. Tolerant of clear and polluted waters; occasionally in water mains. ♀ carries young in ventral chamber. T, ex ?nFS. [♀ 11]

freshwater shrimp *Gammarus pulex* GAMMARIDAE BL ♂ <20 mm, ♀ <12 mm. Body flattened from side to side, when at rest curved in arc; 2 compound eyes not on stalks. Brown-orange. Omnivorous. In rivers, streams, standing water, esp where stony, except where high acidity. Active, swims sideways, scuttles under stones. ♂ often swims grasping ♀. T, ex nBr, Ic, nFi, nSw, No, (but Ir). [12]

crayfish *Austropotamobius pallipes* ASTACIDAE BL <130 mm. 2 compound eyes on stalks; pincers on 3 of the 5 pairs of walking limbs. Omnivorous, seizes food with pincers. Esp in calcareous streams, occasionally in lakes, canals. Crawls; if disturbed moves backwards using abdomen and tail-fan. Seeks refuge under stones. ♀ carries eggs; later, young attached to abdominal limbs. Br, (Ir), wGe, w of Rhine. [13]

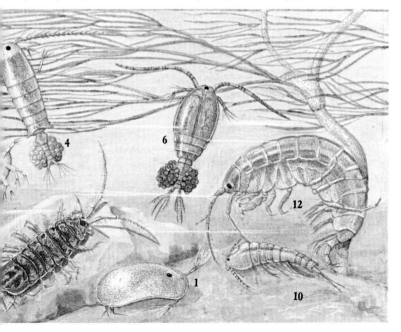

springtail *Podura aquatica* COLLEMBOLA BL <1 mm. Wingless body squat, black; abdomen with retractable spring which enables it to leap. Feeds on detritus on water-surface. Summer; ponds, lakes. Young like miniature adults. CE. WE. [1]

springtail *Sminthurides penicillifer* COLLEMBOLA BL <1 mm, ♀ slightly larger than ♂. Wingless body round, yellow-black. Adult leaps about on water; ♂ has hook on antenna, used to catch on to ♀ antenna; move around hooked together. Feeds on detritus, duckweed, on surface. Summer; lakes, pools. CE, WE, ex Br, Ir. [2]

Mayflies (Ephemeroptera). Usually 2 pairs of gauzy wings, but hindwings often very small; antennae short; 3 long cerci; do not feed. Wings held vertically over body at rest. Subimago emerges from water as 'dun' of fisherman, moults to final winged stage, shinier and sexually mature: moult in adult stage unique in insects. Nymphs aquatic, have 3 long cerci and usually lateral gills, single tarsus and 1 claw.

mayfly *Ephemera danica* EPHEMERIDAE WS 25–40 mm. Antennae short; forewings transparent with olive-brown, interrupted median band, outer margin smoky; hindwings much smaller; abdomen grey-white with black markings. Adult ♂s swarm, rising and falling over water. Apr–Sept; lakes with sand or gravel, rivers, streams. Nymph 20–25 mm long, elongate; wing rudiments pointed; legs large, hairy; gills held over back of 1st few abdominal segments. Plant-feeder. Local. T, ex Ic. [3] [nymph 4]

mayfly *Caenis robusta* CAENIDAE WS 7–8·5 mm. Forewings whitish, hindwings absent; abdomen with greyish marks. Adult ♂s swarm, dancing over water. Summer; slow-moving water with muddy bottoms. Nymph stout, <15 mm long; body often covered with fragments of debris; crawls over surface of mud. Local. T, ex Ic. [5]

mayfly *Ephoron virgo* EPHORIDAE WS ♂ 12–25 mm, WS ♀ 13 mm, cerci 25 mm. ♂ with central cercus smaller than others; ♀ cerci hairy, roughly length of body; wings dull, whitish; abdomen yellow-white; cerci white. Adults emerge in large numbers; dead ones later cover water-surface or lie in heaps like snowflakes. Crepuscular, summer; rivers, lakes. Nymph elongate, lives on muddy bottom. Common. T, ex Br, Ir, Ic. [♂6]

Dragonflies, damselflies (Odonata). Mostly large, with long slender bodies, short antennae; 2 pairs membranous wings, usually with black mark on front margin; large eyes. Prey on other insects, catching them in flight. Nymphs aquatic, predatory, head with specialized mask for catching prey.

Southern Aeshna *Aeshna cyanea* AESHNIDAE WS 100 mm, BL 70 mm. Thorax and most of abdomen green, yellow triangles at top of abdomen; last 3 segments of abdomen pale blue in ♂. Usually hunts near ground but will fly high. Rapid flight. Flies by day and at dusk, Jun–Oct; still water, ponds. Nymph 38–48 mm long, stout, lacking cerci. Widespread. T, ex Ir, Ic. [♂ 7] [nymph 8]

Brown Aeshna *Aeshna grandis* AESHNIDAE WS 102 mm, BL 73 mm. Mostly brown; head yellow at front with black marks; wings yellow-brown with blue spot at base; narrow yellow stripes across abdomen; blue spot at base of abdomen in ♂. Hawks for insects at water's edge. Diurnal and crepuscular, Jul–Oct; ponds, lakes. Nymph similar to *A. cyanea*. Common. T, ex Ic. [♂ 9] [nymph 10]

Broad-bodied Libellula *Libellula depressa* LIBELLULIDAE WS 76 mm, BL 44 mm. Brown with green stripes on thorax; abdomen broad, in ♂ blue with yellow edges. May–Aug; ponds, lakes, canals. Nymph 22–25 mm long, broad, flat, brown, hairy; abdomen with dorsal spines on segments 4–8. Locally common. T, ex Ic. [♀ 11] [nymph 12] Related spp with differently shaped spines.

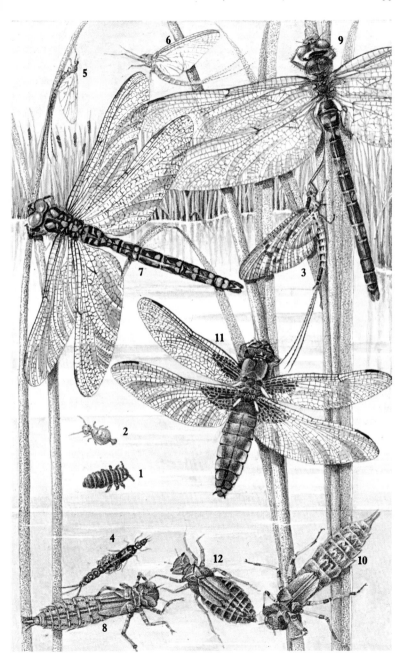

Demoiselle, damselfly *Agrion virgo*
AGRIIDAE WS ♂ 58 mm, ♀ 63 mm, BL
45 mm. Wings purplish-brown, in ♀
duller with white spots at tips; thorax of
♂ blue, of ♀ green; abdomen greenish,
with brown tip in ♀. Fluttery flight,
normally not far from water, ♀ flight esp
feeble. May–Sep; flowing water. Nymph
elongate, 30–35 mm long, brown or
green; 3 cerci; in weed in swift, clear
streams. Locally common. T, ex Ic. [♂ 1]
[nymph 2]

Green Lestes, Emerald Damselfly
Lestes sponsa LESTIDAE WS 20–25 mm,
BL 38 mm. ♂ green with pale brown
pronotum, pale blue at base of wings, tip
of abdomen and all 2nd abdominal
segment; ♀ green with yellow-brown base
to wings. Active in sunshine, Jun–Sep;
reedy ponds, lakes, open ditches, bogs.
Nymph 26–35 mm long, elongate; 3
slender cerci. Locally common. T, ex Ic.
[♂ 3] [nymph 4]

damselfly *Lestes viridis* LESTIDAE
WS 55 mm, BL 41 mm. Head brown;
thorax brown centrally, rest emerald
green; abdomen green with narrow black
stripes; underside yellow. Summer;
stagnant or slow-flowing water. Eggs laid
under bark of twig overhanging water,
cause galls; larvae emerge and fall into
water. Locally common. CE, WE, ex Br,
Ir. [5] [nymph 6]. Similar spp in Br.

Stoneflies (Plecoptera). Adults relatively
weak fliers. Long antennae; 2 pairs gauzy
wings rolled round or held flat over body
at rest; hindwings larger than forewings
with enlarged basal area; abdomen with
2 long cerci. Nymphs aquatic, having
2 long cerci, 3 jointed tarsi with 2 claws;
active swimmers, predatory or herbivorous.

stonefly *Taeniopteryx nebulosa*
TAENIOPTERYGIDAE BL ♂ 7–9 mm, ♀
9–11 mm. Wings smoky grey-brown with
one dark band across forewing; body
black; cerci 2-segmented; ♂ often
short-winged. Adult flies only in still air,
runs over rocks and vegetation by water.
Feb–May; rivers, streams. Nymph
elongate, 8–12 mm long, brown, with 2

long cerci; antennae long; base of legs
with 3-segmented, retractable gill filament;
abdomen with dorsal spine on each
segment; active swimmer; feeds on algae.
Local CE, WE, ex Ir. [7] [nymph 8]

stonefly *Protonemura praecox* NEMOURIDAE
BL ♂ 6–8 mm; ♀ 7–9 mm. Dark, with
dusky wings, identified by 3 short
processes on underside of first segment
behind head; ♂ abdominal cerci short,
rounded. Feb–Jun; swift streams, often
at high altitudes. Nymph elongate,
8–10 mm long, reddish-brown, with 3
sausage-shaped gills on underside of 1st
segment behind head; most abdominal
segments with long bristle on side; tarsi
and antennae yellow; feeds on algae.
Locally common. CE, WE. [9] [nymph 10]

stonefly *Amphinemura sulcicollis*
NEMOURIDAE BL ♂ 4–6 mm; ♀ 5–7 mm.
Similar to preceding sp but wings less
cloudy, held flat over abdomen at rest.
Apr–Sep; running water, esp with stony
bottom. Nymph elongate, 4–6 mm long,
dark brown; antennae long; head
rounded; gills 2 bunches of fringe-like
processes on prothorax; abdomen hairy,
hindleg with patch of long hairs on femur;
feeds on algae. Locally common NE, WE.
[11] [nymph 12]

stonefly *Diura bicaudata* PERLODIDAE
BL ♂ 10–13 mm; ♀ 12–14 mm. Dark
coloured with dorsal yellow line on prothorax; ♂ often short-winged. Apr–Jun;
stony lake shores, streams usually above
300 m. Nymph elongate, 8–17 mm long;
head dark with light coloured marks;
wing buds paler with dark central mark;
abdomen with lighter central area;
predatory. Common. NE, ex De, WE.
[13] [nymph 14]

stonefly *Perla bipunctata* PERLODIDAE
BL ♂ 16–20 mm; ♀ 18–24 mm. Pronotum
pale yellow with black border, dark line
centrally. Apr–June; rivers, streams.
Nymph 16–33 mm long; prothorax wider
than long, yellow and black, strongly patterned; last abdominal segment yellow;
predatory. Common, often abundant. T,
ex Ic, FS. [15] [nymph 16]

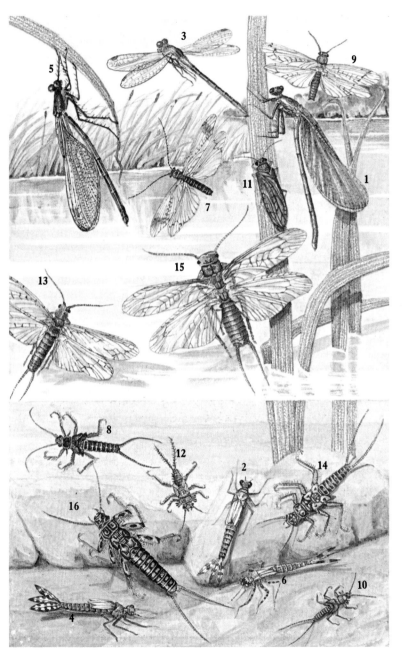

Land- and Water-bugs (Hemiptera-Heteroptera). Minute to large; generally flattened; wings folded flat over body at rest. Mouthparts form rostrum for sucking juice of plants or animals. Forewings (hemelytra) half hardened, half membranous. Metamorphosis incomplete.

Marsh Damsel-bug *Dolichonabis limbatus* NABIDAE BL 7·5–9 mm. Head pointed with stout rostrum below; thorax and short hemelytra grey-brown (rarely long-winged). Jul–Nov; damp meadows, reed-swamps. Adult and nymph prey on other insects. Eggs laid in stems, overwinter; nymphs hatch mid-May. Common, widespread. T, ex Ic. [1] Related spp very similar, also in marshes.

Pondweed Bug *Mesovelia furcata* MESOVELIDAE BL 3–3·5 mm. Wingless; green; thorax slightly darker; legs hairy with claw on tip. Adult lives on floating leaves of water-plants, runs over leaves and into flowers; feeds on small insects on surface film. Jul–Sep; ponds, lakes. Eggs inserted into stems of water-plants, stem sinks in winter, nymphs hatch Apr–May, swim to surface. Widespread. T, ex Ir, Ic. [2]

Sphagnum Bug *Hebrus ruficeps* HEBRIDAE BL 1·2–1·5 mm. Wingless, rarely winged. Adult and nymph in sphagnum on margins of acid lakes or bogs. Adult appears Sep; lays eggs in sphagnum, near base, in spring; dies off June. Common. T, ex Ir, Ic. [3] Related *H. pusillus* usually has wings.

Water Measurer *Hydrometra stagnorum* HYDROMETRIDAE BL 9–12 mm. Very slender; head with long projecting rostrum. Adult walks slowly over water-surface, uses rostrum to catch water-fleas, mosquito larvae, other insects, just below or in surface film. Will jump on surface if disturbed. Gregarious adults found throughout year; ponds, ditches, margins of streams. Nymph smaller, also wingless. Common. T, ex Ic. [4]

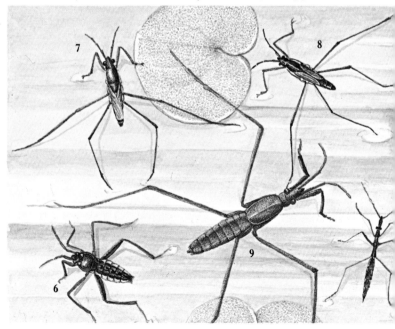

Lesser Water-measurer *Hydrometra gracilenta* HYDROMETRIDAE BL 7–8·5 mm. Very slender, even thinner than *H. stagnorum* and with abdomen shiny above. Habits similar to *H. stagnorum*; Jul–Jun; ponds, lakes. Local. T, ex Ir, Ic. [5]

Water Cricket *Velia caprai* VELIDAE BL 5–7 mm. Wingless, rather stout. Hunts by detecting ripples caused by insect prey on water surface. Often in large numbers. Jul–May; streams, ponds, usually with slow-flowing water but also still pools in mountain streams. Widespread. T, ex Ic. [6]

Little Pond-skater *Gerris argentatus* GERRIDAE BL 6·5–8 mm. Body slender, usually winged; antennae long. Adult skates over water-surface; forelegs used to grasp prey. June–Mar, overwinters; ponds, ditches, esp with reeds. Nymph wingless, smaller. Widespread, locally common. T, ex Ic.

Common Pond-skater *Gerris lacustris* GERRIDAE BL 8–10 mm. Wingless and winged forms. Winged adult flies freely, from pond to pond. Gregarious; skates over surface; jumps if disturbed; preys on insects on surface film, forelegs grasping prey. Jun–Apr, overwinters; ponds, lakes, ditches. Nymph smaller, wingless, predatory. Common and widespread. T, ex Ic. [7] Several very similar related spp.

Toothed Pond-skater *Gerris odontogaster* GERRIDAE BL 7–9 mm. Slender; usually fully winged; ♂ with conspicuous pair of teeth on underside of 7th abdominal segment. Similar habits to *G. lacustris*. Jul–Apr, overwinters; ponds, lakes, rivers. Nymph smaller, wingless, lacks abdominal teeth. Common. T, ex Ic. [8]

River Pond-skater *Aquarius najas* GERRIDAE BL 13–17 mm. Elongate; usually wingless. Hunts prey on surface; skates along and can jump; gregarious. Jun–Apr, overwinters; rivers, streams. Nymph smaller, active; skates and hunts on surface. Common. T, ex Ic. [9] Related sp with yellow line on side of prothorax.

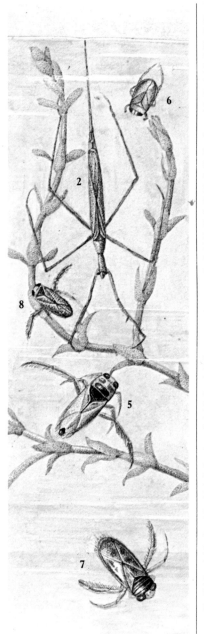

Water Scorpion *Nepa cinerea* NEPIDAE
BL 18–22 mm. Flat, oval, with long tail-tube; wings fully developed but cannot fly; grey-black. Crawls, swims over vegetation; catches young fish, water insects, grasping prey with forelegs. If handled feigns death. Aug–Jun; shallow ponds, lakesides, usually with water-weeds. Nymph smaller, predatory, in shallow water. Widespread. T, ex Ic. [1]

Water Stick-insect *Ranatra linearis* NEPIDAE BL 30–40 mm. Grey-brown with red on top of abdomen; elongate head slender, broader near front; abdomen pointed with long tail-tube. Adult slow moving, usually waits for prey but can swim and fly. Feeds on water insects, tadpoles; grasps prey with forelegs. Will feign death if handled. All year; ponds, lakes, often in deep water. Nymphs short-tailed, wingless, predatory. Common. T, ex Ic. [2]

Saucer Bug *Ilyocoris cimicoides* NAUCORIDAE BL 12–26 mm. Oval; wings fully developed but cannot fly; back slightly arched; thorax pale with 2 reddish patches; hemelytra shining greenish-grey. Moves rapidly over submerged vegetation; feeds on water-fleas and water insects; will 'bite' (stab with proboscis) if handled. May–July, overwinters; muddy ponds, stagnant water, in dense vegetation. Nymph wingless, predatory. Locally common. T, ex Ir, Ic, Fi, No. [3]

water-bug *Aphelochirus aestivalis* APHELOCHIRIDAE BL 9–12 mm. Oval, flattened; winged or wingless; head pointed; hind part of abdomen deeply toothed. Swims well and moves rapidly over bottom, preys on larvae of insects. Will 'bite' if handled. Jul–Mar, overwinters; ponds, slow-flowing rivers, ditches. Nymph wingless, predatory. Local. T, ex Ic. [4]

Backswimmer, Common Water-boatman *Notonecta glauca* NOTONECTIDAE BL 13–16 mm. Hind- and

middle-legs fringed with hairs. Swims
rapidly on back in jerking motion, rowing
with legs. Often hangs upside down below
surface film, with abdomen at surface.
Feeds on water insects; will give painful
'bite' if handled. Aug–Jun, overwinters;
stagnant water, ponds, rivers, ditches.
Nymph smaller. Common. T, ex Ic. [5]
Several very similar related spp.

Water Singer *Micronecta poweri*
CORIXIDAE BL 1·7–2 mm. Pale with brown
markings; head rounded with dark central
line; forewings oval. Gregarious; feeds on
algae, animal debris. Adult ♂ stridulates
loudly by rubbing front legs over ridges
on head. Jun–Sep, 2 generations; lakes,
rivers, in clean shallow water on bottom.
Wingless nymph overwinters. Differs from
next sp in having a clearly visible, small
triangular plate in middle of back.
Common. T, ex Ic, No. [6]

Common Corixa, water-boatman
Corixa punctata CORIXIDAE BL 12–13·5 mm.
Oval; hindlegs fringed with hairs and
enlarged to make oar-blades for rowing
through water; hemelytra and thorax steel
grey-blue with darker patches. Adult flies
freely; swims actively with back
uppermost. Feeds on water-plants, algae.
♂ stridulates, rubbing hair patch on front
legs against head. Comes to surface, hangs
from surface film with head and thorax
uppermost. Hindlegs regularly scrape
along thorax and head in characteristic
corixid action. Jul–Mar, overwinters;
ponds, slow-flowing rivers, ditches.
Nymph wingless, plant-feeder. Common,
often abundant. T, ex Ic, Fi. [7] Several
very similar related spp.

water-boatman *Sigara lateralis* CORIXIDAE
BL 5–6·5 mm. Oval, head rounded; thorax
dark brown; hemelytra paler. Plant-
feeder; flies at night; swims freely. Sep–
Mar, 2 generations, overwinters; cattle
troughs, ditches fouled by cattle. Nymph
wingless, plant-feeder. Common, often
abundant. T, ex Ic. [8] Several very
similar related spp.

Alderflies (Megaloptera), spongeflies and lacewings (Neuroptera). 2 pairs of gauzy net-veined wings, held roof-like at rest; antennae long, slender. Mostly predatory; rather slow-flying. Metamorphosis complete.

alderfly, orlfly *Sialis lutaria* SIALIDAE WS ♂ 18–24 mm, ♀ 23–32 mm. Head and thorax black, antennae long; wings smoky grey-black, front margin slightly protruding with row of straight cross-veins giving ladder-like effect. Crepuscular, but easily disturbed by day, Apr–May; lakes, ponds, slow-moving streams with muddy bottom. Eggs laid on stems overhanging water; larvae drop into water. Young larva 0·7–2·0 mm long; broad head and thorax tapering to abdomen; long, hairy processes from abdomen. Older larvae <26 mm long; broad all along body; prominent jaws; long, hairy processes from abdomen, hairy process nearly as long as abdomen from last segment. Larva feeds on chironomid larvae, other insects; pupates in chamber in clumps of sedges or in damp mud. Complete life cycle takes 2 years. Common. T, ex Ic. [1] [larva 2] Several similar spp.

spongefly *Sisyra fuscata* SISYRIDAE WS 11–13 mm. Hairy; antennae dark all along; 2 pairs grey-brown wings, unpatterned, with relatively few cross-veins. Adults in swarms over water. Crepuscular, May–Sep; streams, rivers, canals. Larva elongate, 0·5–5 mm long; broader near front, tapering behind; short, hairy, lateral processes; long, needle-like jaws which form sucking tube; lives inside freshwater sponge, sucking fluid from it. Larva swims to shore when about to pupate; forms cocoon under bridges, on trees. Locally common. T, ex Ic. [3] Several related spp.

Giant Lacewing *Osmylus fulvicephalus* OSMYLIDAE WS 38–48 mm. Head orange-brown, body black; wings gauzy, net-veined, with dark blotches and iridescence. Adult weak flier, predatory. Crepuscular, Apr–Jun; streams, river-sides. Eggs laid on leaves of plants near water. Young larva lives in damp moss, feeding on insect larvae. Older larva elongate, <15 mm long, with long, slender jaws projecting straight in front of head; hairy, tapering abdomen terminates in short segment with 2 lateral processes; in damp moss, may be semi-aquatic. Locally common. T, ex Ic, FS. [4] [larva 5]

Caddisflies (Trichoptera). Rather moth-like, with 2 pairs hairy, rarely bare, wings, held roof-like at rest. Long filamentous antennae. Rather fluttery flight. Usually dull-coloured adults, brown or grey-brown with some wing markings; live by streams, ponds. Often attracted to light, swarm over water at dusk. Metamorphosis complete. Larvae caterpillar-shaped, with 3 pairs thoracic legs, and claspers at tip of abdomen; aquatic; many spp surround themselves with cases made of sand-grains, twigs, leaf fragments and even empty water-snail shells. Some larvae free-living, make case only to pupate.

caddisfly *Rhyacophila dorsalis* RHYACOPHILIDAE WS 16–28 mm, ♀ larger than ♂. Wings yellow-brown, slightly blotched. Crepuscular, nocturnal, but easily disturbed by day, Apr–Oct; fast-flowing rivers. Larva free-living; small gill tufts laterally; predatory. Pupates in chamber constructed of fragments of stone. Common, widely distributed. T, ex Ic, FS. [6] [larva 7]

caddisfly *Agapetus fuscipes* GLOSSOMATIDAE WS 8–12 mm, ♀ larger than ♂. Wings smoky-grey. Crepuscular, May–Dec; streams, rivers. Larva makes case, 6–8 mm × 4–5 mm, of sand-grains, small pebbles, with 2 openings on ventral side; fastened to rock on pupation. Common. T, ex Ic, FS. [8] [larva 9] [case 10]

caddisfly *Wormaldia occipitalis*
PHILOPOTAMIDAE WS 12–16 mm. Wings
smoky, grey-brown. Crepuscular, Jul–
Oct; fast-flowing water. Larva slender,
without gill tufts on abdomen; free-living;
makes silken net, 5 × 35 mm, on rocks
esp if moss-covered; one end hangs free,
other end closed, catches diatoms, minute
prey. Local. T, ex Ic, FS. [1]

caddisfly *Polycentropus flavomaculatus*
POLYCENTROPIDAE WS 14–24 mm. Wings
smoky-grey. Crepuscular, also by day,
May–Sep; rivers, clear streams, lake-
shores. Larva free-living, predatory,
catches prey in net fixed to stones.
Common. T, ex Ic. [2]

caddisfly *Lype phaeopa* PSYCHOMYIIDAE
WS 10–12 mm. Wings smoky, grey-brown.
Nocturnal, Jun–Sep; ditches, streams,
lakes. Larva makes galleries of silk,
40–50 mm long, on rocks or submerged
branches; becomes covered with silt and
well camouflaged. Common. T, ex Ic. [3]

caddisfly *Hydropsyche angustipennis*
HYDROPSYCHIDAE WS 22–24 mm. Wings
smoky, grey-brown. Crespuscular, Apr–
Oct; streams, rivers. Larva has abdomen
fringed with gills; free-living, predatory;
spins funnel-shaped web of silk under
stones; catches prey as swept into net.
Common. T, ex Ic. [4]

caddisfly *Odontocerum albicorne*
ODONTOCERIDAE WS 26–36 mm, ♀ larger
than ♂. Wings smoky-brown with thin,
dark line across, darker veins. Crepuscular,
Jun–Oct; swift streams. Larva predatory;
lives in tubular case <20 mm long, made
of sand-grains. Common. T, ex Ic. [5]
[case 6]

caddisfly *Phryganea grandis* PHRYGANEIDAE
WS 42–50 mm. Broad smoky-brown wings
usually with darker marks, but sometimes
unmarked. Crepuscular, Jun–Aug; slow-
flowing rivers, streams. Larva makes case,
30–50 mm × 8–9 mm, of leaf fragments;

carries case around; preys on insect larvae,
crustaceans. Common. T, ex Ic. [7] [case 8]

caddisfly *Limnephilus lunatus*
LIMNEPHILIDAE WS 25–35 mm. Wings
patterned, with curved, brown, lunar patch
below yellow-brown outer margin.
Crepuscular, May–Nov; ponds, streams,
lakes. Larva predatory; makes case,
20 × 40 mm, of strips of leaves laid
lengthwise, often with stick incorporated.
Common, widespread. T, ex Ic. [9] [case
10] Other common limnephilids include
L. flavicornis which makes case of sticks
or shells. [case 11]

caddisfly *Mystacides longicornis*
LEPTOCERIDAE WS 17–21 mm. Forewings
slender with dark cross bands; antennae
long. Often swarms by day. Diurnal and
crepuscular, May–Sep; lakes, ponds.
Larva called 'grousefly' by fishermen;
lives in long, slender case made of sand-
grains; swims with case. Common. T, ex
Ic. [12] [case 13]

caddisfly *Molanna angustata* MOLANNIDAE
WS 26–30 mm. Forewings very slender,
smoky-grey with conspicuous veins.
Diurnal and crepuscular, adult often on
water surface by day, May–Sep; lakes,
ponds, slow-moving water. Larva plant-
feeder; lives in case, 26 × 12 mm, hood-
like, with tube below; case attached to
rock. Common. T, ex Ic. [14] [case 15]

caddisfly *Beraea pullata* BERAEIDAE
WS 10–12 mm, ♀ smaller than ♂. Wings
blackish. Diurnal and crepuscular, May;
shallow water, marsh-pools. Larva lives
in curved case, 7 × 1 mm, of sand-grains.
Widespread. T, ex Ic. [16]

caddisfly *Goera pilosa* SERICOSTOMATIDAE
WS 20–24 mm. Forewings yellow-brown.
Crepuscular, May–Sep; streams. Larva
lives in straight-sided case made of sand-
grains, usually with a few larger stones
incorporated; in running water. Common.
T, ex Ic. [17]

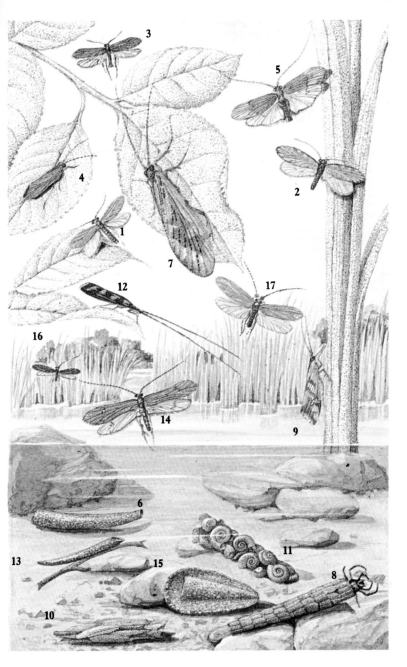

Butterflies and moths (Lepidoptera). Small to large; easily distinguished by covering of fine scales which give colour and pattern; usually proboscis for sucking nectar. Butterflies mostly day-fliers, with clubbed antennae; chrysalis without cocoon. Moths mostly night-fliers with thin, pointed or feathery antennae; cocoon or chamber formed round pupa. Caterpillars feed mostly on plants.

Swallowtail *Papilio machaon* PAPILIONIDAE WS 64–78 mm. Underside similar to upperside, but markings paler. Rapid flight. 2 broods, May and Jul–Aug; damp meadows, marshes. Caterpillar green with red spots on black bands; when disturbed erects orange tube from behind head which releases strong smell; feeds on milk-parsley, wild carrot and other Umbelliferae. Locally common. T, ex Ir, Ic, in Br confined to Fens. [♀ 1]

Marsh Fritillary *Euphydryas aurinia* NYMPHALIDAE WS 33–40 mm. Underside of forewings paler than upperside, of hind wing with greenish tinge; pattern and intensity of colour variable. Active in sunshine, May–Jun; bogs, lake-shores, marshes. Caterpillar black, spotted white, legs red-orange, 2 rows of hairy spines along back of last 9 segments; gregarious, lives in silken webs, feeds on scabious, water-plantains. Local. T, ex Ic, No, but only sSw, sFi. [♀ 2]

Large Copper *Lycaena dispar* LYCAENIDAE WS 36–42 mm. Upperside of both wings of ♂ red-orange with black mark in centre, black outer margins narrower than in ♀, hindwings with darker posterior margin. Underside of ♂ forewings orange with white-edged, black spots, grey margin; of hindwings grey with black, white-edged spots, orange marginal band. Underside of ♀ as ♂. Jun–Jul; marshes, fens. Caterpillar green, slug-like; feeds on water dock. Several ssp; English ssp extinct, but Dutch ssp introduced and established in Fens. Local. Fr, Lu, Be, Ne, Ge, Cz, Po, (Br). [♀ 3]

Pebble Prominent Moth *Eligmodonta ziczac* NOTODONTIDAE WS 38–44 mm. Rapid flight. Nocturnal, May–Sep, 2 broods; marshes, fens. Caterpillar grey, tinged pink, with 2 prominent humps on back, another at end of abdomen; feeds on willow and poplar. Irregular shape of caterpillar aids camouflage. Common. T, ex Ic. [4]

Water Ermine *Spilosoma urticae* ARCTIIDAE WS 38–40 mm. Thorax and head white; abdomen yellow-orange with black spots. Nocturnal, Jun; marshes, fens. Caterpillar hairy, dark red-brown with mauve tinge, black spots each with tufts of long hairs; feeds on yellow loosestrife, water mint, water dock. Local. T, ex Ic, but only sBr. [5]

Round-winged Muslin Moth *Thumatha senex* ARCTIIDAE WS 20–22 mm. Crepuscular and nocturnal, Jul–Aug; marshes, fens. Caterpillar reddish-grey, covered with short hairs; feeds on mosses in wet areas. Local. T, ex Ic. [6]

Dingy Footman *Eilema griseola* ARCTIIDAE WS 32–36 mm. Crepuscular and nocturnal, Jul; fens, marshes. Caterpillar grey-brown, dark line down back and yellowish lines at side, black hairs from dark spots; feeds on lichens on alder, willow. Common. CE, WE, ex Ir. [7]

Cream-bordered Green Pea *Earias clorana* NOCTUIDAE WS 18–22 mm. Nocturnal, adults attracted to light, May–Jun; marshes, bogs. Caterpillar green, smooth except for 2 segments; feeds on osiers. Local. T, ex Ic, but only sBr. [8]

Reed Dagger *Simyra albovenosa* NOCTUIDAE WS 33–37 mm. Hindwings white; body grey-white. Rapid flight. Nocturnal, 2 broods, Jun and Sep; marshes, fens. Caterpillar hairy, black or grey with 2 yellow stripes along back and 1 on each side; feeds on reeds, sedges. Local. CE, WE, ex Ir. [9]

Rosy Marsh Moth *Eugrapha subrosea*
NOCTUIDAE WS 37–41 mm. Nocturnal,
Jul–Aug; marshes, fens. Caterpillar
reddish-grey with yellow spiracles; feeds
on bog myrtle, sallow. Believed extinct in
UK, but recently rediscovered. Local. CE,
WE, ex Ir. [1]

Reed Wainscot *Archanara algae*
NOCTUIDAE WS 33–40 mm. Hindwings
smoky-white, pattern variable. Adult
readily attracted to light. Crepuscular,
Aug–Sep; reed-swamps, marshes.
Caterpillar greenish with black spots;
tunnels in common club-rush stem;
pupates in bulrush stem. Local. CE, WE,
ex Ir. [2] Several similar spp.

Bulrush Wainscot *Nonagria typhae*
NOCTUIDAE WS 38–50 mm. Crepuscular
and nocturnal, Aug–Sep; marshes, water-
margins. Caterpillar pale brown tinged
pink, pale line along side; burrows in
bulrush stem. Locally common. T, ex
Ic, FS. [♂ 3]

Butterbur Moth *Hydraecia petasitis*
NOCTUIDAE WS 42–48 mm. Nocturnal,
Aug–Sep; marshes, river-edges. Caterpillar
feeds in roots and stems of butterbur.
Local. CE, WE. [4]

Silver Hook *Eustrotia uncula* NOCTUIDAE
WS 22–25 mm. Crepuscular, May–Jul;
marshes, bogs. Caterpillar green with
darker green lines on back, pale line on
each side; feeds on grasses and sedges.
Locally common. T, ex Ic. [5]

Marsh Oblique-barred Moth *Hypenodes
turfosalis* NOCTUIDAE WS 13–14 mm.
Crepuscular, Jul–Aug; marshes. Caterpillar
undescribed. Local. CE, WE. [6]

Marsh Carpet *Perizoma sagittata*
GEOMETRIDAE WS 24–27 mm. Crepuscular,
Jun–Jul; marshes, fens. Caterpillar
yellowish-green with pinker sides, dark
stripe along side; feeds on seeds of
meadow-rue. Local. CE, WE. [7]

crambid moth *Calamotropha paludella*
PYRALIDAE WS 21–26 mm. Head with

prominent, beak-like palps, upper palp
roughly triangular when viewed from side.
Rests with head upwards and wings
closely folded round body. Crepuscular,
Jul–Aug; marshes, swamps. Caterpillar
grey-white with darker line along back;
feeds on leaves of bulrushes; later tunnels
into leaf, mining towards base. Locally
common. T, ex Ic. [8]

reed moth *Chilo phragmitellus* PYRALIDAE
WS ♂ 23–28 mm, ♀ 29–37 mm. Head with
prominent beak-like palps, upper palp
triangular when viewed from side; ♂
forewings less pointed than ♀, darker
brown; hindwings white. Rests with head
upwards and wings held tightly round
body. Crepuscular, Jun–Jul; marshes,
swamps. Caterpillar whitish-brown; feeds
inside stems of reeds, reed sweet-grass,
often below water-level; silken cocoon
made in stem at water-level. Locally
common. T, ex Ic. [♀ 9]

pyralid moth *Schoenobius gigantellus*
PYRALIDAE WS ♂ 23–28 mm, ♀ 38–42 mm.
Head with prominent, beak-like palps;
♂ forewings dark brown, with black spots
and darker lines, some paler streaks, but
variable, apex rounded; hindwings grey-
white, veins darker; Rests with wings
along side of body. Crepuscular and
nocturnal, Jul–Aug, sometimes 2 broods;
marshes, swamps. Caterpillar burrows into
shoots of reeds, reed sweet-grass; after
feeding in stem, cuts off piece and floats
to surface on this; when drifts near new
stem climbs on and continues feeding;
burrows actively in stem. Locally
common. CE, WE, ex Ir. [♀ 10]

pyralid moth *Schoenobius forficellus*
PYRALIDAE WS 23–27 mm. ♀ forewings
reddish-brown, reddish lines along wing
often with dark streaks, apex strongly
pointed, slightly concave outer margin;
hindwings white. Slow flier. Crepuscular,
Jun–Jul; marshes, bogs. Caterpillar feeds
on young shoots of reed sweet-grass,
reeds, sedges; when finished bites
off piece and floats on it to new
shoot. Locally common. CE, WE.
[♂ 11]

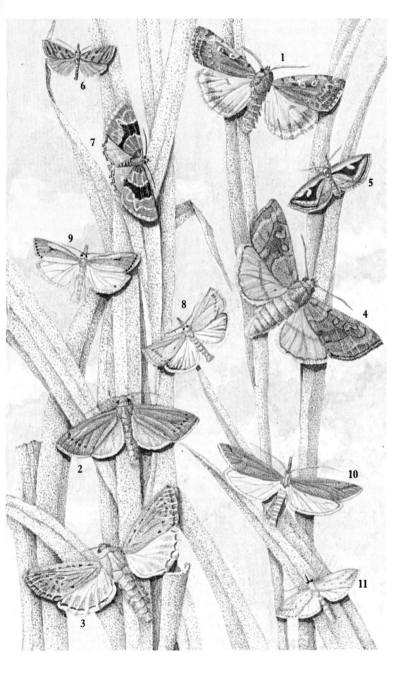

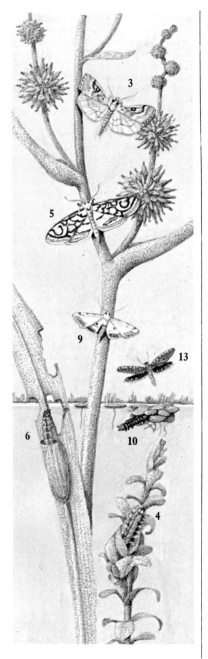

Water Moth *Acentria nivea* PYRALIDAE
WS 12–16 mm, winged ♀s larger, <22 mm,
although ♀s usually wingless. ♂ forewings
greyish-white with pointed apex; hindwings white. ♂ rests by day on rocks
or floating reeds; at night flies rapidly
round and round, often touching water;
wingless ♀ lives below surface, swims
using middle- and hind-legs which have
hairy fringe; mating takes place on surface,
♂ sometimes carries ♀ for short distances;
♀ lays 100–200 eggs on water-plants.
Habits of winged ♀s not known. Nocturnal,
Jul–Sep; ponds, lakes. Caterpillar feeds on
pondweeds, algae, Canadian waterweed;
spins leaves together; lives totally
submerged; pupates under water. Local.
CE, WE. [♂ 1] [caterpillar 2]

Ringed China-mark *Parapoynx
stratiotata* PYRALIDAE WS 20–25 mm.
♀ brown, wings narrower than in ♂; black
spot with white centre on forewings, white
lines along veins, paler outer margin;
hindwings white with 2 prominent bands
near margin. Rather fluttery flight.
Nocturnal but easily disturbed by day,
Jul–Aug; marshes, lakes, stream-sides.
Caterpillar feeds on Canadian waterweed,
hornwort; spins leaves and stems together
into web; has 8 long gill filaments on
each side of body, undulates body in web
to assist respiration. Locally common. CE,
WE. [♂ 3] [caterpillar 4]

Beautiful China-mark *Parapoynx
stagnata* PYRALIDAE WS 19–23 mm. Slow
flier. Nocturnal, but easily disturbed by
day, Jul–Aug; rivers, streams, lakes.
Caterpillar feeds below water-surface on
bur-reed, water-lily; bores into stem when
young, overwinters; in spring spins bits
of leaves together to form case; feeds on
leaves on surface. Locally common. T,
ex Ic. [5] [caterpillar 6]

Brown China-mark *Nymphula
nympheata* PYRALIDAE WS 23–30 mm.

Nocturnal, Jun–Aug; slow streams, ponds, Caterpillar feeds on pondweeds, frogbit, bur-reed; at early stage mines into leaf mid-rib; at later stage makes flat, oval case of pieces of leaves and lives in case near water-surface; body undulates to aid respiration; overwinters. Locally common. CE, WE. [7] [caterpillar 8]

Small China-mark *Cataclysta lemnata*
PYRALIDAE WS 17–21 mm, ♂ smaller than ♀. ♀ forewings brown, black spot near apex, some darker patterns; hindwings white, base brown, with darker markings, margin with 4–5 black, white-centred spots in yellow marginal band. Crepuscular, Jun–Aug; ponds, lakes. Caterpillar feeds on duckweed, on or under water-surface; makes well-camouflaged, irregularly-shaped case of pieces cut from duckweed; hibernates; enlarges case as grows; pupates below surface. Common. CE, WE. [♂ 9] [caterpillar 10]

plume-moth *Platyptilia isodactyla*
PTEROPHORIDAE WS 21–23 mm. Incision on outer margin of forewings forming 2 lobes; hindwings with 2 incisions giving 3 lobes; legs long with prominent spines. 2nd brood paler and smaller than 1st. Sits with wings outstretched, rolled, like letter T. Slow, fluttery flight. Crepuscular and nocturnal, but easily disturbed by day; 2 broods, Jun and Aug–Sep; marshes. Caterpillar feeds on underside of leaves of marsh ragwort; older caterpillar burrows in stems. Local. CE, WE. [11]

micro-moth *Orthotaelia sparganella*
YPONOMEUTIDAE WS 21–28 mm. Palps under head long, curved upwards. Nocturnal, Jul–Aug; marshes. Caterpillar mines in stems of iris, bur-reed. Local. T, ex Ir, Ic. [12] Several similar spp.

micro-moth *Glyphipterix thrasonella*
GLYPHIPTERIGIDAE WS 12–25 mm. Crepuscular, Jun–Jul; marshes. Caterpillar feeds on rushes. Common. CE, WE. [13]

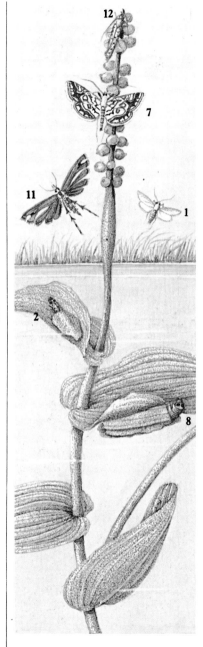

Bees, Wasps, Ants, Ichneumons
(Hymenoptera). 2 pairs of wings.
Metamorphosis complete; larvae usually
legless. Hymenoptera are common in
drier areas but very few spp are adapted
to aquatic life.

parasitic wasp *Prestwichia aquatica*
TRICHOGRAMMATIDAE BL 0·3 mm. Minute;
♂ wings short or vestigial. Adult ♀ enters
water to lay eggs inside eggs of water-
bugs, water-beetles; wasp larva develops
inside host egg. Summer, ponds, lakes.
Local. CE, WE, ex Ir. [1] Related spp
with similar habits.

Flies (Diptera) Tiny to large; slender to
stout; 1 pair transparent wings and small,
knob-like halteres (balancers) in place of
hindwings. Mouthparts for sucking or
piercing. Metamorphosis complete. Larvae
(maggots, grubs) legless.

crane-fly, daddy-long-legs *Tipula
maxima* TIPULIDAE WS 65 mm, BL 32 mm.
Slow flier, hangs delicately on vegetation.
Summer; marshes, lake-sides. Larva
semi-aquatic in pond-margins, shallow
pools; respiratory gills in rosette at tip of
abdomen, comes to surface for air or uses
gills under water; plant-feeder; pupates
on shore. Locally common. CE, WE.
[2]

fly *Ptychoptera contaminata* PTYCHOPTER-
IDAE BL 6–9 mm. May–Oct; adult stays
near water, ponds, marshes. Larva
narrow, elongate, with long, whip-like tail
which is respiratory process; in shallow
water, mud, leaf-litter. Common.
CE, WE. [3]

Common Anopheles Mosquito
Anopheles labranchiae (*maculipennis*)
CULICIDAE BL 5–9 mm. Wings spotted, legs
with pale ring; rests with body sloping,
head lower than abdomen; buzzes or
whines softly in flight. Crepuscular and
nocturnal, summer; above ditches, ponds;
♂s in swarms, feed on plant juices; ♀s in
houses, suck blood. Larva hairy, active,
lives in water; lies horizontally to water-
surface. Common. T. [4] [larva 5]

mosquito, Common Gnat *Culex pipiens*
CULICIDAE BL 5–6 mm. Wings unspotted;
rests with abdomen sloping downwards;
buzzes or whines softly in flight.
Crepuscular and nocturnal, summer; above
still water. Feeds as *Anopheles*. Larva
hangs down from water-surface by tail,
swims down jerkily if disturbed; in ponds,
ditches, water butts, even tins filled with
water. Abundant. T. [6] [larva 7]

phantom fly *Chaoborus crystallinus*
CHAOBORINIDAE BL 6 mm. Like a
mosquito, but very plumose antennae.
Non-biting. Crepuscular, summer; ponds,
lakes. Larva transparent (hence name),
has 2 air containers which help it float
horizontally in water; jerky movement;
predatory, uses antennae for grasping
water-fleas, other prey. Common, often
abundant. T, ex Ic. [8] [larva 9]
C. flavicans similar sp.

gnat, non-biting midge *Chironomus
plumosus* CHIRONOMIDAE BL 10–12 mm.
Antennae hairy, thorax humped. Swarms
after dusk. Crepuscular, May–Jun; ponds,
lakes. Larva ('bloodworm') worm-like,
<2 cm long, red; in mud; swims by
curling up and extending sharply.
Common, often abundant. Br, Ir, Fr, Lu,
Be, Ne, Ge, FS. [10] [larva 11]

black-flies *Simulium* SIMULIIDAE BL 2 mm.
♀ has vicious bite; ♂ feeds on nectar.
Diurnal and crepuscular, summer; rivers,
lakes, streams. Larva <1·5 mm long,
slender; hind-end expanded and attached
to stone or plant; 2 fans of bristles strain
food particles from water. Common. T.
[12] [larva 13]

fly *Hilara maura* EMPIDAE BL 4–5 mm,
WS 10 mm. Adult swarms low over water,
weaving in and out just above surface;
preys on smaller flies. Summer; ponds,
ditches. Larva lives in humus at water's
edge. Common. T, ex Ic. [14]

fly *Hydrellia albilabris* EPHYDRIDAE
BL 10 mm. Adult runs over water surface.
Diurnal, Aug; ponds, ditches. Larva lives
under water, mining in water-plants.
Common. T, ex Ic. [15] Many related spp.

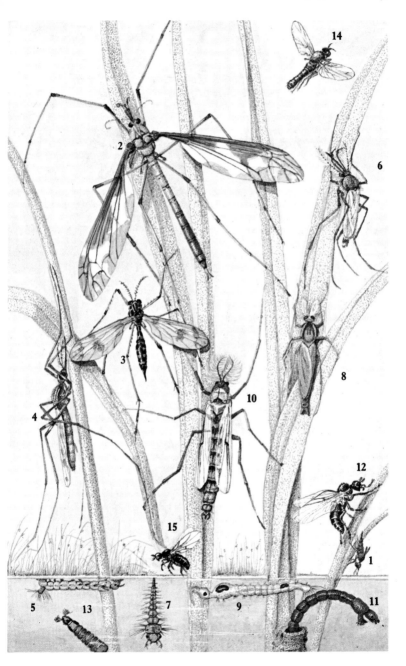

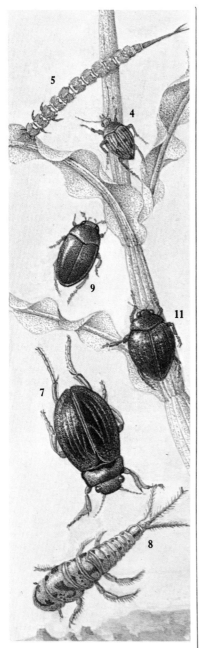

Beetles (Coleoptera). Mostly compact with tough skins; biting mouthparts; usually strong legs; no cerci; forewings hardened to form non-overlapping, horny elytra which protect membranous hindwings and abdomen. Many fly readily, others flightless. Metamorphosis complete; larvae varied.

ground-beetle *Chlaenius nigricornis* CARABIDAE BL 10–11 mm. Head coppery-green; thorax brown, broader at front; elytra greenish-yellow with coppery-black patches on sides, black apex and pair of black spots; legs yellow and black. Spring, summer; marshes, water-margins. Adult and larva predatory on other insects. Larva elongate, hairy. Local. T, ex Ic. [1]

water-beetle *Peltodytes caesus* HALIPLIDAE BL 3·5–4 mm. Body oval; antennae long, slender; legs hairy for swimming; pale yellow with black stripes; elytra strongly spotted. Summer; silty ponds. Adult and larva feed on algae. Larva aquatic, with 2 long cerci and long, hairy processes from all abdominal segments. Local. T, ex Ic. [2] [larva 3]

water-beetle *Haliplus ruficollis* HALIPLIDAE BL 2–2·5 mm. Oval, with pointed posterior; yellow-brown with darker stripes and black spots on elytra. Adult predatory. Spring-autumn; ponds, lakes. Larva aquatic, with long process on each side of body. Common. T, ex Ic. [4] [larva 5]

water-beetle *Haliplus fulvus* HALIPLIDAE BL 3·5–4·5 mm. Oval; dark reddish-brown; darker marks on elytra. Adults inactive, creep around on substrate. Summer; silty ponds. Larva and adult feed on algae. Larva aquatic, similar to *H. ruficollis*. Widespread. T, ex Ic. [6]

Screech Beetle *Hygrobia hermanni* HYGROBIIDAE BL 9–12 mm. Head and body

reddish-brown; elytra with black fore-
and hind-margins; underside of abdomen
covered with fine, short hairs. Feeds on
worms, insect larvae. Screeching sound
produced by ♂ and ♀, by rubbing apex of
abdomen against file-like structure below
elytra. Mar–Oct; ponds, esp with muddy
bottoms. Larva aquatic, with 3 cerci,
broad head and thorax; feeds on *Tubifex*
worms in mud; pupates out of water.
Common. CE, WE. [7] [larva 8]

water-beetle *Noterus clavicornis*
DYTISCIDAE BL 4–5 mm. Antennae dilated;
elytra with distinct indentations
posteriorly; hindlegs modified for
swimming; yellow-brown or reddish-
brown, glossy. Spring-autumn; stagnant
waters, ponds, with rich vegetation. Larva
aquatic, elongate, predatory. Local. T,
ex Ic, but only sFS. [9]

water-beetle *Laccophilus hyalinus*
DYTISCIDAE BL 4–5 mm. Oval; yellow-
brown with lighter patches on elytra;
hindlegs hairy, used for swimming.
Spring-autumn; ponds. Larva aquatic,
with long, thin legs, predatory. Common.
T, ex Ic, but only sFS. [10]

water-beetle *Hyphydrus ovatus*
DYTISCIDAE BL 4–5 mm. Oval with
pointed posterior; ♂ elytra strongly
punctured, ♀ less so; hindlegs fringed
with hairs; reddish-brown; thin dark lines
down elytra. Predatory. All year; ponds,
lakes, with vegetation. Larva aquatic,
yellowish, with darker cross bands,
predatory. Local, sometimes common.
T, ex Ic, but only sBr, sIr. [11]

water-beetle *Hydroporus palustris*
DYTISCIDAE BL 3–4 mm. Oval; blackish-
brown with yellow edges; hindlegs fringed
with hairs. Predatory. Spring-autumn;
ponds, lakes. Larva aquatic, elongate,
yellow-brown with prominent jaws,
predatory. Common. T, ex Ic. [12]

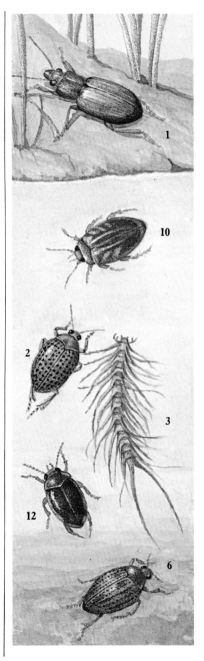

water-beetle *Agabus bipustulatus*
DYTISCIDAE BL 10–11 mm. Oval, shiny
black; reddish marks on head; antennae
reddish-brown; narrow grooves on
prothorax and elytra; elytra with slightly
darker lines. Flies freely. Mar–Sep; ponds,
stagnant water. Adult and larva predatory;
larva hunts over bottom of pond, comes
to surface. Common. T. [1] Several
similar spp.

water-beetle *Platambus maculatus*
DYTISCIDAE BL 7–8 mm. Head and thorax
yellow-brown; elytra brown with
prominent yellow marks on outer edges;
hindlegs fringed with hairs. Predatory.
Most of year; running water with stony
bottoms. Larva aquatic, predatory;
overwinters. T, ex Ic, but only sFS, ? Ir.
[2] [larva 3]

water-beetle *Acilius sulcatus* DYTISCIDAE
BL 16–18 mm. Bronzy reddish-brown,
heavily spotted; brown between yellow-
black patches on head; thorax with black
lines; elytra brown and smooth in ♂, red-
brown with longitudinal ridges in ♀.
Predatory. Mar–Nov; gravelly ponds,
lakes. Larva aquatic; slender in front,
with humped outline when viewed from
side; head more elongate than *Dytiscus*
larvae. Common. T, ex Ic. [♂ 4]

Great Diving-beetle *Dytiscus marginalis*
DYTISCIDAE BL 27–33 mm. Elytra ridged in
♀, smoother in ♂; shiny olive-black or
brownish-black with yellow edges.
Predatory, very voracious, will attack
young fish, newts and water insects; feeds
in water by day, flies by night. Feb–Nov;
ponds, still waters, sometimes rivers.
Larva aquatic; brown, elongate, with 2
short cerci; long, curved jaws; lives
amongst pondweeds; feeds on young fish,
newts. Common. T, ex Ic. [♂ 5] [larva 6]
Several similar spp.

diving-beetle *Dytiscus dimidiatus*
DYTISCIDAE BL 33–37 mm. ♂ smooth, ♀
with ridges along elytra, usually with
posterior part smooth; margins of
head and elytra yellow, margins of

thorax are less yellow than in
D. marginalis. Active, flies at night; preys
on small fish, newts. Nocturnal, May–
Oct; ponds, lakes. Larva brownish,
elongate, with sickle-shaped jaws; lives
amongst pondweeds; preys on small fish,
newts, insects. Local. T, ex Ir, Ic, No,
rare Fi. [♂ 7]

whirligig-beetle *Gyrinus natator*
GYRINIDAE BL 4·5–7 mm. Oval; elytra
narrower posteriorly; eyes divided into 2
parts for vision in air and water, upper
part separated from lower part by
antennae; middle- and hind-legs short,
paddle-like, for swimming; forelegs grasp
prey. Gregarious; swims in active
gyrations and curves on surface; dives
below when alarmed. Jun–Oct; ponds,
slow streams. Larva elongate, with pair of
long, pointed processes on each abdominal
segment and 4 processes from last
abdominal segment; lives at edge of
ponds in underwater vegetation; preys on
aquatic insects; pupates in cocoon out of
water. Common, often abundant. T, ex Ic,
rare No. [8] [larva 9] Several closely
allied spp.

Hairy Whirligig-beetle *Orectochilus
villosus* GYRINIDAE BL 5–6 mm. Oval; more
elongate than *Gyrinus*; eyes similarly
divided; hind- and middle-legs short,
paddle-like. Gregarious; swims actively in
circles, mainly at night; hides by day;
dives if threatened; preys on insects. Jul–
Oct; lakes, rivers. Larva elongate with 4
processes at apex of abdomen and feathery
processes on each abdominal segment;
amongst stones in lakes, rivers.
Widespread, common. T, ex Ic, rare FS.
[10]

water-beetle *Helophorus aquaticus*
HYDROPHILIDAE BL 5–9 mm. Palps longer
than antennae; parallel-sided elytra each
with 10 rows of black spots. Plant-feeder;
crawls over water-plants; rarely swims.
Spring-summer; ponds, ditches. Larva
aquatic; legs short, long hairy processes
from tip of abdomen; plant-feeder.
Widespread. T, ex Ic. [11]

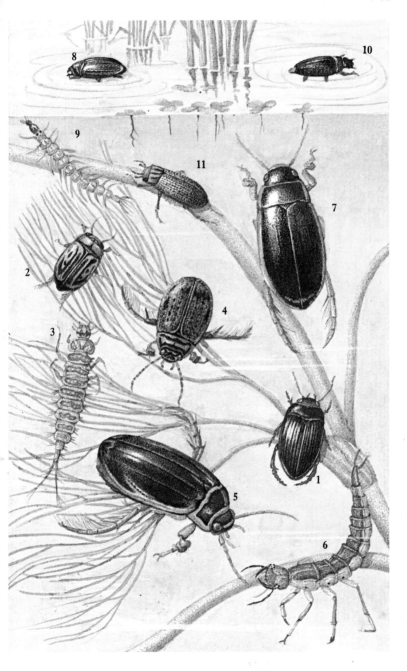

water-beetle *Hydrobius fuscipes*
HYDROPHILIDAE BL 6–7 mm. Palps as long
as or slightly longer than antennae; each
elytra with 11 rows of black spots.
Predatory; clambers over water-plants;
flies freely. Spring–autumn; ponds,
stagnant pools. Larva aquatic; squat, legs
short, thorax and head brown; tip to
abdomen with brown patch, sides hairy;
feeds on small crustaceans, usually near
water-surface. Common, T, ex Ic. [1]

water-beetle *Hydrochara caraboides*
HYDROPHILIDAE BL 14–18 mm. Shiny,
greenish-black; palps longer than black-
tipped antennae; elytra with 5 rows of
black spots. Predatory, also feeds on plant
debris; crawls over water-plants. Summer;
ponds, lakes. Larva aquatic; hangs from
surface film by tip of abdomen; predatory.
Widespread. T, ex Ic, rare Fi, No. [2]

Great Silver Water-beetle *Hydrophilus*
piceus HYDROPHILIDAE BL 34–48 mm.
Elytra with lines which join together;
palps longer than slightly clubbed
antennae. Feeds on algae, water-plants.
♀ lays eggs, encloses them in silken bag at
surface with part of bag protruding
through surface. Spring–summer; ponds,
lakes, usually over muddy bottoms. Larva
aquatic; elongate, with prominent jaws,
no processes on abdomen; crawls over
vegetation; preys on small fish, tadpoles,
insects, water snails. Locally common. T,
ex Ic, rare Fi, No. [3]

water-beetle *Enochrus coarctatus*
HYDROPHILIDAE BL 3·5–4 mm. Palps
longer than clubbed antennae. Crawls over
water-plants; eggs laid in small triangular
silk bag, often attached to duckweed.
Summer; ponds, lakes. Larva short,
flattened, head and 1st segment of thorax
narrower than next 2 segments; crawls
over submerged vegetation; plant-feeder.
Widespread. T, ex Ic. [4]

water-beetle *Berosus signaticollis*
HYDROPHILIDAE BL 5–6 mm. Elytra brown
with rows of spots. Swims well; usually

predatory; sound produced by rubbing
elytra on abdomen. Summer; ditches,
ponds. Larva feeds on water-plants.
Common. T, ex Ic. [5]

water-beetle *Heterocerus fenestratus*
HETEROCERIDAE BL 3–5 mm. Body oval,
very hairy; head large, eyes half-hidden;
legs stout, tibia of forelegs strongly spiny;
thorax black, elytra yellow-brown with
dark brown band centrally and black-
brown patch near margin. Flies evening.
Summer; ponds, streams; lives in galleries
in mud at edge or below water-margin.
Larva has prominent jaws; thorax broad
with narrower abdomen; burrows in mud.
Local. T, but only sBr, sFS. [6]

13-spot Ladybird *Hippodamia*
tredecimpunctata COCCINELLIDAE
BL 4–7 mm. Not as oval as commoner
ladybirds; elytra yellow-brown with 13
black spots; head black with yellow
centre; thorax with black patch centrally
and 2 lateral spots. Apr–Sep; lakes,
marshes. Adult and larva prey on
aphids. Local, sometimes common. T,
ex Ic. [7]

beetle *Prasocuris phellandri* CHRYSOM-
ELIDAE BL 5–7 mm. Greenish iridescence,
black and yellow stripes; thorax broader
near middle with yellowish edge and
iridescent, black, central band. Aug–Jun,
overwinters; edges of lakes, marshes,
amongst Umbelliferae, esp water-
dropwort. Larva feeds on water-dropwort,
when older burrows into stem. Common.
T, ex Ic. [8]

Reed-beetle *Donacia aquatica*
CHRYSOMELIDAE BL 6–10 mm. Iridescent;
head green; thorax bronzy-brown, lightly
spotted, with expanded front margin;
elytra bright green at sides, broad reddish-
purple or violet stripe centrally, not
reaching tip; hind tibia enlarged, with
spine. Feeds on water- and marsh-plants.
Mar–Aug; ponds, lakes, marshes. Larva
burrows into stems of aquatic plants
including bur-reed. Local. T, ex Ic. [9]

Many spp of spiders are associated with fresh, brackish or sea water and marshland, but *Argyroneta aquatica* is the only sp in the world which spends most of its life under water.

spider *Clubiona phragmitis* CLUBIONIDAE BL 5–11 mm. Carapace reddish-brown with darker head region; abdomen dark brown, noticeably silky. Apr–Nov; in sedges and reeds near water's edge; hunts at night for insects; in daytime sometimes found in silk retreat-sac. T, ex Ic. [1]

wolf-spider *Arctosa cinerea* LYCOSIDAE BL 12–14 mm. Large size; carapace dark brown or grey with radiating markings; abdomen dark, brownish, with red-brown lanceolate stripe and black markings. All year; among stones in river-beds, lake-sides; builds silken tube which usually opens under a stone; remains in tube during winter months even if river rises. Hunts for insects. T, ex Ic. [2]

wolf-spider *Pirata piraticus* LYCOSIDAE BL 4·5–9 mm. Forked mark on carapace distinctive; abdomen with stripe down middle and white spots conspicuous in living spider. ♂ Apr–May, ♀ all year; in wet places; runs quickly across water; hunts prey, but builds retreat-tube often in bog-moss. Egg cocoon white, carried attached to ♀'s spinnerets (as in all wolf-spiders). Associated with hot springs in Ic. T. [♀ 3]

Marsh Spider *Dolomedes fimbriatus* PISAURIDAE BL ♂ 9–13 mm, ♀ 13–20 mm. Large size, handsome; deep, rich brown, with conspicuous bright yellow or white bands. Apr–Jun; near and on surface of water, may climb down plant stems beneath water-surface if disturbed. Mistakenly called 'raft spider' because sometimes on floating leaves, but does not build raft. T, ex Ic. [4]

Water Spider *Argyroneta aquatica* AGELENIDAE BL 8–16 mm. Large, brownish. All year; in lakes, ponds and ditches; swims under water clothed in bubble of air which shines like quicksilver; lives in diving bell of silk filled with air. Hunts aquatic animals. Mates within bell, eggs laid in upper part of chamber. Unique spider because aquatic, rarely leaves water. T, ex Ic. [5] [bell 6]

spider *Antistea elegans* AGELENIDAE BL 2·5–3 mm. Transverse row of 6 spinnerets distinctive; carapace and legs orange to bright yellow-brown; abdomen mousy, greyish-brown, with long hairs. May–Aug; in wet places; builds small sheet web in bog-moss or in dips in ground. T, ex Ic, Sw, No. [7]

spider *Tetragnatha extensa* TETRAGNATH-IDAE BL 8–12 mm. Slender, with long, narrow abdomen, very long legs and protruding jaws; carapace light brown; abdomen greenish with silvery markings and dark veins. Abundant, Jun–Aug; close to water; spins fine orb web on reeds and shrubs. At rest it lies inconspicuous along stems with outstretched legs. T. [8]

spider *Araneus cornutus* ARANEIDAE BL 5–8 mm. Carapace light brown with darker radiating streaks; abdomen usually cream with brown, pink or reddish leaf-like pattern, but colour variable. All year; near water; builds orb web on plants; lives in silken retreat connected to web by signal thread which detects prey. Both sexes sometimes together in retreat. T. [9]

money-spider *Gnathonarium dentatum* LINYPHIIDAE BL 2·5–3 mm. Carapace brown to dark brown; abdomen grey to black, with indistinct, longitudinal, white band. Apr–Oct; in wet areas, stream- and lake-sides; builds minute sheet web. T, ex Ic. [10]

spider *Floronia bucculenta* LINYPHIIDAE BL *c*4 mm. Carapace light brown, with blackish marginal markings; abdomen rather globular esp in ♀, grey-brown with white spots and black markings posteriorly. Able to change colour: when disturbed, drops from sheet web to ground, white spots contract and abdomen becomes dull brown. Jun–Oct; on river-banks, pond- and lake-sides; also in heather. T, ex Ic. [♀ 11]

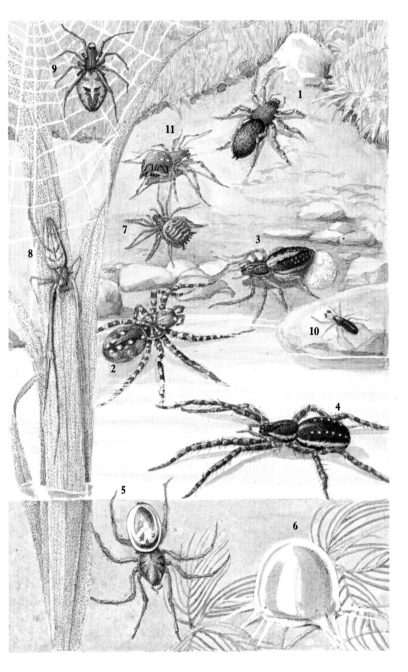

Lampern *Lampetra fluviatilis* PETROMY-
ZONIDAE BL <50 cm. Snake-like body,
sucker disc with few sharply pointed teeth;
dorsal fins separate. Greenish-brown above
merging with yellow belly. On coastlines
and in rivers. Migrates from sea in winter-
spring. Adult sucks blood of bony fishes.
Juv lives in mud of rivers 2–3 years, not
parasitic. T, ex Ic, eGe, ePo, Cz, eFi, No.
[1]

Brook Lamprey *Lampetra planeri*
PETROMYZONIDAE BL <25 cm. Snake-like
body, sucker disc with few blunt teeth;
dorsal fins united at base. Dark brown to
slate grey above, yellowish below. Spawns
in spring in gravel. Adult does not feed.
Br, Ir, Fr, Be, Ne, De, nGe, nPo, Fi, Sw.
[2]

Sturgeon *Acipenser sturio* ACIPENSERIDAE
BL 350 cm. Elongate body, asymmetrical
tail; 5 rows of bony plates on back, sides
and belly. 2 pairs of barbels around small
mouth. Greenish-brown above, lighter
below. Spawns late spring on gravel
bottom; young stay in river for 2–3 years
then migrate to sea. Feeds on molluscs,
worms, crustaceans, bottom-living fishes.
Virtually exterminated in N Europe.
Vagrant nGe, Baltic. [3]

Eel *Anguilla anguilla* ANGUILLIDAE
BL <1 m. Snake-like body, lower jaw
longer than upper; pectoral fins rounded.
Greenish-brown above, golden-yellow to
silvery below. Juv enters rivers in spring
from mid-Atlantic spawning grounds;
lives in freshwater for up to 20 years then
migrates to sea. Feeds on invertebrates,
scavenges on waste. T, ex nIc, SC, (eGe,
Po). [4]

Twaite Shad *Alosa fallax* CLUPEIDAE
BL <55 cm. Herring-like, but with deep
body, serrated edge on belly, deep notch
in middle of upper lip. 40–60 rakers on
1st gill arch. Deep blue above, intense
silvery sides, row of dusky spots along
upper side. Lower reaches of coastal rivers.
Spawns in spring in lower river.
Migrates to sea after 6 months to feed
on crustaceans, small fishes. T,
ex nIc, nNo. [5]

Powan *Coregonus lavaretus* COREGONIDAE
BL <20–70 cm (varies with populations).
Herring-like, but with fleshy fin on back,
upper jaw longer than lower, reaching to
eye; 33–39 rakers on 1st gill. Light grey-
green above, silvery on sides. Mainly
confined to mountain lakes. Spawns in
winter on gravelly shallows. Feeds on
small crustaceans. nWales, nScotland,
De, nGe, nwPo, Fi, Sw. [6]

Houting *Coregonus oxyrinchus*
COREGONIDAE BL <50 cm. Herring-like,
but with fleshy fin on back; snout very
long and pointed; 35–44 rakers on 1st
gill arch. Greenish-blue above, silver
sides. Lowland rivers, estuaries, lakes.
Spawns in autumn-winter. Feeds on
planktonic crustaceans. Extinct in North
Sea. nPo, Fi, Sw. [7]

Salmon *Salmo salar* SALMONIDAE
BL <1·5 m. Cigar-shaped body, fleshy fin
on back; tail stalk narrow, tail fin
shallowly forked; upper jaw reaches to
eye. Young (parr) dark above, 8–11
rounded dusky marks on sides with
orange spots; adults steel blue above,
silvery below. Spawns in winter in gravel
shallows high up rivers. Migrates to sea to
feed on crustaceans, fishes. T, ex Ge,
Cz, Po. [8]

Brown Trout *Salmo trutta* SALMONIDAE
BL <23–100 cm (varies with populations).
Cigar-shaped body, fleshy fin on back;
tail stalk deep, tail fin straight-edged;
upper jaw reaches past eye. Brownish
above with numerous black and reddish
spots; in large lakes silvery. Spawns in
winter in river gravel. Some forms (sea
trout) migrate to sea. Feeds on small
crustaceans, water insects; large
specimens eat fishes. T. [9]

Rainbow Trout *Salmo gairdneri*
SALMONIDAE BL <1 m. Cigar-shaped body,
fleshy fin on back; tail stalk moderately
deep. Brownish-green above, cream below,
body and fins with dense small black
spots, clear rainbow band along sides.
Feeds on crustaceans, water insects. Few
natural breeding populations. (W ex Ic,
Fi, No, from nw N America.) [10]

Arctic Charr *Salvelinus alpinus*
SALMONIDAE BL <25–100 cm (varies with
populations). Cigar-shaped body, fleshy
fin on back; body scales very small. In
rivers, steel blue above, silvery on sides
with reddish spots; in lakes, greenish-
brown above, lighter below; leading edges
of pectoral, pelvic and anal fins light.
Spawns winter-spring in gravel. Feeds on
planktonic crustaceans; migrants to sea
eat fishes. Mountain lakes Br, Ir, FS;
rivers Ic, nNo. [1]

Brook Charr *Salvelinus fontinalis*
SALMONIDAE BL <75 cm. Cigar-shaped
body, fleshy fin on back; body scales very
small. Olive-green to brown above, with
creamy spots making wavy lines, sides
lighter. Spawns in winter. Feeds on
insects, insect larvae, crustaceans. (Br,
Ge, Sw, from eN America.) [2]

Grayling *Thymallus thymallus*
THYMALLIDAE BL <50 cm. Elongate body,
fleshy fin on back; body scales large;
dorsal fin long and high. Steel blue above,
silvery green on sides, with faint violet
stripes; dorsal fin with dusky spots. Clean,
cool rivers and mountain lakes. Spawns
early spring in gravel. Bottom-feeder, on
insect larvae, molluscs, crustaceans. T,
but local, ex nBr, Ir, Ic, No. [3]

Pike *Esox lucius* ESOCIDAE BL <1·3 m.
Elongate head and body; dorsal and anal
fins opposite, placed near tail. Greenish-
brown above, yellowish on sides and
below; flecked with light golden spots and
lines. Slow streams, lakes amongst
vegetation. Spawns early spring in weed-
beds, flooded water-meadows. Feeds on
fishes, occasionally water-birds, mammals,
amphibians; juv on insects, crustaceans.
T, ex Ic, nNo. [4]

European Mudminnow *Umbra krameri*
UMBRIDAE BL <13 cm. Small, stout body,
with pronounced scales; dorsal fin
opposite pelvic fin base. Greenish-brown
above, with dusky vertical bars, yellowish
below. Swamps, overgrown ponds and
streams where dissolved oxygen is low.
Spawns in spring. Feeds on insect larvae,
crustaceans, molluscs. Ge, Cz. [5]

Carp *Cyprinus carpio* CYPRINIDAE
BL <90 cm. Stout, heavy body; dorsal
fin long-based, high in front; 2 pairs of
barbels on lips. Scaleless and partly scaled
forms occur. Brownish-green above,
shading to golden below. Warm, slow
weedy rivers, lakes. Feeds on bottom-
living insect larvae, snails, crustaceans,
plants. Spawns late spring amongst
water-plants. Cz, (Br ex Scotland, Ir,
Fr, Lu, Be, Ne, De, Ge, Po, Fi,
Sw). [6]

Crucian Carp *Carassius carassius*
CYPRINIDAE BL <40 cm. Deep body;
dorsal fin long-based, of uniform height;
no barbels on lips. Olive-green to reddish-
brown above, yellowish below. Still
waters, even marshy pools. Spawns May–
June, eggs attached to water-plants. Feeds
on plants, insect larvae. seBr, Fr, Lu, Be,
Ne, De, Ge, Cz, Po, Fi, sSw. [7]

Tench *Tinca tinca* CYPRINIDAE
BL <70 cm. Thickset body, deep tail;
dorsal and anal fins short-based and
rounded; single barbel each side of

mouth; scales small. Deep greenish-brown
above, lighter below. Mainly in still
waters and lowland rivers, in dense
vegetation. Spawns early summer amongst
water-plants. Feeds on insect larvae,
worms. T, ex nBr, Ic, Fi, nSw, No. [8]

Bream *Abramis brama* CYPRINIDAE
BL <80 cm. Deep body, with steep back;
long-based anal fin (24–30 principal rays);
mouth down-turned, extensible. Dark
brown or greyish above, golden sides;
young silvery. Slow-flowing rivers, lakes,
ponds; spawns late spring-summer
amongst weeds. Bottom-feeder, on worms,
insect larvae. T, ex nBr, Ic, nSw, No.
[9]

Zope *Abramis ballerus* CYPRINIDAE
BL <36 cm. Very narrow body; back with
shallow curve; long-based anal fin (36–43
principal rays); dorsal fin short-based but
high. Dark blue-green above, sides silvery
with yellowish tinge. Lowland rivers and
lakes, schools in open water. Spawns Apr–
May in dense weed growth. nGe, Cz, Po,
sFi, sSw. [10]

Zährte *Vimba vimba* CYPRINIDAE
BL <40 cm. Slender body, smoothly
curved back; dorsal fin short-based but
high; anal fin (18–21 principal rays);
snout long. Grey-blue above, yellowish
sides; spawning fish reddish-orange below.
Bottom-living in lowland rivers, estuaries,
lakes. Migrates up river to spawn May–
July on stony bottom. nwGe, Cz, nwPo,
sFi, sSw. [1]

Silver Bream *Blicca bjoerkna* CYPRINIDAE
BL <25 cm. Rather deep body; steep
back; dorsal fin high, anal fin long-based
(21–23 principal rays); eye larger than
snout length. Light olive-brown above,
sides bright silver. Schools in lowland
rivers, lakes, ponds. Spawns summer
amongst water-plants. Feeds on plants,
insect larvae, crustaceans. seBr, Fr, Lu,
Be, Ne, De, Ge, Cz, Po, sFi, sSw. [2]

Bleak *Alburnus alburnus* CYPRINIDAE
BL <15 cm. Slender body; head small,
mouth upturned, lower jaw prominent,
eye large; anal fin long-based (16–20
principal rays). Blue-green above,
brilliant silvery sides. Schools in surface
waters of lowland rivers. Feeds on small
crustaceans, insects. Spawns May–Jun in
shallows among stones or plants. T, ex w
and nBr, Ir, Ic, No. [3]

Asp *Aspius aspius* CYPRINIDAE BL <60 cm.
Slender, compressed body, with sharp
keel below; head pointed, lower jaw long;
scales small. Greenish on back, sides
silvery; ventral fins deep red. In moderate
currents in rivers, large lakes. Spawns
Apr–May over stony bottom. Feeds on
fishes; young on crustaceans. Ge, Cz, Po,
sFi, sSw. [4]

Barbel *Barbus barbus* CYPRINIDAE
BL <60 cm. Elongate, rounded body,
flattened on belly. 2 pairs of barbels on
upper lip; dorsal fin short-based, high,
with serrated spine. Warm green-brown
above, yellowish below. Bottom-living on
clean gravel in lowland rivers. Generally
crepuscular. Spawns late spring over
gravel. Feeds on invertebrates. seBr, Fr,
Lu, Be, Ne, sGe. [5]

Gudgeon *Gobio gobio* CYPRINIDAE
BL <16 cm. Elongate, rounded body,
flattened on belly. A barbel at each corner
of mouth; scales large. Greenish-brown
above, creamy below; series of blotches
along sides. Bottom-living in rivers and
lakes in small schools. Spawns early
summer amongst plants, stones. Feeds on
insect larvae, crustaceans, molluscs. T, ex
nBr, Ic, nFi, nSw, No. [6]

Bitterling *Rhodeus sericeus* CYPRINIDAE
BL <7 cm. Deep, plump body; small
head; dorsal fin moderately long-based;
lateral line on first 5–6 scales. Grey-brown
above, sides silvery with pink flush and
bright metallic streak near tail. Lowland
lakes and backwaters of rivers. Spawns
Apr–Jun, ♀ lays eggs inside freshwater
mussel. Feeds on planktonic crustaceans.
Fr, Lu, Be, Ne, Ge, Cz, Po, (Br). [♂ 7]
[♀ 8]

Dace *Leuciscus leuciscus* CYPRINIDAE
BL <25 cm. Slender body, narrow head,
small mouth; edges of dorsal and anal fins
concave. Greenish-olive above, bright

silvery sides; lower fins pale yellow.
Schools in rivers where current moderate.
Spawns early spring in gravel shallows.
Feeds on larval and flying insects, crusta-
ceans. T, ex nBr, Ic, nSw, No; (Ir). [9]

Ide *Leuciscus idus* CYPRINIDAE BL <50 cm.
Fairly slender body, humped back, blunt
head; scales small (56–61 in lateral line);
anal fin concave. Greenish-brown above,
sides and belly silvery. Bright orange
variant called 'orfe'. Lower rivers, lakes
and brackish estuaries in deep water.
Spawns in shallows over gravel. Feeds on
insect larvae, crustaceans, small fishes.
Ne, De, Ge, Cz, Po, Fi, Sw. [10]

Chub *Leuciscus cephalus* CYPRINIDAE
BL <50 cm. Fairly slender body, broad
head and 'shoulders'; head and mouth
large; scales large (44–46 in lateral line);
dorsal and anal fins convex. Greenish- or
grey-brown above, sides silvery, each
scale dusky-edged. Rivers and large lakes;
schooling when young. Spawns May–Jun
on gravel. Feeds on invertebrates, fishes.
T, ex nBr, Ir, Ic, nFi, nSw, No. [11]

Ziege *Pelecus cultratus* CYPRINIDAE
BL <40 cm. Elongate body, with deep
belly; jaws turned upwards; pectoral fin
long and pointed; lateral line wavy.
Greenish-blue above, sides silvery with
pinkish tinge. Estuaries and brackish
water in schools at surface. Spawns May–
Jul in freshwater. Feeds on fish,
crustaceans, insects. nwPo, sFi. [1]

Minnow *Phoxinus phoxinus* CYPRINIDAE
BL <8 cm. Cigar-shaped body, blunt
head; short-based, rounded fins; minute
scales. Olive-brown above, creamy below;
series of dusky blotches on sides.
Breeding ♂ red below, with black throat.
Schools in upland rivers and lakes. Spawns
May–Jul on gravel shoals. Feeds on
planktonic crustaceans, insects. T, ex nBr,
Ic, No, (Ir). [2]

Roach *Rutilus rutilus* CYPRINIDAE
BL <35 cm. Moderately deep body,
small head, dorsal fin origin above pelvic
fin base. Greenish-brown above, sides
silvery; ventral fins orange to red; iris of
eye red. Lowland rivers and lakes in
schools. Spawns Apr–Jun in water-plants,
often forms hybrids with related spp.
Feeds on plant material, insect larvae,
crustaceans. Br, Fr, Lu, Be, Ne, De, Ge,
Cz, Po, Fi, Sw, (Ir). [3]

Rudd *Scardinius erythrophthalmus*
CYPRINIDAE BL <40 cm. Moderately deep
body, small head, mouth oblique; dorsal
fin origin behind pelvic fin base. Greenish-
brown above, bronze sides; fins blood
red; iris of eye golden. Lowland rivers,
marshes and lakes in schools close to
surface. Spawns Apr–Jun in vegetation.
Feeds on insects and their larvae, crustaceans. T, ex nBr, Ic, nFi, nSw, No; (Ir). [4]

Stone Loach *Noemacheilus barbatulus*
COBITIDAE BL <11 cm. Slender body but
cylindrical anteriorly; head moderate with
6 long barbels round mouth. Greenish-
brown above, yellowish below; sides
yellowish, with dusky blotches. Upland
and lowland rivers, clean lakes; usually
under stones or in weed-beds. Crepuscular.
Spawns Apr–Jun; eggs laid among stones.
T, ex nBr, Ic, nFi, nSw, No. [5]

Spined Loach *Cobitis taenia* COBITIDAE
BL <11 cm. Slender body, with flattened
sides; small head, numerous short barbels
round mouth, spine hidden under each
eye. Light brown above, creamy below,
dusky patches on sides. Lowland rivers
and lakes, burrows in soft mud and
blanket weed. Spawns Apr–Jun amongst
algae. Bottom-feeder, on crustaceans.
e England, Fr, Lu, Be, Ne, De, Ge, Cz,
Po, Fi, sSw. [6]

Weatherfish *Misgurnus fossilis* COBITIDAE
BL <14 cm. Slender body but cylindrical;
small head, 5 pairs of barbels round
mouth. Grey-brown above, yellowish-
brown below with lengthwise dark stripes
on sides. Lowland ponds and marshes
often overgrown; gulps air at surface.
Spawns Apr–Jun; eggs shed on water-
plants. Fr, Lu, Be, Ne, Ge, Cz, Po. [7]

Wels *Silurus glanis* SILURIDAE BL <1·5 m.
Elongate body; broad head with 3 pairs
barbels, upper ones long; dorsal fin small;
anal fin long. Dull brown or green above,
mottled yellowish on sides. Deep lowland
rivers and lakes. Nocturnal. Spawns May–
Jul in hollow in bottom. Feeds on fishes,
occasional ducklings, water voles.
Ne, Ge, Cz, Po, sFi, sSw, (Br, Fr). [8]

Black Bullhead *Ictalurus melas*
ICTALURIDAE BL <25 cm. Stout body;
fairly broad head; 4 pairs of barbels,
longest on snout; long, low fleshy fin on
back, anal fin with 17–21 rays. Dark
brown above, sides with golden sheen; fin
membranes black. Lowland rivers and
ponds. Spawns in nest on bottom; parents
guard nest. (Br, Fr, Ne, Be, De, Ge, Po,
from eN America). [9]

Burbot *Lota lota* GADIDAE BL <50 cm.
Cigar-shaped body; single chin barbel;
long second dorsal and anal fins. Dull
green above, cream below; sides mottled
with yellow. Lowland rivers and lakes
under banks, tree roots, in weed-beds.
Crepuscular. Spawns Dec–Mar on mud or
gravel bottoms. Feeds on insect larvae,
crustaceans, fishes. T, ex Ir, Ic, nwNo,
but probably extinct Br. [10]

Stickleback *Gasterosteus aculeatus*
GASTEROSTEIDAE BL <5 cm. Moderately
slender body, flattened sides; 2 large,
separate, dorsal spines, heavy spine in
each pelvic fin. Brown-green above, sides
silvery; breeding ♂ with red throat and
belly. Lakes, rivers, estuaries, usually in
shallow, clear water; spawns spring-
summer in nest on bottom, not in mountainous areas. Feeds on crustaceans, worms,
insects. T, ex Ic, Sw, No. [♂ 1] [♀ 2]

Nine-spined Stickleback *Pungitius
pungitius* GASTEROSTEIDAE BL <6 cm.
Slender body; 8–10 short spines on back;
tail stalk long. Dark olive-green, paler
below; breeding ♂ with black throat, light
pelvic spines. Lowland rivers, ponds,
marshes. Spawns summer in nest built
in weed-bed off bottom. Feeds on
crustaceans, insect larvae, T, ex Ic,
central Fr, Ge, mountainous FS. [3]

Four-horn Sculpin *Myoxocephalus
quadricornis* COTTIDAE BL <30 cm. Slender
body but broad head; 4 sharp spines on
each gill cover; rounded spongy knobs on
top of head. Grey-brown above, yellowish
below. Isolated lakes and brackish areas.
Spawns in early winter. Feeds on
crustaceans, fishes. FS. [4]

Bullhead *Cottus gobio* COTTIDAE
BL <8 cm. Rather slender body; broad,
flattened head; short spine on each gill
cover; pelvic fin rays equal length,
relatively short. Brownish or greenish,
darker mottled above, creamy below.
Small rivers and lakes in shallows, under
stones or in weed-beds. Nocturnal.
Spawns Mar–May under stones. Feeds on
freshwater shrimps, insect larvae. T, ex
nBr, Ir, Ic, De, No. [5]

Alpine Bullhead *Cottus poecilopus*
COTTIDAE BL <8 cm. Rather slender body;
broad, flattened head; short spine on each
gill cover; inner pelvic ray shorter than
others, all rather long. Greenish-brown
above, with dusky crossbars, lighter below.
Small, upland rivers and shallows of
larger rivers, usually hidden among
stones. Spawns spring under stones. Feeds
on crustaceans. De, nGe, Po, sFi, Sw. [6]

Large-mouth Bass *Micropterus salmoides*
CENTRARCHIDAE BL <50 cm. Moderately
slender body with flattened sides; large
head; jaw reaches past eye; dorsal fins
almost separate. Deep olive above, white
below, irregular dark stripe along sides.
Rivers and lakes, esp where large weed-
beds. Feeds on fishes. (Br, Fr, Lu, Be,
Ne, De, Ge, from eN America.) [7]

Pumpkinseed *Lepomis gibbosus*
CENTRARCHIDAE BL <20 cm. Rather deep
body with flattened sides; dorsal fins
continuous; scales large. Golden-brown to
olive above, sides with wavy blue lines
and flecks, black spots on gill cover with
red edge. Small lakes and lowland rivers,
in shallow weedy water. Feeds on insects,
crustaceans, worms. (Br, Fr, Lu, Be, Ne,
Ge, Cz, Po, from eN America). [8]

Perch *Perca fluviatilis* PERCIDAE
BL <35 cm. Moderately deep body;
dorsal fins separate, 1st fin spiny.
Greenish-brown above, cream below,
dusky vertical bars across sides, intense
black spot low on 1st dorsal fin, ventral

fins red. Rivers and lakes, usually near
tree roots, weed-beds, in schools. Spawns
Apr–May, eggs in strings round plants.
Feeds on invertebrates and fishes; juv
on invertebrates. T, ex Ic, nNo. [9]

Ruffe *Gymnocephalus cernua* PERCIDAE
BL <20 cm. Rather slender body; dorsal
fins united, 1st fin spiny; hollows under
skin on head. Pale greenish-brown flecked
with dark brown above, yellow below,
ventral fins yellow. Lowland lakes and
rivers in small schools. Spawns Mar–May,
eggs stuck to plants or stones. Feeds near
bottom on insect larvae, crustaceans. T,
ex w and nBr, Ir, Ic, nNo. [10]

Zander *Stizostedion lucioperca* PERCIDAE
BL <70 cm. Slender body; head pointed,
several large fangs in jaws; dorsal fins
separate, 1st fin spiny. Greyish-green to
brown above, creamy below, faint vertical
bars on sides. Lowland rivers and lakes,
in schools in mid-water. Spawns Apr–Jun
over stony bottoms or plants. Feeds on
fish, hunts at dawn and dusk. Ge, Cz, Po,
Fi, Sw, (Br, Fr, Lu, Be, Ne, De). [11]

Amphibians are cold-blooded; in winter dormant on land or at bottom of pond. Larvae aquatic: either miniature adults with gills (newts, salamanders) or tadpoles (frogs, toads).

Common Frog *Rana temporaria* RANIDAE L 7–9 cm. Smooth skin. Colour variable, pale with dark markings; dark pads on forelimbs of breeding ♂. Soft, purring croak during mating. Damp places in fields, meadows, woods, gardens. Breeds Mar–Apr; in ponds; eggs in clumps. Food insects, worms. T, ex Ic. [1]

Marsh or **Lake Frog** *Rana ridibunda* RANIDAE L <15 cm. Pointed snout. Brown with dark markings; may be green in places; back of thighs white. ♂ produces variety of croaks, usually in chorus. Ponds, ditches, streams and lakes, favours open water. Active by day, often basks in sun. Breeds Apr–May; eggs in clumps. Food insects, slugs, occasionally fish, amphibians, lizards, mice. Ge, Cz, Po, (se Br). [2]

Edible Frog *Rana esculenta* RANIDAE L <12 cm. Pointed snout. Green to brown with dark markings; pale green stripe along middle of back; back of thighs yellow or orange with dark markings. ♂ makes growl-like croak. Ponds and lakes; hibernates in mud at bottom of pond. Breeds Apr–May. Eggs in clumps. Food insects, slugs. T, ex Ir, Ic, nSw, No, (sBr). [3] Pool frog *R. lessonae* similar, but smaller (L <9 cm). T, ex Ir, Ic, nSw, No, (sBr).

Parsley Frog *Pelodytes punctatus* PELOBATIDAE L <5 cm. Small, agile, long-limbed. Eyes prominent, vertical pupils. Grey or olive with green spots; orange warts on flanks. ♂ makes deep croak under water; weak squeak in air. In and around ponds with dense vegetation. Active by night; hides under stones or in burrow by day. Climbs walls, bushes. Breeds Feb–May and Sep–Oct; eggs in broad bands. Food worms, insects. Fr, wBe. [4]

Mud Frog, Common Spadefoot *Pelobates fuscus* PELOBATIDAE L <8 cm. Eyes large with vertical pupils; skin smooth. Large pale 'spade' on hind foot; lump on head behind eyes. Grey, pale brown, yellowish or white with brown markings; small orange spots on sides. ♂ makes repeated clicking call, alarm call squeal-like. Lowland areas, cultivated land esp where asparagus. Active by night; burrows by day. Usually on land; enters water to breed, Apr–May; eggs in bands. Food invertebrates. Smells of garlic. T, ex Br, Ir, Ic, FS. [5]

Common Tree Frog *Hyla arborea* HYLIDAE L <5 cm. Smooth skin; long limbs; adhesive pads at end of fingers and toes. Bright green, yellow or brown, with dark stripe along each flank. ♂ makes rapid-pulsed call, very loud chorus. Trees, bushes or reeds around water. Enters water to breed, May–Jun. Food insects. T, ex Br, Ir, Ic, wNe, nSw, No. [6]

Common Toad *Bufo bufo* BUFONIDAE L <12 cm. Plump; rounded head; warty skin. Colour variable, brown, green or reddish. Croaking call during mating. Damp places in woods, gardens, fields. Breeds Mar–May; in ponds; eggs in strings. Food insects, worms, slugs. T, ex Ir, Ic, nFS. [7]

Fire-bellied Toad *Bombina bombina* DISCOGLOSSIDAE L <5 cm. Back dark brown, sometimes with green markings. Belly black and red, white spots. ♂ calls 'oop, oop . . . ' in chorus, usually evening. Shallow water in lowland areas; hibernates on land. Breeds May–Jun; eggs single or in small clumps. Food insects, worms. Exposes belly and exudes distasteful secretion if attacked. De, Ge, Cz, Po, ? extinct sSw. [8]

Yellow-bellied Toad *Bombina variegata* DISCOGLOSSIDAE L <5 cm. Back grey, brown, yellowish or olive. Belly black and yellow markings. ♂ calls 'poop, poop . . . ' in chorus, usually evening. Ponds, ditches, lowland and upland areas; hibernates on land. Breeds May–Sep; eggs single or in small clumps. Food insects, worms. Exposes belly and exudes distasteful secretion if attacked. Fr, Lu, Be, Ge, Cz. [9]

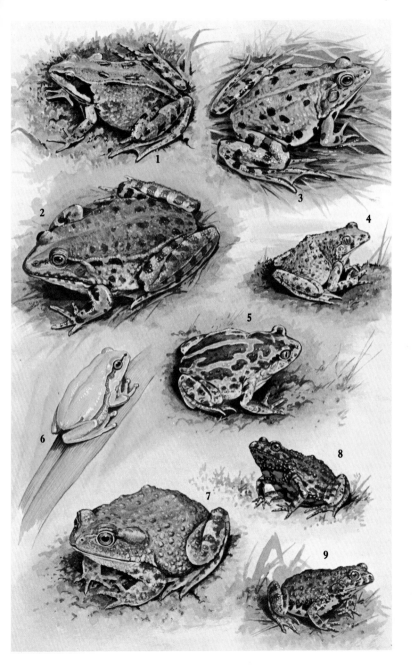

Warty or **Crested Newt** *Triturus*
cristatus SALAMANDRIDAE L <14 cm. Warty
skin. Dark grey or brown above with large
black spots; belly orange with black spots.
Breeding ♂ has large, toothed crest,
white stripe on tail. Deeper pools, lakes,
slow-flowing streams. Breeds Mar–Jun;
elaborate courtship display. Food worms,
snails, insect larvae. Exudes musty-
smelling, distasteful, white secretion when
handled. T, ex Ir, Ic, nSC. [♂ 1]

Smooth Newt *Triturus vulgaris*
SALAMANDRIDAE L <10 cm. Colour variable.
Breeding ♂ has toothed, dorsal crest and
tail; pale green, brown or grey with black
spots; orange belly; blue and red stripes
at base of tail. Breeding ♀ yellow or
brown; yellow belly; small dark spots all
over. In spring in ponds, ditches; rest of
year on land, in damp places, *eg* under
logs. Mates Feb–Jun; ♀ wraps eggs
individually in leaves. Food small insects,
frog spawn, tadpoles. T, ex Ic, nFS. [♂ 2]

Alpine Newt *Triturus alpestris*
SALAMANDRIDAE L ♂ <9 cm, ♀ <12 cm.
♂ has low, black and white crest, more
spots than ♀. In spring in ponds, mostly
in hilly country; rest of year on land,
hiding by day, wandering by night.
Enters water after spring thaw,
mates Mar–May. Food small crustaceans,
insects and larvae, worms, slugs.
Exudes distasteful secretion when
handled. neFr, Lu, Be, Ne, sDe, Ge, Cz,
Po. [♂ 3]

Marbled Newt *Triturus marmoratus*
SALAMANDRIDAE L <14 cm. Green above
with irregular black markings; belly grey.
Breeding ♂ has large black and white
vertically striped crest and pale stripe on
tail. Breeding ♀ has orange or red stripe
along middle of back. Deeper pools, lakes
and slow-flowing streams in lowland areas.
Breeds Mar–Jun; elaborate courtship
display. Food worms, snails, insect larvae.
wFr. [♂ 4]

Reptiles are cold-blooded, but can control body temperature to a limited extent, *eg* by basking in sun. Of the N European snakes only the adder (viper) is poisonous. Internal fertilization: ♂ with penis. Eggs with shells, laid in dry places, fewer than in amphibians; or young born alive. Young are like miniature adults.

Grass Snake *Natrix natrix* COLUBRIDAE L ♂ <120 cm, ♀ larger. Colour variable; upperside dark brown or green, with yellow or white 'collar' and jaws. Good swimmer. Dense undergrowth near water in open woodlands, farmland, hedges. Hibernates Oct–Apr. Mates Apr–May; eggs laid Jul–Aug. Food frogs, toads, newts. If grasped secretes a noxious slime. T, ex nBr, Ir, Ic, nFS n of 67°N. [5]

Dice Snake *Natrix tessellata* COLUBRIDAE L <150 cm. Narrow, pointed head. Grey, brown or green above with darker spots; underside white, yellow, pink or red with dark markings. In or near water; winters on land. Mates Mar–Apr; eggs laid Jul–Aug. Food fishes, amphibians. Ge, Cz. [6]

Water or **Viperine Snake** *Natrix maura* COLUBRIDAE L <100 cm. Broad head; thick body. Brown or grey, sometimes tinged with yellow, red or olive; usually 2 rows of dark markings which may form cross-bar or zigzag stripes; 1 or 2 inverted V marks on head. In or near still or flowing water, also brackish water, mountain streams. Mates Mar–Apr; eggs Jun–Jul. Food fishes, amphibians. Fr. [7]

European Pond Terrapin *Emys orbicularis* EMYDIDAE L <20 cm, rarely <30 cm. Oval-shaped carapace, black or brown with pale spots and streaks. Still or slow-flowing water with rich vegetation; also swamps. Mates May–Jun; eggs hatch Aug–Sep, or in following spring. Food worms, snails, fish, frogs, newts. eGe, Cz, Po. [8]

Little Grebe *Tachybaptus ruficollis*
PODICIPEDIDAE L 25–29 cm. Small, dumpy, with short bill, short neck, blunt-ended body, no white wing-patches like other 4 grebes; in summer, chestnut cheeks and throat, yellow-green patch at gape; in winter, white throat, grey-brown rear. High, whinnying trill. Shallow lakes, meres, ponds, gravel pits, slow rivers, marshes; winters open freshwater, estuaries. Nest soggy floating heap of water-plants, anchored to vegetation or trailing twigs, 4–6 eggs, Feb–Sep. Food insects and larvae, molluscs, crustaceans, tadpoles, small fish. T, ex Ic, Fi, all but extreme sSC, but only summer Cz, ePo, sSC. [summer 1] [winter 2]

Great Crested Grebe *Podiceps cristatus*
PODICIPEDIDAE L 46–51 cm. Large, with pink dagger bill, long thin neck; in summer, black crest, chestnut and black tippets, white face and underparts; in winter, tippets lost, crest reduced, white-headed look due to stripe above eye; juv broken stripes on head, neck. Harsh, nasal or guttural calls. Shallow lakes, reservoirs, gravel pits, quiet rivers, with reeds, sedges; winters also coasts. Locally colonial; nest much larger than little grebe, similarly anchored, or built up on mud, 3–5 eggs, Feb–Sep. Food mainly fish, also invertebrates, tadpoles. T, ex nBr, Ic, all but sFS, but mainly summer Cz, Po, Fi, Sw. [summer 3] [winter 4] [juv 5]

Red-necked Grebe *Podiceps grisegena*
PODICIPEDIDAE L 41–46 cm. Largish, stocky, with stout yellow-based bill, bulbous head, thickish neck; in summer, pale grey throat and cheeks, chestnut neck and breast; in winter, told from great crested by shape, bill colour, black crown to eye-level, greyer neck; juv like pale summer ad, but striped head. Loud wailing. Shallow lakes, quiet rivers, with extensive reed-beds; winters estuaries, coasts. Nest like great crested, 4–5 eggs, Apr–Jul. Food as smaller grebes, esp insects. Summer De, Ge, Po, Fi, sSw, irregular Cz; winter eBr, nFr, Be, Ne, De, Ge, sSC, rare nPo. [summer 6] [juv 7]

Slavonian Grebe *Podiceps auritus*
PODICIPEDIDAE L 31–36 cm. Larger than
little grebe, with straight bill, flattish
head, thin erect neck; in summer, golden
'horns' on sides of black head, black
hindneck and upperparts, chestnut foreneck
and flanks; in winter, told from black-
necked grebe by bill and head shape,
blackish crown extending only to eye-level,
white on cheeks crossing to nape, white
foreneck. Loud, accelerating trill. Shallow,
northern lakes, meres, pools, slow rivers,
with reeds, horsetails; winters mainly
estuaries, coasts. Solitary to colonial;
nest rather larger than little grebe, 4–5
eggs, May–Aug. Food as little grebe. Local
summer nBr, Ic, FS; winter Br, Ir, wIc,
Fr, Be, Ne, De, Ge, Po, sSw, No. [summer 8]

Black-necked Grebe *Podiceps nigricollis*
PODICIPEDIDAE L 28–33 cm. Just smaller
than Slavonian, with squarer head, rounder
back, thin uptilted bill; in summer, also told
by black neck, golden 'fan' over cheeks; in
winter, by more rounded head, less erect
neck, blackish crown extending to ear-
coverts, white smudge behind not crossing
to nape, duskier foreneck. Soft, rippling
trill. Shallow lakes, meres, reservoirs,
slow rivers, floodlands; also coasts in
winter. Colonial, often with gulls, terns;
nest like little grebe, usually in reeds,
sedges, 3–4 eggs, Apr–Jul. Food as little
grebe. Summer De, Ge, Cz, Po, rare nBr,
Fr, Be, Ne, sSw; winter sBr, Fr, Be, Ne,
wGe. [summer 9] [winter 10]

Cormorant *Phalacrocorax carbo*
PHALACROCORACIDAE L 80–100 cm. Large,
heavy, goose-like in flight, wings often
hanging open when perched, with longish
neck, hook-tipped bill; mainly black, fore-
cheeks and chin white; in summer, white
thigh-patch and ephemeral hoary feathering
on head; imm brown above, mainly whitish
below. Sea-cliffs, estuaries, rivers, lakes.
Colonial; flattish nest of sticks, grass, in
tree, bush, reeds (or of seaweed on cliff),
3–4 eggs, Mar–Aug. Food fish. Mainly
coastal Br, Ir, wIc, nFr, De, sSw, nNo, and
winter Be, Ne, sNo; inland summer Ne,
nGe, sCz, nPo. [summer 11] [winter 12]

Bittern *Botaurus stellaris* ARDEIDAE
L 70–80 cm. Stocky, mainly golden-brown mottled with black, striped red-brown below. Skulking, crepuscular; hides in reeds with bill vertical; owl-like flight on broad, rounded wings, neck retracted (as all herons). ♂ song deep, resonant boom 'oh-boomp', like distant fog-horn, audible < 3–5 km. Swamps, marshes, with dense reed-beds. Nest flat heap of reeds, sedges, in old reeds, 4–6 eggs, Apr–Aug. Food fish, amphibians, invertebrates, birds, mammals. sBr, Fr, Be, Ne, De, only summer Ge, Cz, Po, sFi, sSw. [1]

Little Bittern *Ixobrychus minutus* ARDEIDAE L 33–38 cm. Tiny, dark above but for pale forewings, light below; ♂ black and pale buff, tinged pink on wing-coverts; ♀ browner above with darker buff wing-panels, streaked below; juv duller, all heavily streaked. Behaviour as bittern; flight much faster, interspersed with glides. ♂ song low, far-carrying croak, repeated at 2-sec intervals. Reed-beds in wooded swamps, by ponds, lakes, rivers. Nest of reeds, rushes, twigs, < 3 m up in reeds, bush, willow, 5–6 eggs, May–Aug. Food as bittern, but smaller. Summer Fr, Lu, Be, Ne, Ge, Cz, Po. [♂ 2] [♀ 3] [juv 4]

Night Heron *Nycticorax nycticorax* ARDEIDAE L 58–65 cm. Small, stocky, with stout bill, shortish legs; black, grey and white, with 2–3 long drooping white plumes; juv like small dark bittern, but spotted above with whitish-buff. Crepuscular. Hoarse, raven-like croak in flight. Lakes, ponds, rivers, swamps, esp with trees, tangled scrub. Colonial; nest of twigs, in tree, shrub, 3–5 eggs, Apr–Aug. Food much as bittern. Rare/local summer Fr, Ne, sGe, sCz, sPo. [ad 5] [juv 6]

Little Egret *Egretta garzetta* ARDEIDAE L 55–65 cm. Small, white heron, with long thin neck, long black bill and legs, yellow feet; in summer, 2 long crest-feathers, elongated plumes on breast and back. Breeds S Europe; otherwise, open shallow lakes, rivers, marshes, estuaries. Food much as bittern. Summer marginally nFr; annual spring Br, Ir, Ne, Ge, Cz. [summer 7]

Grey Heron *Ardea cinerea* ARDEIDAE L 90–98 cm. Large, dagger-billed, with long neck and legs; grey, with white head, neck and underparts, black markings; juv more uniformly grey. Flies with retracted head, bulging neck, trailing legs, slow flaps of bowed wings. Flight-call harsh, coughing squawk 'frarnk'. Shallow lakes, rivers, swamps, estuaries, even rocky coasts; nests may be several km from water. Colonial; large nest of sticks, lined twigs, lvs, grass, high in tree, on cliff-ledge, among rocks, or of reeds in reed-bed, 3–5 eggs, Feb–Aug. Food much as bittern. T, ex Ic, but only sFS, coastal No, only summer Cz, ePo, Fi, inland Sw. [ad 8] [juv 9]

Purple Heron *Ardea purpurea* ARDEIDAE L 78–90 cm. Thin head and neck, narrow body, long toes; told from larger grey heron by serpentine shape, darker combination of dark grey, chestnut and black, and in flight by lower, more angular neck-bulge and large feet; juv paler, tawny above, more uniform buff below. Skulking, generally in cover. Flight-call higher-pitched, less loud 'krrank'. Marshy wetlands with extensive reeds, rushes, willows. Colonial; nest loose pile of dead reeds in reed-bed, or of sticks in tree, 4–5 eggs, Apr–Aug. Food much as bittern. Scarce/local summer Fr, Ne, sGe, Cz, sPo, has bred Be. [ad 10] [juv 11]

Spoonbill *Platalea leucorodia* THRES-KIORNITHIDAE L 80–90 cm. Large, heron-like, with long spatulate bill, long neck and legs extended in flight; all-white but for yellow-tipped black bill, black legs, bare yellow skin on throat and round eyes; in summer, crest and yellow-buff collar; juv like winter ad, but wing-tips black, bill and legs pinkish. Shallow marshes, lagoons, with dense reed-beds; winters also estuaries. Colonial; nest heap of reeds, twigs, lined grass, lvs, in reeds, adjacent willow, 3–4 eggs, Apr–Aug. Food small fish, insects, crustaceans, molluscs, worms, leeches, tadpoles. Summer Ne, irregularly De, sCz, has bred Fr, wGe, formerly Br; few winter swBr, sIr, Ne; passage also eBr, Fr, Be, wGe. [summer 12]

Bean Goose *Anser fabalis* ANATIDAE
L 66–84 cm. Large, upstanding, browner
than other *Anser*; bill orange and black,
legs orange-yellow, head and long neck
dark brown, forewings brown. Loud, clear
'ung-unk' like donkey bray. Open forest,
birch scrub, stony uplands with few trees,
tundra, but near water; winters grassy
wetlands, crops, arable. Nest low heap of
grass, lvs, moss, lined down, on hummock,
among tree roots, 4–6 eggs, May–Jul.
Food green plants, berries, seeds; in
winter, grasses, grain, potatoes. Summer
nFS; passage/winter Fr, Be, Ne, De, Ge,
Po, sFS, scarce Br, Lu, Cz. [1]

Pink-footed Goose *Anser brachyrhynchus*
ANATIDAE L 60–75 cm. Smaller than bean
goose, with shorter bill, neck; bill pink
and black, legs pink, head and neck dark
brown contrasting with pale grey back
and forewings; juv darker, less grey above,
with yellowish-pink legs. Calls higher-
pitched than bean goose: honking 'ang-
ank', shriller 'wink-wink'. Rock outcrops,
river gorges, islets, tundra; winters
lakes, marshes, estuaries, stubble, potato
fields. Often colonial; nest low heap of
grass, sedge, moss, lined down, on rock
ledge, hummock, 3–5 eggs, May–Jun. Food
much as bean goose. Summer Ic; winter
Br, Ne, De, wGe, scarce Ir, nFr, Be;
passage SC. [ad 2, 3]

White-fronted Goose *Anser albifrons*
ANATIDAE L 65–78 cm. Medium-sized,
grey-brown, including forewings, with
white forehead, black-barred belly, orange
legs; Eurasian ssp pink bill, Greenland ssp
longer orange-yellow bill, darker head
and body; juv lacks white forehead, black
bars. Calls faster, higher, more musical
than other *Anser*: laughing 'kow-lyow'.
Breeds arctic tundra USSR/America;
winters water-meadows, lowland pastures,
arable, Greenland ssp on bogs in wBr, Ir.
Winter food grasses, clover, cereals,
potatoes. Winter sBr, Ir, Be, Ne, scarce Fr;
mainly passage Ic, De, Ge, Cz, Po, FS.
[Eurasian ad 4, 5] [Greenland ad 6] [juv 7]

Lesser White-fronted Goose *Anser
erythropus* ANATIDAE L 53–66 cm. Smaller,

daintier than white-front (also darker
than Eurasian ssp) with brighter pink
bill, white forehead extending to crown,
yellow eye-ring, shorter neck, folded
wing-tips usually extending beyond tail;
juv lacks white forehead, black bars, but
shows eye-ring. Calls faster, higher,
squeakier, less loud: 'kyu-yu' (♂), 'kow-
yow' (♀). Wooded tundra, thickets,
foothills, by swamps, streams; passage
water-meadows, lakes, rivers, pastures,
crops. Nest low heap of grass, moss, lined
down, on hummock, rock outcrop, 4–6
eggs, May–Jul. Food green plants, willow
shoots, cottongrass. Summer nFS; passage
eGe, Cz, Po, sFi, sSw, vagrant elsewhere,
ex Ic, Lu. [ad 8]

Greylag Goose *Anser anser* ANATIDAE
L 75–90 cm. Large, heavy, grey-brown,
with large, pale bill, big head and thick
neck no darker than body, variable black
spots (not bars) on breast, pinkish legs,
pale grey forewings; W European ssp
orange bill, E European pink bill, paler
body. Loud, deep, cackling honk like
farmyard goose 'aang-ung-ung', distant
flock suggesting baying hounds. Swamps,
lakes with reed-beds or islands, boggy
thickets, moorland bogs; winters also
floods, reservoirs, grassland, arable,
estuaries. Often colonial; nest heap of
grass, rushes, moss, heather, lined scanty
down, on ground, in reeds, under bush,
4–6 eggs, Mar–Jun. Food shoots, lvs,
stems, berries, roots, grain, potatoes,
turnips. nBr, De, wGe, (also sBr, nIr, Be)
only summer Ic, eGe, Cz, Po, FS, only
winter sBr, Ne. [W European 9, 10]

Canada Goose *Branta canadensis* ANATIDAE
L 90–100 cm. Large, long-necked, grey-
brown, with black bill, legs, head and neck,
white patch from throat to cheeks, whitish
breast. Loud, clear, mellow trumpeting
'ah-honk', rising on 2nd syllable. Lakes
with islands, gravel pits, marshes, adjacent
parkland; also estuaries in winter. Social;
nest low heap of grass, reeds, lvs, lined
down, in thick cover, under bush, 5–6
eggs, Mar–Jun. Food grass, clover, cereals,
grain, water-plants. (Br, nIr, sSC, from
N America; also winter Ne, De, Ge.) [11]

Mute Swan *Cygnus olor* ANATIDAE L 145–160 cm. Large, heavy, with rounded head, long curved neck, often arched wings; bill orange with black base and knob (♂ knob larger, esp in spring); juv dingy brown above, with knobless grey (then pinkish) bill. Less vocal than other swans: hissing, snoring, snorting; wings make loud, throbbing hum. Lakes, rivers, gravel pits, marshes, ponds, also estuaries. Nest huge heap of reeds, water-weeds, on island or bank, in reed-bed or marsh, 2–8 eggs, Mar–Jun. Food water-plants, seeds, grasses, also amphibians, invertebrates. Br, Ir, Ne, De, Ge, local Fr, Be; largely summer Po, sSw (coastal in winter), local Cz, swFi, sNo. [♂ **1**] [juv **2**]

Bewick's Swan *Cygnus columbianus* ANATIDAE L 115–127 cm. Smaller than other 2 swans, with rounded head, shorter erect neck; bill black with yellow base not reaching nostrils; juv paler and greyer above than juv whooper, but bill similar until tip darkens. Flight more goose-like than other swans, head

and neck shape distinctive. Musical babble when settled; short, sharp honking notes in flight. Breeds arctic tundra USSR/America; winters flooded grasslands, with adjacent lakes, reservoirs, rivers, also visiting arable. Food water-plants, grass, clover, potatoes. Winter sBr, Ir, Ne, De, fewer Fr, Be, wGe; passage also eGe, nPo, Fi, sSw. [ad **3**] [juv **4**]

Whooper Swan *Cygnus cygnus* ANATIDAE L 145–160 cm. Large, with flattened forehead, long erect or kinked neck; bill black with yellow base extending in wedge to below nostrils; juv grey-brown above, with pink (then white) base to bill. Loud, clear trumpeting 'whoop-whoop', deeper and stronger than Bewick's. Lakes, swamps, upland ponds, rivers, estuaries; winters flooded grasslands, arable, sheltered coasts. Nest large heap of moss, reeds, grass, on lake shore, islet, 2–7 eggs, May–Jul. Food water-plants, also grain, potatoes, grass. Summer Ic, Sw, fewer Fi, nNo; winter nBr, Ir, sIc, neFr, Be, Ne, De, nGe, nPo, sSC. [ad **5**] [juv **6**]

Mandarin *Aix galericulata* ANATIDAE
L 41–49 cm. Large-headed, long-tailed
perching-duck; exotic ♂ has sheened
crown and drooping crest, broad white
band from red bill to nape, orange 'side-
whiskers' and wing 'sails', maroon breast
edged with black and white stripes; ♀
olive-brown above, with oval grey head,
white 'spectacles' and 'moustache', rows
of large white spots on brown breast and
flanks. ♂ sharp whistles, snorts; ♀ coot-
like and softer notes. Lakes, ponds,
streams, in wooded areas. Nest in tree-
hole, lined down, 9–12 or more eggs, Apr–
Jun. Food insects, snails, seeds, nuts. (sBr,
from E Asia.) [♂ 7] [♀ 8]

Wigeon *Anas penelope* ANATIDAE L 45–
51 cm. Medium-sized, short-necked
dabbling-duck, with small bill, narrow
wings, pointed tail; ♂ yellow blaze on
chestnut head, grey body, pinkish breast
and, in flight, large white patches on inner
wings, white belly contrasting with black
undertail; ♀ rufous, or greyer on back,
with white belly, green-black wing-patch
between whitish bars, dull blue bill. ♂
loud whistle 'whee-oo', ♀ purring growl.
Shallow lakes, large pools, slow rivers,
in marshes, moorland, tundra, open forest;
winters lakes, reservoirs, floods, estuaries,
salt-marshes. Nest like mallard, in thick
cover, 7–9 eggs, Apr–Jul. Food pondweeds,
algae, grasses, eelgrass, some seeds.
Summer nBr, Ic, FS, local sBr, neGe,
nPo; winter Br, Ir, swIc, Fr, Lu, Be, Ne,
De, wGe, Cz, sSC. [♂ 9] [♀ 10]

Gadwall *Anas strepera* ANATIDAE L 46–56
cm. Slight, rather drab dabbling-duck;
♂ greyish, with black stern and, in flight,
white rectangle behind chestnut and black
wing-coverts; ♀ like slender ♀ mallard,
but orange side-panels to bill, white
wing-patch, white belly. ♂ low whistles,
grunts; ♀ diminuendo quacks. Lakes, slow
rivers, marshes with pools, esp where
reeds. Nest like mallard, in thick cover,
usually by water, 8–12 eggs, Apr–Jul. Food
mainly water-plants. Local summer Br,
eIr, nIc, Fr, Ne, De, Ge, Cz, Po, seSw;
winter Br, Ir, Fr, Be, Ne. [♂ 11] [♀ 12]

Teal *Anas crecca* ANATIDAE L 34–38 cm.
Small, short-necked dabbling-duck with
oval head, narrow wings; ♂ grey, with
chestnut head, green eye-patch, spotted
breast, white stripe above wing, black and
buff stern; ♀ mottled brown. In flight,
green and black wing-patch between 2
white bars. ♂ high, musical, far-carrying
whistle 'prrit'; ♀ quacks. Rushy pools
in moorland, tundra, also small lowland
lakes, isolated ponds, slow streams,
marshes; passage/winter lakes, reservoirs,
esp where reeds, also estuaries. Nest like
mallard, in thick cover, 8–11 eggs, Apr–
Jun. Food water-plants, seeds, insects,
molluscs, worms. T, but mainly summer
Ic, ePo, FS. [♂ 1] [♀ 2]

Mallard *Anas platyrhynchos* ANATIDAE
L 55–64 cm. Large, heavy dabbling-duck;
♂ yellow bill, green head, white collar,
purplish breast, black and white stern;
♀ mottled brown, with olive-brown bill
(often dull orange at sides). In flight,
purple wing-patch between 2 white bars.
♂ low 'yaarb', loud whistle; ♀ quacks. Any
freshwater from pools and marshes to
rivers, lakes, reservoirs, in open or forest,
even towns; many winter on sea, estuaries.
Nest hollow lined lvs, grass, down, in thick
or thin cover, by or well away from water,
even in tree-hole, pollard willow, building,
old crow nest, 9–13 eggs, mainly Mar–Jul
(Feb–Oct). Food water- and land-plants,
invertebrates, fish, amphibians. T, but
only summer most FS. [♂ 3] [♀ 4]

Pintail *Anas acuta* ANATIDAE L 51–66 cm
+ <10 cm elongated tail of ♂. Slender,
long-necked, narrow-winged dabbling-duck
with pointed tail; ♂ chocolate head, white
neck-stripe and underparts, black and
white stern; ♀ told from ♀ mallard by
shape, paler colour, blue-grey bill, whitish
belly. ♂ quiet 'whee' and teal-like whistle;
♀ quacks. Shallow lakes, pools, with drier
shores, in open grassland, moorland;
coastal in winter. Nest like mallard, but
rather open in short grass, rushes, heather,
often on islet, 7–9 eggs, Apr–Jul. Food
seeds, water- and land-plants, cereals,
potatoes, also invertebrates. Summer
Ic, Po, FS, local/irregular Br, Ir, Fr, Ne,

De, Ge; winter Br, Ir, Fr, Be, Ne, De,
wGe; passage also Lu, Cz. [♂ 5] [♀ 6]

Garganey *Anas querquedula* ANATIDAE
L 37–41 cm. Teal-sized, slender-necked
dabbling-duck; ♂ white superciliary, brown
body with grey flanks, long drooping
shoulder feathers of grey, black, white;
♀ told from ♀ teal by paler plumage, more
stripy head, white throat. In flight, ♂
forewings blue-grey, ♀'s greyish. ♂ soft,
crackling rattle; ♀ quacks. Shallow freshwater with adjacent grassland, water-
meadows, marshes. Nest like mallard, in
coarse grass, rush tussock, near water, 8–11
eggs, Apr–Jun. Food invertebrates, fish,
water-plants. Summer sBr, Fr, Lu, Be,
Ne, De, Ge, Cz, Po, sFi, sSw, has bred
Ir. [♂ 7] [♀ 8]

Shoveler *Anas clypeata* ANATIDAE
L 44–52 cm. Heavy-bodied, short-necked
dabbling-duck with flattened head, huge
spatulate bill; ♂ black and white, with
green head, chestnut flanks and belly; ♀
like ♀ mallard, but shape very different,
swims with front end low in water. In
flight, ♂ forewings bright blue, ♀'s duller.
♂ quiet, hoarse 'took'; ♀ low quacks.
Shallow muddy lakes, reedy meres,
marshland pools; passage/winter also lakes,
reservoirs. Nest like mallard, but rather
open in short grass, rushes, near water,
9–11 eggs, Apr–Jul. Food mainly molluscs,
crustaceans, insects, water-plants. T, ex
Lu (passage), but only summer Ic, De,
Ge, Cz, Po, FS. [♂ 9] [♀ 10]

Ruddy Duck *Oxyura jamaicensis* ANATIDAE
L 35–43 cm. Dumpy stiff-tailed duck with
large bill, oft-cocked tail; ♂ has black
crown, white cheeks and undertail; in
summer, bill blue, body chestnut, but in
winter, bill grey, body dark brown above,
barred paler below; ♀ much like winter ♂,
but line across greyer cheeks, undertail
barred. Rattling sounds produced by bill.
Reservoirs, gravel pits, with reedy edges.
Nest bulky platform of reeds, rushes,
woven among reeds in water, 6–10 eggs,
Apr–Sep. Food mainly insect larvae, seeds
of water-plants. (Br, from N America).
[summer ♂ 11] [♀ 12]

Red-crested Pochard *Netta rufina*
ANATIDAE L 53–57 cm. Large, plump
diving-duck with rounded head; ♂ red bill,
golden-chestnut head, black neck, breast
and stern, contrasting white flanks; ♀
pale brown, with dark crown, grey-white
cheeks. Lakes, pools, brackish lagoons,
with extensive reeds, sedges. Nest hollow
lined grass, lvs, rushes, down, in dense
reeds, under bush, 8–10 eggs, May–Jul.
Food water-plants, some invertebrates,
frogs, small fish. Scarce summer Ne, De,
Ge, Cz, has bred Be, Po, (rare feral Br);
passage also Fr, Lu. [♂ 1] [♀ 2]

Pochard *Aythya ferina* ANATIDAE L 42–49
cm. Stocky, short-necked diving-duck with
large, blue-banded bill, sloping forehead,
high crown; ♂ grey, head chestnut, breast
and stern black; ♀ grey-brown, with hoary
face, dull yellow-brown head and breast.
Lakes, gravel pits, with islets, reeds;
winters also reservoirs, estuaries. Nest
platform of reeds, sedges, lvs, down, in
waterlogged tussock, or lined hollow on
ground, 8–10 eggs, Apr–Jul. Food water-

plants, grasses, invertebrates, frogs,
small fish. Summer T, ex Lu, nFi, nSw,
No, local Ic, Fr; winter T, ex Ic, ePo, Fi,
all but sSC. [♂ 3] [♀ 4]

Ferruginous Duck *Aythya nyroca*
ANATIDAE L 38–42 cm. Small, neat diving-
duck with flat forehead, high crown; ♂
dark reddish-chestnut, with greenish-
black back, white undertail, white eyes;
♀ duller, browner above, paler below, eyes
brown. Shallow lakes, ponds, with floating
weeds, dense reeds. Nest like pochard, 8–10
eggs, May–Jun. Food mainly water-plants,
also tadpoles, small fish, invertebrates.
Mainly summer eGe, Cz, Po, irregular Ne
(some feral), wGe, has bred Be. [♂ 5] [♀ 6]

Tufted Duck *Aythya fuligula* ANATIDAE
L 40–47 cm. Small, compact diving-duck
with round head, drooping crest; ♂ black
with white flanks; ♀ dark brown or blackish
upperparts and breast, often some white
round base of bill, yellow-brown to rufous
flanks with white markings, whitish undertail. Lakes, reservoirs, gravel pits, slow

rivers, often fairly free of reeds. Often social; nest hollow lined grass, sedges, down, in tussock, under bush, 8–11 eggs, May–Aug. Food much as scaup. T, but local as breeder Fr, Be, Ne; mainly summer Ic, Cz, ePo, Fi, inland SC. [♂ 7] [♀ 8]

Scaup *Aythya marila* ANATIDAE L 42–51 cm. Round-headed, broad-bodied diving-duck with large bill; ♂ looks black at ends, white in middle, though back pale grey; ♀ brown, paler below, with white face and, in summer, whitish patch on ear-coverts. Lakes, pools, rivers, in moorland, tundra, open forest, also islets in Baltic; winters coasts. Nest like tufted duck, 8–11 eggs, May–Aug. Food molluscs, insects, crustaceans, fish eggs, pondweeds, seeds. Summer Ic, nFS, Baltic coasts of Fi, Sw, has bred Br; winter Br, Ir, swIc, Fr, Be, Ne, De, nGe, nPo, sSC. [♂ 9] [♀ 10]

Harlequin *Histrionicus histrionicus* ANATIDAE L 38–45 cm. Small, dark sea-duck with small bill, pointed tail; ♂ dark grey-blue (black at distance) with chestnut flanks, 'harlequin' pattern of black-edged white marks; ♀ brown, with 2 pale patches before eye, white circle behind. Rushing rivers, by waterfalls; winters off rocky coasts. Nest hollow lined twigs, grass, down, in thick cover, among rocks, 5–7 eggs, May–Jul. Food insects, larvae; in winter, crustaceans, molluscs. Ic. [♂ 11] [♀ 12]

Long-tailed Duck *Clangula hyemalis* ANATIDAE L 40–47 cm + < 13 cm pointed tail of ♂. Small-headed sea-duck with short, high-based bill, narrow wings; ♂ mainly brown in summer (whitish face-patch, flanks to undertail), mainly white in winter (brown cheek-patch, breast-band, mid-back, tail, wings); duller ♀ changes correspondingly, but retains dark crown and upperparts in winter. Tundra lakes, coastal islands; winters on sea. Nest hollow scantily lined plants, down, usually in thick cover, 6–9 eggs, May–Jul. Food invertebrates, small fish. Summer Ic, sFi, nFS; winter nBr, nIr, Ic, Ne, De, Ge, Po, sSw, No. [summer ♂ 13] [summer ♀ 14]

Common Scoter *Melanitta nigra*
ANATIDAE L 44–54 cm. Squat, dark sea-
duck with deep bill, pointed tail; ♂ all-
black but for orange-yellow patch in front
of bill-knob; ♀ brown, with defined
whitish-brown cheeks, throat. Large lakes,
esp on tundra, moors; winters on sea. Nest
hollow lined grass, moss, lichens, down, in
thick cover, usually near water, 6–8 eggs,
May–Jul. Summer food insect larvae, fish
eggs, seeds, molluscs. Summer nBr, nIr,
nIc, nFS; winter Br, Ir, Fr, Be, Ne, De,
Ge, Po, sSw, No. [♂ 1] [♀ 2]

Velvet Scoter *Melanitta fusca* ANATIDAE
L 51–58 cm. Heavy-headed, dark sea-duck,
with long deep bill, pointed tail, white
wing-patches, red feet; ♂ black with white
below eyes, orange-yellow *sides* to swollen
(not knobbed) bill; ♀ dark brown with 2
whitish cheek-patches. Lakes, rivers, on
wooded tundra, moors, also wooded islets
of Baltic; winters on sea. Nest as common
scoter, 7–9 eggs, May–Jul. Summer food
similar, but more molluscs, crustaceans.
Summer FS; winter Br, eIr, Fr, Be, Ne,
De, Ge, Po, sSw, No. [♂ 3] [♀ 4]

Barrow's Goldeneye *Bucephala islandica*
ANATIDAE L 42–53 cm. ♂ told from goldeneye ♂ by flat crown to purple-glossed, oval
head, with white *crescent* before eye, also
by spur of black in front of wing, white
blobs at sides of blacker upperparts; ♀ by
richer brown, oval head, stubbier bill with
more yellow on top, less white on wings.
Lakes, rivers, even torrents; also sheltered
bays in winter. Nest hollow lined down in
rock-crevice, building, or also grass, lvs, in
thick scrub, 8–11 eggs, May–Jun. Food
insect larvae, molluscs, crustaceans, fish
eggs, seeds. Ic. [♂ 5]

Goldeneye *Bucephala clangula* ANATIDAE
L 42–50 cm. Smallish, stocky, short-billed
diving-duck with peak to triangular head;
♂ boldly pied, with green-glossed head,
white circle before eyes, streaky white
shoulders; ♀ chocolate head, whitish collar,
grey-mottled upperparts, breast. Forest
lakes; winters lakes, reservoirs, coasts.
Nest hollow lined wood chips, down, in
tree-hole, nestbox, 8–11 eggs, May–Jul.

Food molluscs, crustaceans, insect larvae,
fish, also seeds, plants. Summer FS, rare
nBr, Ge, Cz, Po; winter T, ex Fi, nSC,
but local Ic, Fr, Cz. [♂ 6] [♀ 7]

Smew *Mergus albellus* ANATIDAE L 38–44
cm. Small, compact sawbill-duck with
short, grey bill; pied ♂ looks all-white at
distance, but for black eye-patch; ♀
mainly greyish, but chestnut cap contrasts
with white cheeks, throat. In flight, ♂
looks darker above. Forest lakes, pools,
backwaters; winters lakes, reservoirs,
rivers, estuaries. Nest hollow lined mainly
down, in tree-hole, nestbox, 7–9 eggs,
May–Jul. Food mainly insects, larvae, fish.
Summer nFS; winter T, ex Ic, Fi, but
only sBr, sSC, rare Ir. [♂ 8] [♀ 9]

Red-breasted Merganser *Mergus serrator*
ANATIDAE L 52–58 cm. Rakish sawbill-duck
with narrow red bill, double crest; ♂
green-black head, wide white collar, black-
spotted chestnut breast; ♀ red-brown head
merging into whitish foreneck, brown-grey
upperparts. Open or forest lakes, rivers,
also bays, estuaries; winters sheltered
coasts. Nest hollow lined grass, down, in
thick cover, hole, rabbit burrow, 8–10
eggs, May–Jul. Food fish, also crustaceans,
molluscs, worms, insects, plants, seeds.
Summer nBr, Ir, Ic, De, FS, local nGe,
nPo; winter T, ex Lu, Cz, Po, Fi, nSw.
[♂ 10] [♀ 11]

Goosander *Mergus merganser* ANATIDAE
L 58–66 cm. Long-bodied, bulky sawbill-
duck with narrow red bill, bulbous head;
♂ green-black head, black back, creamy
underparts giving clean look quite unlike
shaggy-headed, dark-breasted merganser,
whole inner wings also white; ♀ resembles
♀ merganser, but also cleaner-looking, with
whiter throat and sharp demarcation of
chestnut neck from whiter chest and greyer
back and flanks. Lakes, rivers, usually
in forest; winters on large open waters,
rarely estuaries. Nest hollow lined down,
in hole in tree, house, rock, bank, nestbox,
8–11 eggs, Apr–Jul. Food as merganser.
T, but only summer Fi, nSC, only winter/
passage sBr, Ir (rare), Fr, Lu, Be, Ne,
wDe, wGe, Cz, sPo. [♂ 12] [♀ 13]

Black Kite *Milvus migrans* ACCIPITRIDAE
L 55–60 cm. More compact than red kite;
tail shorter, less forked, triangular when
spread; dark brown, with greyish head,
pale diagonal across inner wings. Thin,
whinnying, gull-like squeal, chattering
notes, esp when nesting. Farmland with
trees, open woods, esp near lakes, rivers.
Often social; nest of sticks, dung, moss,
paper, rags, in tree, 2–3 eggs, May–Aug.
Food dead fish, carrion, garbage, small
mammals, reptiles, frogs, pond snails,
insects. Summer Fr, Lu, Ge, Cz, Po, sFi;
passage Be, Ne, De, sSw. [1]

White-tailed Eagle *Haliaeetus albicilla*
ACCIPITRIDAE L 70–95 cm, ♂ smaller than
♀. Huge, with rectangular wings, massive
yellow bill, large pale head and short,
wedge-shaped, white tail; juv brown,
centres of tail-feathers later whitish. Shrill
chatter, gull-like croak. Forest lakes, sea-
cliffs; winters also estuaries, coasts.
Nest of sticks, heather, lined wood-rush,
grass, on tree, ledge, islet, 2 eggs, Mar–
Aug. Food fish, carrion, mammals, birds.

wIc, nGe, Po, wFi, eSw, No; winter also
Ne, De, Cz. [ad 2] [imm 3]

Marsh Harrier *Circus aeruginosus*
ACCIPITRIDAE L 48–56 cm, ♂ smaller than
♀. Larger than other harriers, with broader
wings; ♂ mainly dark brown above, redder
below, with contrasting grey on upper-
wings and tail, and white on underwings
with dark grey trailing edge; ♀/imm dark
chocolate with or without yellowish crown,
shoulders, throat. Plaintive 'quee-oo'
in display. Fens, swamps, marshes, with
dense reed-beds. Nest of reeds, sedges,
sticks, lined grass, among reeds, 4–5 eggs,
Apr–Aug. Food frogs, small mammals,
reptiles, eggs, sick birds, carrion. Mainly
summer T, ex Ir, Ic, No, but local/scarce,
only seBr, sSw, swFi. [♂ 4] [♀ 5]

Hen Harrier *Circus cyaneus* ACCIPITRIDAE
L 43–51 cm, ♂ smaller than ♀. Slim, with
long narrow wings, long tail; ♂ grey
above with white rump, white below with
grey head, wings with black tips, blackish
trailing edges; ♀/imm dark brown, with

owl-like face, white rump, banded tail, streaked underparts. Chatters, squeals, when breeding. Marshes, moors, heaths, crops. Ground nest of reeds, sedges, heather, grasses, 4–6 eggs, Apr–Jul. Food birds, mammals, esp pipits, voles. T, ex Ic, but only summer Fi, nSC, only winter sBr, De, ePo. [♂ 6] [♀ 7]

Montagu's Harrier *Circus pygargus*
ACCIPITRIDAE L 40–46 cm, ♂ smaller than ♀. Narrower-winged than hen harrier; ♂ differs in grey rump, rusty streaks on flanks, black bar in mid wing; ♀/imm very like ♀ hen harrier, but less owl-like face, dark crescent on cheeks, less white on rump. Softer, higher-pitched chattering near nest. Reed-marshes, heaths, conifer plantations, crops. Ground nest of sedges, grasses, 4–5 eggs, May–Jul. Food frogs, reptiles, eggs, small birds, mammals. Summer Fr, Lu, Be, Ne, De, Ge, Cz, Po, rare sBr, sSw. [♂ 8] [♀ 9]

Spotted Eagle *Aquila clanga* ACCIPITRIDAE
L 65–75 cm. Bulky, in flight with broad wings bulging at rear, short tail, small head; dark brown; imm with bold white U above tail, whitish line along wings, rows of large white spots on coverts. Dog-like yapping, mainly when breeding. Wooded river valleys, marshes with woods or scattered trees. Nest of sticks, lined grasses, green sprays, in tree, 1–2 eggs, Apr–Aug. Food frogs, reptiles, fish, also small mammals, birds, carrion. Scarce summer eCz, ePo, swFi; passage Ge, wCz, wPo, sFi, sSw. [ad 10] [imm 11]

Osprey *Pandion haliaetus* PANDIONIDAE
L 51–58 cm. Long, gull-like wings; uniformly dark above, whitish head and underparts contrast with black mask and carpal patches; imm paler above, speckled creamy. Repeated, shrill, cheeping whistle. Lakes, reservoirs, rivers, coasts. Nest of branches, reeds, heather, lined grass, moss, on tree (esp pine, spruce), ledge, 3 eggs, Apr–Aug. Food fish, rarely frogs, mice, birds. Summer neGe, nPo, FS, rare nBr, De; passage T, ex Ic, but rare Ir. [ad 12]

Water Rail *Rallus aquaticus* RALLIDAE
L 27–29 cm. Long red bill (3 crakes have
short bills), blue-grey face and breast,
black and white bars on flanks, whitish
undertail, flesh-brown legs; juv similar,
but throat and breast mottled buff and
brown. Skulking, crepuscular, often only
heard, esp remarkable 'sharming':
alternating grunts and pig-like squeals,
later falling in pitch, followed by deeper
groans; also loud, harsh 'kik-kik-kik-kik'.
Reed-beds, fens, bogs, overgrown edges of
lakes and rivers. Nest like small moorhen's,
of dead reeds, hidden in reeds, rushes,
sometimes well above water, 6–11 eggs,
Apr–Jul. Food insects, crustaceans,
molluscs, worms, leeches, roots, seeds.
T, ex nFS, but mainly summer Cz, Po,
Fi, Sw. [ad 1]

Spotted Crake *Porzana porzana* RALLIDAE
L 22–24 cm. Told from water rail by short,
mainly yellowish bill, white speckles on
back and on greyish throat and breast,
duller brown and whitish bars on flanks,
buff undertail, green legs; juv buffish,
hardly spotted on breast. Skulking,
crepuscular; main calls explosive whistling
'hwet, hwet, hwet' (whiplash) and harder,
sharper 'trik-trak' (ticking clock). Habitat
and nest much as water rail, but more in
sedges; nest usually in tussock, 8–12
eggs, May–Aug. Food insects, molluscs,
seeds. Mainly summer T, ex Ir, Ic, nFS,
but rare Br. [ad 2]

Little Crake *Porzana parva* RALLIDAE
L 18·5–19·5 cm. Small, with red-based
green bill, green legs, sexes dissimilar:
♂ olive-brown above, streaked blackish,
slate-grey below, with barred undertail
but only faintly barred flanks; ♀ white
throat, buff underparts. ♂ slow series of
coot-like squawks, also repeated 'quek'
dropping in scale and accelerating to short
trill; ♀ irregular higher-pitched notes
like moorhen. Habitat and nest like other
crakes, esp in reeds, bulrushes, floating
vegetation; nest hidden in tussock, 7–8
eggs, May–Aug. Food insects, spiders,
molluscs, seeds, worms. Summer Ge, Cz,
Po, local Fr, irregular Ne, has bred Sw.
[♂ 3] [♀ 4]

Baillon's Crake *Porzana pusilla*
RALLIDAE L 16–17 cm. Tiny, sexes alike,
similar to ♂ little crake, but green bill
lacks red base, legs greyish-pink, upperparts
redder-brown streaked white, flanks barred
black and white. Main call of ♂ recalls
little crake's accelerating trill, but quicker,
higher-pitched, falling more. Habitat and
nest like other crakes, esp in sedges,
rushes, smaller pools, 6–8 eggs, Apr–Aug.
Food as little crake. Summer Fr, Cz,
irregular Be, Ne, Ge, has bred Br, Po. [5]

Moorhen *Gallinula chloropus* RALLIDAE
L 31–34 cm. Blackish, with white streak
along flanks, white undertail, red frontal
shield, yellow-tipped red bill, green legs
with red garters; juv grey-brown with
whitish throat and belly, green-brown bill
and shield. Loud croaks, many disyllabic.
Rivers, lakes, ponds, marshes, adjacent
grassland. Bulky nest of reeds, sedges, over
or near water, on ground or in shrub, 5–11
eggs, Mar–Sep. Food seeds, grass, lvs, moss,
insects, worms, slugs. T, ex Ic, but only sFS,
mainly summer Cz, Po, FS. [ad 6] [juv 7]

Coot *Fulica atra* RALLIDAE L 36–40 cm.
Black, with bold white frontal shield and
bill; juv brown-grey with whitish throat
and breast, greenish bill. Short, explosive
squawks, many monosyllabic. Lakes,
reservoirs, reedy rivers; also estuaries in
winter. Bulky nest of reeds, bulrushes,
hidden in water vegetation or in open,
4–8 eggs, Mar–Aug. Food water-plants,
also fish, tadpoles, molluscs, leeches,
insects. T, ex nFS, but only summer Cz,
ePo, Fi, mainly winter Ic. [ad 8] [juv 9]

Crane *Grus grus* GRUIDAE L 107–117 cm.
Long neck extended in flight, long legs;
grey, but for black and white head (red
inconspicuous), with blackish flight-
feathers, drooping plumes over tail; juv
darker, with brown head and neck.
Trumpeting call. Bogs, marshes, wooded
swamps; passage also riversides, grasslands,
arable. Nest heap of sedges, rushes, 2 eggs,
Apr–Jun. Food grain, berries, lvs, insects,
worms, frogs, young birds, voles. Summer
Ge, Po, FS, rare De; passage also Fr,
Lu, Be, Ne, Cz. [ad 10] [juv 11]

Little Ringed Plover *Charadrius dubius*
CHARADRIIDAE L 15–16 cm. Told from
larger ringed plover by thinner, mainly
dark bill, yellow eye-ring, white line over
black forehead, longer pinkish or yellowish
legs and, in flight, lack of wing-bar; juv
by proportions, pinkish legs, no wing-bar.
Shrill, piping whistle 'pee-u'; in 'butterfly'
display-flight, whistle rapidly repeated,
then creaky 'tree-a, tree-a'. Gravel pits,
river shingle, silt tips. Nest scrape lined
pebbles, in open, 4 eggs, Apr–Aug. Food
insects, larvae, molluscs. Summer T,
ex nBr, Ir, Ic, nFS. [ad **1**] [juv **2**]

Ringed Plover *Charadrius hiaticula*
CHARADRIIDAE L 18–20 cm. Small, plump,
with stubby, orange-based bill and orange
legs; black breast-band, black-and-white
head-pattern, white wing-bar; juv duller,
looks scaly, no black, browner breast-band
often broken, dark bill, yellowish legs.
Soft whistle 'poo-i'; trilling song repeated
'qui-lee-yu'. Local by rivers, lakes, gravel
pits, on fallow, heaths, tundra, but commonest on coast. Nest scrape bare or lined
pebbles, debris, in open or among plants,
3–4 eggs, Apr–Aug. Food molluscs, crustaceans, insects, also worms. Summer T, ex
Lu, Cz (passage); winter Br, Ir, Fr.
[ad **3**] [juv **4**]

Lapwing *Vanellus vanellus* CHARADRIIDAE
L 29–32 cm. Looks pied, with long crest,
metallic green back, red-buff undertail;
throat white in winter; juv duller, with
buff feather-edges, short crest. In flight,
black-ended white tail and undersides of
rounded, slow-flapped wings; display-flight
erratic, tumbling. Familiar 'pees-weet'.
Marshes, rushy fields, gravel pits,
farmland, moors; winters fields, marshes,
estuaries. Nest scrape lined grass (thickly
in wet sites), on open ground, 3–4 eggs,
Mar–Jul. Food insects, molluscs, worms,
also seeds, grass lvs, cereals. T, ex Ic, nFS,
but mainly summer Cz, Po, FS. [summer **5**]
[winter **6**]

Little Stint *Calidris minutus* SCOLOPACIDAE
L *c*14·5 cm. Tiny, with short bill, black
legs; in summer, rufous and white; in

winter, much greyer; juv paler than summer ad, with 2 large whitish Vs on back. Short 'trit' or twitter. Breeds in arctic grassy marshes, tundra; passage on coasts and by freshwater inland. Food insects, larvae, molluscs, crustaceans, worms, seeds. Summer nNo; passage T, ex Ic, but mainly in autumn; few winter sBr, wFr. [summer 7] [juv 8]

Temminck's Stint *Calidris temminckii* SCOLOPACIDAE L *c*14 cm. Told from little stint by more uniform grey upperparts, grey breast, greenish or brown legs and, in flight, white (not grey) outertail; juv uniform grey above but for scaly buff feather-edges. Short, high-pitched trill; song prolonged trill, rising and falling, in moth-like flight or on ground. Grass, sedge, thin scrub, by lakes, rivers, pools; passage on marshes, lake edges, also coastal creeks. Nest scrape variably lined grass, lvs, in short vegetation, 4 eggs, May–Aug. Food mainly insects, larvae, also worms. Summer nFS, rare nBr; passage T, ex Ir, Ic. [summer 9] [juv 10]

Curlew Sandpiper *Calidris ferruginea* SCOLOPACIDAE L 18–20 cm. Larger, more upright than dunlin, with longer, finer downcurved bill, longer neck and legs, white rump; in summer, head and underparts russet, face whitish; in winter, grey-brown above, white below; juv upperparts darker, more scaly, breast buff. Soft 'chirrip'. Breeds tundra NE Asia; passage and food as little stint. Passage T, ex Ic, but mainly in autumn. [summer 11] [juv 12]

Dunlin *Calidris alpina* SCOLOPACIDAE L 17–19 cm. Small, hunched, with straight or slightly downcurved bill; in summer, black-streaked chestnut crown and back, black belly-patch; in winter, brown-grey above, white below with greyish breast. Nasal 'tree'. Breeds on moors, tundra, salt-marshes, lowland mosses; winters on coasts, estuaries, but passage also by freshwater inland. Food insects, molluscs, crustaceans, worms. Summer nBr, Ir, Ic, De, nGe, nPo, FS; passage T; winter Br, Ir, Fr, Be, Ne, De, Ge, swSC. [winter 13]

Black-winged Stilt *Himantopus himantopus*
RECURVIROSTRIDAE L 37–39 cm. White
with black bill, back, wings (underwings
also black, contrasting in flight with
underbody), and absurdly long, pink legs;
♂ more or less black on crown and back of
neck (sometimes mottled just on nape);
♀ and juv browner backs, juv brown head
to below eyes. Shrill, monotonous 'kyik-
kyik-kyik', esp when nesting. Lakes,
lagoons, marshes, floods, esp with weedy
shallows. Colonial; nest scrape scantily
lined grass on mud or tussock, or substan-
tial heap of plant debris in shallow water,
3–4 eggs, May–Jul. Food insects, larvae,
small molluscs, worms, tadpoles. Summer
wFr, nFr, irregular Be, Ne, has bred Br,
Ge, ?Cz. [♂ 1] [♀ 2]

Ruff *Philomachus pugnax* SCOLOPACIDAE
L ♂ 28–31 cm, ♀ 22–25 cm. Summer ♂
unmistakable with erectile ruff and ear-
tufts in varied combinations of black,
purple, chestnut, buff and white, barred
or unbarred; ♀ and winter ♂ grey-brown
above, scaled with pale feather-edges on
wings, white below washed grey on breast,
oval white patch on each side of dark
tail, orange-red or pinkish legs and base
to shortish bill; juv smaller, browner
above with richer buff scaling, breast
pinkish-buff, bill brown, legs green or
yellow-brown. ♂s congregate on display-
ground, scuttling about, crouching,
quivering wings, with ruffs expanded; ♀
visits, selects ♂. Sometimes low 'chut-it' in
flight. Marshes, fens, water-meadows,
tundra; also lake-edges and estuaries on
passage. Nest scrape lined grass, in thick
grass, sedges, 4 eggs, May–Jul. Food insects,
also worms, molluscs, crustaceans, seeds.
Summer Ne, De, nGe, nPo, FS, rare or
irregular Br, Fr, Be; passage T, ex Ic; winter
sBr, nFr, Be, Ne. [summer ♂s 3–6] [juv 7]

Jack Snipe *Lymnocryptes minimus*
SCOLOPACIDAE L c19 cm. Small, with short
bill; skulks, seldom flies far if flushed;
dark central crown-stripe, 2 light stripes
and purplish gloss on back, no barring on
flanks. Usually silent, but summer song
like cantering horse in sky. Bogs, in open
forest, scrub, tundra; passage/winter on

marshes, swamps, rushy fields, boggy lake
edges. Nest scrape lined grass, 4 eggs,
Jun–Aug. Food worms, molluscs, insects,
seeds. Summer nFS; passage T, ex Ic;
winter Br, Ir, Fr, Be, Ne. [8]

Snipe *Gallinago gallinago* SCOLOPACIDAE
L 26–27 cm. Skulking; long bill held down
in zigzag flight; mottled black and
rufous, with buff stripes, some white at
sides of tail. Rasping 'scaap'; song 'chip-
per, chip-per'; bleating 'drumming' by
spread tail in display-flight. Marshes,
rushy fields, wet moors, tundra; also
salt-marshes in winter. Nest scrape lined
grass, sedges, in tussock, 4 eggs, Apr–
Aug. Food worms, also insects, molluscs,
crustaceans, seeds. T, but only summer
Cz, Po, FS. [9]

Great Snipe *Gallinago media* SCOLOPACI-
DAE L 27–29 cm. Bulkier than snipe, with
broader wings, shorter bill held up in
straighter flight; mealy head, heavily
barred underparts, white tail-corners;
juv barred even on belly, less white on
tail. Usually silent; bubbling chorus of
♂s on display-ground. Swamps, marshes,
waterside meadows, tundra scrub; passage
on marshes, stubble, heaths. Nest scrape
lined grass, 4 eggs, May–Jul. Food worms,
also molluscs, insects. Scarce summer
nePo, sFi, nSw, No; passage eFr, Be, Ne,
De, Ge, Cz, Po, sSw. [ad 10] [juv 11]

Black-tailed Godwit *Limosa limosa*
SCOLOPACIDAE L 37–44 cm. Tall, with long,
pinkish bill slightly upturned, long
legs, black-ended white tail, white wing-
bar; in summer, head and breast reddish
(♀ duller), flanks and belly white with
blackish bars; in winter, grey-brown and
whitish; juv rufous-buff head, breast,
back-markings. Loud 'weeka-weeka-weeka';
song musical 'krr-wit-tew'. Water-meadows,
marshes, fens, locally scrub, heaths;
passage/winter also lakes, estuaries, salt-
marshes. Nest scrape well lined grass,
sedges, in lush vegetation, 4 eggs, Apr–
Jul. Food crustaceans, molluscs, worms,
insects. Summer Ic, Ne, De, Ge, Cz, Po,
local Br, nwFr, Be, sSw; passage T, ex
FS; winter sBr, Ir, wFr. [summer ♂ 12]

Spotted Redshank *Tringa erythropus*
SCOLOPACIDAE L 29–31 cm. Taller,
slenderer than redshank, bill and legs
longer, no wing-bar, but white wedge up
back; black in summer with dark red legs,
grey and whitish in winter with orange
legs, spotted white above. 'Tchu-eet'.
Breeds open marshy forests; passage/
winter estuaries, marshes, lakes. Food
insects, molluscs, shrimps, worms,
tadpoles, small fish. Summer nFS; passage
T, ex Ic; some winter sBr, sIr, wFr, Ne.
[summer 1] [winter 2]

Redshank *Tringa totanus* SCOLOPACIDAE
L 27–29 cm. Brown and whitish, with
orange-based bill, orange-red legs; in
flight, white crescent on hindwings, white
rump. Shy, restless, often bobbing. Noisy,
esp piping 'tu', yelping 'teuk', down-
slurred 'tlu-hu-hu'. Marshes, water-
meadows; winters estuaries. Nest usually
in tussock, 4 eggs, Apr–Jul. Food as spotted
redshank, also grasses, seeds, algae.
Summer T, ex Lu, but local Fr, Be; passage T; winter Br, Ir, Ic, Fr, Be, Ne. [3]

Greenshank *Tringa nebularia* SCOLO-
PACIDAE L 30–32 cm. Larger, taller than
redshank with slightly upturned, blackish
bill, green legs, no wing-bar, but white
wedge up back; in summer, dark brown
and white, streaked and spotted; in
winter, greyer above, white face and
underparts. Loud 'tew-tew-tew'. Breeds
moors, open forest; passage/winter and
food as spotted redshank. Summer nBr,
nFS; passage T, ex Ic; winter sBr, Ir,
wFr. [winter 4]

Green Sandpiper *Tringa ochropus*
SCOLOPACIDAE L 22–24 cm. Dark olive-
brown above (spotted whitish in summer),
with green legs; in flight, upperparts and
underwings look black against white rump,
belly. Ringing 'weet, weet-weet'. Woodland
lakes, streams, marshes; passage/winter
ponds, streams, marsh drains. Uses old
tree nest of another bird, 4 eggs, Apr–Jul.
Food insects, other invertebrates, algae.
Summer eDe, Ge, Cz, Po, FS, has bred
Br; passage T, ex Ic; winter sBr, Fr, Be.
[summer 5] [winter 6]

Wood Sandpiper *Tringa glareola*
SCOLOPACIDAE L 19–21 cm. Slenderer,
paler, less contrasted than green sandpiper
(but boldly spotted white in summer),
with longer yellowish legs, pale underwings,
whitish rump. Shrill 'chiff-iff-iff'. Marshes
in forest, tundra; passage marshes, lake
edges, boggy pools. Nest scrape lined
grass, lvs, rarely in old tree nest, 4 eggs,
May–Jul. Food invertebrates. Summer
De, FS, rare nBr, nGe, ?Po; passage T,
ex wIr, Ic. [summer 7] [winter 8]

Common Sandpiper *Actitis hypoleucos*
SCOLOPACIDAE L 19–20 cm. Short legs,
constant bobbing, low flight with bowed
wings flicking; olive-brown above (dark-
barred in summer), white-sided tail.
Shrill 'twee-wee-wee'. Streams, rivers,
lakes, esp upland; passage/winter by
freshwater, salt-marshes. Nest scrape
lined plants, debris, 4 eggs, Apr–Jul.
Food invertebrates, esp insects. Summer
T, ex seBr, Ic, Lu, has bred Be, Ne, De;
passage T, ex Ic; winter sBr, eIr, wFr.
[summer 9] [winter 10]

Red-necked Phalarope *Phalaropus
lobatus* PHALAROPIDAE L 16·5–18 cm,
♂ smaller, duller than ♀. Dainty, tame,
swims habitually; bill black, needle-like;
in summer, orange patch contrasts with
grey head, white throat and underparts.
Low 'whit'. Marshy lakes, boggy pools.
Nest lined grass, in tussock, 4 eggs,
May–Jul (♂ incubates). Food insects,
tiny molluscs, worms. Summer Ic, nFS,
rare nBr, nwIr; passage T, ex Lu, Cz,
but coastal, scarce. [summer ♂ 11]
[summer ♀ 12]

Grey Phalarope *Phalaropus fulicarius*
PHALAROPIDAE L 19–21 cm, ♂ smaller,
duller than ♀. Told from red-necked
phalarope in summer by yellow-based
bill, white sides of head, chestnut underparts. Shrill 'twit'. Open pools, coastal
lagoons. Nest scrape lined grass, in
open or tussock, 4 eggs, Jun–Jul
(♂ incubates). Food tiny crustaceans,
molluscs, insects, worms. Summer Ic;
passage Br, Ir, Fr, Be, Ne, De, wGe,
swNo, but coastal. [summer ♀ 13]

Little Gull *Larus minutus* LARIDAE L 27–29 cm. Smaller than black-headed gull, with tern-like flight, white-tipped grey primaries, blackish undersides to more rounded wings, *black* head in summer, dark bill in winter; imm has kittiwake-like black zigzag on wings, pale underwings, black-ended tail; juv crown and back blackish. Low 'kek-kek-kek'. Marshes, lakes; passage/winter also coasts. Colonial; nest heap of dead rushes, sedges, in tussock, among plants in shallows, on islet, 2–3 eggs, May–Jul. Food small fish, molluscs, crustaceans, worms, insects. Scarce summer nDe, nPo, sFi, sSw, has bred eBr; passage/winter T, ex Ic, most of SC. [summer 1] [imm 2]

Black-headed Gull *Larus ridibundus* LARIDAE L 35–38 cm. In flight, broad white front edge to pointed black-tipped wings; smallish, white and grey, with red bill and legs, *brown* hood (not back of neck) in summer, white head with blackish marks round eyes in winter; juv mottled brown on crown and back, black-tipped tail, yellower bill and legs. Noisy when breeding, *eg* harsh 'kwarr', short 'kuk'. Lakes, meres, gravel pits, bogs, moorland pools, coastal marshes; in winter, freshwater and fields inland, coasts, estuaries. Colonial; nest bare scrape to heap of vegetation, 2–3 eggs, Apr–Jul. Food as little gull, also seeds, roots, moss, refuse. T, ex nFS, but only summer Fi, most SC. [summer 3] [imm 4]

Common Gull *Larus canus* LARIDAE L 39–42 cm. White and grey, with white-spotted, black tips to long, thin wings, slender greenish-yellow bill and legs, head strongly streaked in winter; juv/imm grey-brown above, with broad black tail-band, blackish bill, brownish-pink legs. Shrill 'kee-yah'. Lakes, rivers, bogs, moors; winters fields, lakes, coasts. Usually colonial; nest lined scrape to heap of vegetation, 2–3 eggs, Apr–Jul. Food as black-headed gull. Summer nBr, nIr, wIc, Ne, De, nGe, nPo, FS, few sBr, nFr, Be; winter T, ex Fi, nSw. [summer 5] [imm 6]

Lesser Black-backed Gull *Larus fuscus* LARIDAE L 51–60 cm. Like herring gull, but black slate-grey (Br, Ir, Ic, Fr, Ne, wGe) to black (De, eGe, FS), legs yellow in summer (but may fade to yellowish-pink in autumn), head closely streaked in winter; imm like herring gull, but darker-backed. Calls deeper. Coasts, also lakes, bogs; passage/winter coasts, inland. Colonial; nest as herring gull, but inland also of moss, heather, 2–3 eggs, May–Jul. Food fish, worms, crustaceans, molluscs, insects, rodents, birds, eggs, carrion, refuse, grain. Summer T, ex Lu, Be, Cz, Po; inland esp nBr, nIr, sIc, Fi, wNo; passage T, some winter ex Ic, FS. [winter 7] [imm 8]

Herring Gull *Larus argentatus* LARIDAE L 53–64 cm. Larger than common gull, with heavier, yellow bill (red spot near tip), pink legs (yellow Fi), fiercer look, broader wings, head less streaked in winter; juv mottled brown with darker primaries and tail, blackish bill, becoming paler over 3 yrs. Loud 'keew', trumpeting 'kyow-kyow-kyow'; rhythmic 'gag-gag-gag' near nest. Mainly coastal WE, but lakes, bogs in sFi, sSw; winters coasts, reservoirs, lakes, rivers. Colonial; nest lined scrape to heap of grass, litter, 2–3 eggs, Apr–Jul. Food as lesser black-back, but also grass, seeds, berries, potatoes, turnips. T, but breeding rare Be, Po, only passage Lu, Cz. [winter 9] [imm 10]

Great Black-backed Gull *Larus marinus* LARIDAE L 64–79 cm. Larger than lesser black-back, upperparts black, legs whitish-pink, head sparsely streaked in winter; juv/imm head and underparts whitish, back and wings chequered, 4 yrs to adult. Deep, barking, disdainful 'owk', guttural 'uk-uk-uk'. Mainly coasts, but locally lakes, bogs; winters coasts, estuaries, but also reservoirs, lakes. Often single pairs; nest large pile of grass, heather, twigs, litter, 2–3 eggs, Apr–Jul. Food as lesser black-back, but more birds. Summer Br, Ir, Ic, nwFr, De, FS; winter/non-breeding T, ex Lu, Cz, N Baltic. [winter 11] [imm 12]

Terns are slender, narrow-winged, graceful fliers with pointed bills, short legs, forked tails. The 7 N European 'sea terns', 3 of which also nest inland, are white and grey, with black caps in summer, white foreheads and streaked crowns in autumn; juvs as autumn adults, but mottled brown above. They mostly fish by plunging, whereas the 3 'marsh terns' pick food from the surface. These are dark-bodied in summer, but more like sea terns in autumn; juvs as autumn, but with dark 'saddles' on backs.

Common Tern *Sterna hirundo* STERNIDAE L 33–35·5 cm. Told from arctic tern by black tip to orange-red bill, shorter tail-streamers not projecting beyond closed wing-tips, translucent innermost primaries overhead; autumn/juv by blacker shoulder-patches. Long-drawn, grating 'keeee-yaah', also 'kikikikik', 'kirri-kirri'. Coasts, rivers with shingle, lakes with islets, gravel pits. Colonial; nest scrape often lined grass, in open, 2–4 eggs, May–Sep. Food fish, crustaceans, molluscs, insects. Summer T, ex Ic, nFS. [summer 1] [juv 2]

Arctic Tern *Sterna paradisaea* STERNIDAE L 35–38 cm. Told from common tern by entirely blood-red bill, shorter legs (looks 'legless'), longer tail-streamers, greyer underparts, wholly translucent primaries overhead. Calls similar, but shorter 'kee-yah' with emphasis more on 2nd syllable, whistling 'kee-kee' with rising pitch. Habitat and food similar, but less inland. Nest as common tern, 1–3 eggs, May–Aug. Summer Br, Ir, Ic, Ne, De, Ge, FS, rare nwFr; inland nBr, nIr, Ic, De, FS; passage also Be, Po. [summer 3] [juv 4]

Little Tern *Sterna albifrons* STERNIDAE L 23–25 cm. Tiny, with black-tipped yellow bill, yellow legs, white forehead contrasting with black crown and eye-stripe; juv brownish-yellow bill and legs. Persistently hovers; rapid beats. Sharp 'ki-tuk', rasping 'kree-ik', chattering 'kirri-kikki, kirri-kikki'. Coasts, rivers, lakes, with sand or shingle. Loosely

colonial; nest scrape in open, 2–3 eggs, May–Aug. Food crustaceans, worms, also fish. Summer T, ex Ic, Lu, Fi (passage), No, but local Sw; inland Fr, Ne, De, Ge, Cz, Po. [summer **5**] [juv **6**]

Whiskered Tern *Chlidonias hybridus* STERNIDAE L 24–26 cm. Dark grey with contrasting white cheeks, underwings and undertail, black cap, red bill and legs; in autumn, told from black tern by lack of breast-patches, less black on head, paler upperparts; from white-winged black by longer (blackish) bill, greyish nape, grey rump; juv mottled 'saddle'. Rasping 'ky-ik'. Marshy lagoons, shallow lakes, with reeds, sedges. Colonial; floating nest of reeds, weeds, anchored to vegetation, 2–3 eggs, May–Jun. Food insects, also shrimps, leeches, tadpoles, small fish. Local summer wFr, has bred Be, Ne, Ge, Po. [summer **7**] [juv **8**]

Black Tern *Chlidonias niger* STERNIDAE L 23–25 cm. All blackish-grey, darkest on head and underbody, but for white undertail, pale grey underwings, red-brown legs; in autumn, forehead, neck and underparts white, but crown and nape blackish, upperparts dark grey, black patch at sides of breast; juv black-brown 'saddle'. Squeaky 'kik, kik'. Habitat and food as whiskered tern. Nest also similar, or lined scrape on ground by water, 2–3 eggs, May–Jul. Local summer Fr, Be, Ne, De, Ge, Cz, Po, sSw; has bred Br, Ir, sFi, where also passage. [summer **9**] [juv **10**]

White-winged Black Tern *Chlidonias leucopterus* STERNIDAE L 22–24 cm. Jet-black, including underwings, but for white shoulders, rump and tail, red bill and legs; in autumn, told from black tern by same characters as whiskered tern and stubbier (blackish) bill; from whiskered also by blacker nape, white collar, paler rump, squarer tail; juv black-brown 'saddle' contrasting with pale grey wings, white rump. Hoarse 'kerr'. Habitat and nest as whiskered tern, 2–3 eggs, May–Jul. Food mainly insects. Summer ePo, has bred Be, Ge; passage Cz. [summer **11**] [juv **12**]

Cuckoo *Cuculus canorus* CUCULIDAE L 32–
34 cm. Tail long, graduated, wings pointed;
upperparts and throat blue-grey, underparts whitish, barred dark grey; juv has
white nape-patch, strongly barred red-
brown or faintly marked grey-brown
upperparts. ♂ far-carrying 'cuc-coo'; ♀
bubbling chuckle. Woods, farmland with
hedgerows, to moors, tundra, including
marshes, reed-beds. ♀ lays in nests of other
spp, esp pipits, wagtails, warblers, dunnock,
robin, specializing on 1 host, 6–18 eggs,
May–Jul. Food mainly insects, esp larvae;
♀ eats 1 of host's eggs. Summer T, ex Ic.
[♂ 1] [♀ at reed warbler nest 2] [juv 3]

Short-eared Owl *Asio flammeus* STRIGIDAE
L 36–39 cm. Mainly diurnal, settling on
open ground or flying low with frequent
glides on raised wings; wings long and
narrow with dark patch at 'elbows', ear-
tufts barely visible; tawny-buff blotched
with dark brown above, streaked on neck
and breast; fierce whitish face darkening
round yellow eyes. Resonant 'boo-boo-
boo', barking, wing-clapping, only when
breeding. Marshes, fens, bogs, moors,
heaths, dunes. Nest bare scrape among
tall vegetation, 4–8 eggs, Mar–Jul. Food
small mammals, esp voles; also small
birds, insects. Summer T, ex sBr, Ir, sFS;
winter T, ex most FS. [4]

Swift *Apus apus* APODIDAE L 16–17 cm.
Wings scythe-shaped, tail short, forked;
sooty-black with pale throat; juv whiter
throat, white-edged wing-feathers. Rapid
beats of stiff wings. Screaming, chasing,
when breeding. Exclusively aerial, over
urban areas, open country, often many over
water. Social; nest of aerially collected
plant fragments, feathers, in hole in
building, cliff, tree, 2–3 eggs, May–Aug.
Food insects, spiders, caught on wing.
Summer T, ex Ic, nSC. [ad 5] [juv 6]

Kingfisher *Alcedo atthis* ALCEDINIDAE
L 16–17 cm. Stumpy, short-tailed, with
large head, long dagger bill; iridescent
blue and green above, chestnut below, with
white throat and neck-patch, small red
feet. Perches, often bobbing, or hovers,
then plunges into water; flight low, rapid.

Loud, shrill 'chee' or 'chee-ee'; song
trilling medley of whistles. Streams, rivers,
gravel pits, lakes; winters also estuaries,
rocky shores. Nest tunnel < 150 cm in
sand or earth bank, ending in circular
chamber, 5–7 eggs, Mar–Aug. Food mainly
fish, insects, tadpoles. T, ex nBr, Ic, No,
but only sFi (summer), sSw. [7]

Sand Martin *Riparia riparia* HIRUN-
DINIDAE L 11·5–12·5 cm. Slender, tail
barely forked; brown above, white below
with brown breast-band; juv light-edged
feathers on upperparts, buff-washed throat.
Erratic, fluttering flight. Hard, trilling
twitter 'trri-trri-trri'; song weak
twittering. Largely aerial, usually near
lakes, rivers, sand pits, railway cuttings.
Colonial; nest tunnel, with flattened
entrance, < 1 m in sand, earth or peat
bank, ending in round chamber lined plant
down, stems, feathers, 4–5 eggs, May–Aug.
Food insects, caught on wing. Summer T,
ex Ic. [ad 8]

Swallow *Hirundo rustica* HIRUNDINIDAE
L 17–19 cm. Long wings, tail-streamers;
upperparts and breast-band dark blue,
forehead and throat chestnut-red, underparts creamy-white; juv duller, with
shorter streamers. Twittering 'tswit-
tswit-tswit'; song similar, mixed with
trilling warble. Largely aerial over open
country, often many over lakes, rivers.
Cup nest of mud and straw, lined grass,
feathers, on ledge in cowshed, boathouse,
under bridge, 4–6 eggs, May–Sep. Food
insects, caught on wing. Summer T, ex
Ic, nFS. [ad 9] [juv 10]

House Martin *Delichon urbica* HIRUN-
DINIDAE L 12–13 cm. Tail slightly forked;
upperparts blue-black (juv browner), rump
and underparts white. More chirruping
than swallow, hard 'tchirrp'; song weak,
prolonged twitter. Largely aerial over
farms, villages, towns, locally cliffs,
often many over lakes, rivers. Colonial;
nest ½-cup of mud mixed with plant fibres,
lined fine grass, feathers, under eaves,
bridge, cliff overhang, 4–5 eggs, May–Oct.
Food insects, caught on wing. Summer T,
ex Ic. [ad 11]

Meadow Pipit *Anthus pratensis*
MOTACILLIDAE L 14–15 cm. Olive-brown above, whitish to buff below, heavily streaked blackish; white-sided tail, pale brown legs. 'Tseep', 'tissip'. Breeds rough pastures, moors, coastal marshes, dunes; winters lowland marshes, farmland, coasts. Food insects, spiders, seeds. T, but only summer Ic, Cz, Po, FS. [1]

Water Pipit *Anthus spinoletta*
MOTACILLIDAE L 16–17 cm. Mountain ssp of coastal rock pipit. Larger, longer-billed than meadow pipit, with white superciliary; brown above (greyish in summer), brown-streaked whitish below (unstreaked pinkish in summer); white-sided tail, dark legs. Breeds mountain pastures; winters lowland marshes. Food insects, snails, seeds. Summer eFr, sGe, Cz, sPo, winter west to sBr, Fr, Be, Ne. [winter 2]

Yellow Wagtail *Motacilla flava*
MOTACILLIDAE L 16–17 cm. Long-tailed, slim, with yellow underparts, greenish back; ♂ yellow ssp *M. f. flavissima* (Br, local nFr, nNe, nwGe, swNo) greenish crown and cheeks, yellow superciliary; ♂ blue-headed *M. f. flava* (T, ex Br, Ir, Ic, nFS) bluish crown and cheeks, white superciliary and chin; ♂ grey-headed *M. f. thunbergi* (nFS) slate-grey crown, blackish cheeks, no superciliary; ♀s/autumn ♂s duller and browner above, paler below. Drawn-out, musical 'tswee-ip'. Water-meadows, marshes, gravel pits, fields, moors, tundra. Cup nest of grass, roots, lined hair, wool, in hollow, under plant, 5–6 eggs, May–Aug. Food insects, small molluscs. Summer T, ex Ic, irregular Ir. [♂ yellow 3] [♂ blue-headed 4] [♂ grey-headed 5] [♀ 6]

Grey Wagtail *Motacilla cinerea* MOTA-CILLIDAE L 17–18 cm. Told from yellow wagtails by blue-grey back, longer tail; throat whitish, but ♂'s black in summer. Short, metallic, high-pitched 'tzitzit'. Rocky hill-streams, lowland rivers with weirs, locally lakes, quarries, ruins; winters lowland freshwater, coasts. Cup nest of moss, grass, twigs, roots, lined hair, on ledge, in crevice, over or near

water, 4–6 eggs, Mar–Jul. Food mainly insects. T, ex Ic, Fi, all but sSC, but scarce Ne, mainly summer Cz, Po, SC. [summer ♂ 7] [♀ 8]

White/Pied Wagtail *Motacilla alba* MOTACILLIDAE L 17–18 cm. ♂ boldly black, grey, white; ♀ greyer, less black on head, breast. Pied ssp *M. a. yarrellii* (Br, Ir, erratically Ne, De, nwGe, swNo) has black rump, ♂ also black back, where Continental white ssp *M. a. alba* grey. Shrill 'tchizzik'. Often by water, in open country, farmland, hill streams, also towns, quarries, coasts. Cup nest of moss, grass, twigs, roots, lined hair, wool, feathers, in recess in wall, rock, bank, haystack, ivy, tree, old nest, 5–6 eggs, Apr–Aug. Food mainly insects. T, but only summer Ic, Ne, De, Ge, Cz, Po, FS. [summer ♂ white 9] [♂ pied 10]

Dipper *Cinclus cinclus* CINCLIDAE L 17–18 cm. Plump, short-tailed, blackish, breast white, belly chestnut (esp Br) to blackish (nFS); juv slate-grey above,

whitish mottled with dark brown below. Bobs constantly; wades or plunges in to swim or walk under water. Loud 'zit'; in flight, metallic 'clink'; song mixture of deep grating and higher clear notes. Rocky streams, slower rivers with weirs, also coasts in winter. Domed nest of moss with grass cup, lined dead lvs, in crevice or on ledge over torrent, 4–6 eggs, Feb–Aug. Food larvae, small molluscs, crustaceans, worms. Br, Ir, eFr, Lu, Be, Ge, Cz, sPo, nFi, SC, rare De, has bred Ne; winter T, ex Ic. [nFS ad 11] [Br ad 12]

Wren *Troglodytes troglodytes* TROGLO-DYTIDAE L c9·5 cm. Tiny, stumpy; tail short, cocked; red-brown, closely barred blackish, with paler superciliary, under-parts. Hard ticking or churring; song loud, clear phrase of shrill notes with final trill. Almost ubiquitous, including watersides, marshes, reed-beds esp in winter. Domed nest with side-entrance, of lvs, moss, grass, lined feathers, in any fork, cranny, 5–6 eggs, Apr–Aug. Food insects, spiders, seeds. T, ex nFS, but only summer Fi. [13]

Grasshopper Warbler *Locustella naevia*
SYLVIIDAE L 12–13 cm. Dark-streaked
yellowish-brown above, lightly streaked
on breast, with rounded tail. Song
prolonged, high-pitched, insect-like trill,
audible < ½ km. Bushy marshes, reed-beds,
osiers, heaths, moors, young plantations.
Cup nest of grass, in tussock, rushes,
bramble, gorse, 5–6 eggs, May–Aug. Food
insects, also spiders, woodlice. Summer
T, ex Ic, No, but only sFi, sSw. [1]

River Warbler *Locustella fluviatilis*
SYLVIIDAE L 12–13 cm. Told from grasshopper warbler by unstreaked dark brown
upperparts, blurred streaks on breast.
Trilling song softer, slower, more rhythmic
and chuffing. Watersides with rank herbage,
damp woods. Nest similar, in thick cover,
5–6 eggs, Jun–Aug. Food mainly insects.
Summer Ge, Cz, Po, has bred sFi. [2]

Savi's Warbler *Locustella luscinioides*
SYLVIIDAE L 13·5–14·5 cm. Like large
reed warbler, dark red-brown above, buff-
white below, no streaking. Song like
grasshopper warbler, but lower-pitched,
more rattling, often less prolonged,
preceded by accelerating ticking notes.
Reedy swamps with sedges, sweet-grass,
scattered bushes. Cup nest of sweet-grass,
sedge, in thick cover, 4–6 eggs, May–Aug.
Food mainly insects. Summer Fr, Ne, Ge,
Po, rare seBr, Be, De, Cz, has bred sFi. [3]

Aquatic Warbler *Acrocephalus paludicola*
SYLVIIDAE 12–13 cm. Like sedge warbler,
but greyer above in summer, yellower in
autumn, with broad buff crown-stripe,
bolder black streaks extending to rump;
in summer, dark streaks on breast, flanks.
Song similar, but phrases shorter, faster,
less varied. Open sedge-marshes, with
scattered bushes; reed-beds on passage.
Cup nest of grasses, plant down, spider
webs, lined feathers, in sedges, low shrub,
5–6 eggs, May–Jul. Food mainly insects.
Summer neGe, Cz, nPo, occasional Ne;
regular autumn sBr, Fr, Be, Ne. [4]

Sedge Warbler *Acrocephalus schoenobaenus*
SYLVIIDAE L 12–13 cm. Bold creamy superciliary, dark-streaked crown and back,
contrasting with plain tawny rump in flight;

juv yellower, with faint breast-spots, sometimes ill-defined crown-stripe (*cf* aquatic
warbler). Song loud, hurried, without reed
warbler's 'jag-jag-jag', combining musical
and harsh notes with trills and imitations.
Rank vegetation with scattered bushes by
lakes, reed-beds, rivers, locally hedgerows,
crops. Bulky cup nest of moss, grass, lined
plant down, feathers, hair, bound to sedges,
reeds, nettles, 5–6 eggs, May–Aug. Food
insects, spiders, berries in autumn. Summer
T, ex Ic, central FS. [ad 5] [juv 6]

Blyth's Reed Warbler *Acrocephalus
dumetorum* SYLVIIDAE L 12–13 cm. Very like
reed and marsh warblers, but greyer above,
with longer-looking bill and tail, short
rounded wings, clearer superciliary, darker
legs than marsh warbler. Song like marsh
warbler, but generally even louder, richer,
more varied; sings more from trees and by
night. Marshy thickets of willow, alder,
also dry wood-edges, often near water. Cup
nest, neater than marsh warbler's, of grass,
plant down, lined roots, hair, bound to
tall herbage, 4–5 eggs, Jun–Jul. Food
mainly insects. Summer sFi. [7]

Marsh Warbler *Acrocephalus palustris*
SYLVIIDAE L 12–13 cm. Very like reed
warbler, but plumper, more olive-brown
above, with whiter throat, pinkish legs.
Song typically much richer, more varied,
strongly mimetic, esp canary-like trills
and nasal, greenfinch-like imitations.
Osier beds, bushy areas, with nettles or
meadowsweet, by rivers, lakes; locally also
crops, hedgerows, scrub. Loose cup nest of
grass, lined rootlets, hair, suspended by
'basket handles' from nettles, meadowsweet,
4–5 eggs, May–Jul. Food as sedge warbler.
Summer eFr, Lu, Be, Ne, De, Ge, Cz, Po,
sSw, rare sBr, sFi, has bred sNo. [8]

Reed Warbler *Acrocephalus scirpaceus*
SYLVIIDAE L 12–13 cm. Brown above with
redder rump, buff below with whiter throat.
Harsh, repetitive song, slower than sedge
warbler's, esp 'jag-jag-jag', churring
'chirruc-chirruc-chirruc'. Reed-beds, osiers.
Cylindrical cup nest of grass, reed-fls, plant
down, woven round reed-stems, shrub fork,
3–5 eggs, May–Aug. Food as sedge warbler.
Summer T, ex Ir, Ic, but only sBr, sFS. [9].

Great Reed Warbler *Acrocephalus arundinaceus* SYLVIIDAE L 18–20 cm. Brown above, buff below with whitish throat, like reed warbler, but much larger, with long stout bill, bold superciliary. Song loud, guttural, croaking, with frog-like 'karra-karra', 'gurk-gurk'. Reeds, bulrushes, by lakes, rivers, marshes. Deep, cylindrical cup nest of reeds, sedges, lined reed-fls, plant down, woven round 3–5 stems of reeds, 4–6 eggs, May–Jul. Food insects, larvae, spiders. Summer Fr, Lu, Be, Ne, De, Ge, Cz, Po, rare sFi, sSw. [1]

Cetti's Warbler *Cettia cetti* SYLVIIDAE L 13·5–14·5 cm. Red-brown, greyish below, with whitish superciliary, graduated tail. Recalls small nightingale; equally skulking, best located by song: sudden, loud, rich outburst 'chee, cheweechoo-weechoo-weechoo-wee'. Low tangles, reedy thickets, brambles, by streams, rivers, swamps. Untidy cup nest of grasses, fibres, on base of dead lvs, lined fine stems, hair, reed-fls, feathers, in rank herbage, reeds, hedge, 3–4 eggs, Apr–Jul. Food insects, larvae, small molluscs, seeds. Fr, spreading to sBr, Be, Ne, wGe. [2]

Fan-tailed Warbler *Cisticola juncidis* SYLVIIDAE L c10 cm. Like tiny, short-tailed sedge warbler, heavily streaked above, whitish and rufous-buff below, but white and black tips to tail-feathers, no pale superciliary. Skulking, usually seen in song-display: rasping 'dzeep' at each rise in high, dipping flight. Marshes, swampy meadows, grasslands, cornfields. Nest deep, pear-shaped purse with top-entrance, of fine grass, plant down, bound with spider webs, in grass, rushes, 4–6 eggs, Mar–Aug. Food insects, larvae, seeds. Fr, spreading to Be, Ne, wGe. [3]

Bearded Tit *Panurus biarmicus* TIMALIIDAE L 16–17 cm. Not true tit. Tawny above, white to pinkish-grey below, with long, tawny tail; ♂ blue-grey head, black moustache and undertail-coverts; juv like ♀, but paler, with black on mid-back, wing-coverts, tail-sides (juv ♂ also black before eye). Shrill, twanging 'pieng,

pieng', interspersed with 'tick' or 'tew'. Large reed-beds. Nest of dead reeds, sedges, lined reed-fls, low in thick cover near edge of reed-bed, 5–7 eggs, Apr–Aug. Food insects, larvae; reed seeds in winter. Local seBr, Fr, Be, Ne, De, Ge, Cz, Po; wanders in winter. [♂ 4] [♀ 5]

Penduline Tit *Remiz pendulinus* REMIZIDAE L 10·5–11 cm. Tiny; grey-white head and throat, black mask, chestnut back; juv browner-grey above, lacks black and chestnut. Soft, plaintive, robin-like 'tsee-oo', more tit-like 'tsi-tsi-tsi'. Thickets of willow, poplar, by ponds, marshes, streams, rivers; also dry scrubby woodland. Domed nest with side-entrance tube, of plant down, fibres, in outer twigs of bush or tree, often over water, 6–8 eggs, Apr–Jul. Food insects, larvae, seeds. eGe, Cz, Po, local De, wGe, has nested Ne, sSw; wanders in winter. [ad 6] [juv 7]

Scarlet Rosefinch *Carpodacus erythrinus* FRINGILLIDAE L 14–15 cm. Dumpy, with largish, round head, bright dark eyes, 2 pale bars on dark wings; ad ♂ head, breast and rump rosy-red, belly white; ♀/1st yr ♂ yellow-brown above, buff below, streaked brown. Soft, canary-like 'twee-eek'; song loud, clear piping. Swampy woods, riverside thickets. Warbler-like nest of grass, lined roots, hair, in shrub, small tree, 4–5 eggs, May–Jul. Food seeds, buds; young fed on insects, larvae. Local summer eGe, eCz, Po, sFi, sSw. [♂ 8] [♀ 9]

Reed Bunting *Emberiza schoeniclus* EMBERIZIDAE L 15–16 cm. ♂ black head and throat, white collar, whitish underparts, streaked flanks, but pattern obscured by brown mottling in winter; ♀/juv brown head, blackish moustache, buff superciliary, streaked breast and flanks, white tail-sides. Grating 'tseep'; song 2–3 wheezy squeaks and short, tuneless trill 'tseep-tseep-tserrr'. Rushy pastures, reed-beds, lakes, rivers, young conifers. Cup nest of dry grass, sedges, lined fine grass, hair, on or near ground in reeds, shrub, 4–5 eggs, Apr–Sep. Food seeds, small molluscs, insects, larvae. T, ex Ic, but only summer Cz, ePo, Fi, most SC. [summer ♂ 10] [♀ 11]

Water Shrew *Neomys fodiens* SORICIDAE
BL 70–90 mm, TL 50–75 mm. Pointed
snout; underside of tail and sides of hind
feet fringed with stiff white hairs.
Distinguished from other, non-aquatic,
shrews also by large size and black
upperparts. Slow streams, rivers, lake-
margins, marshes, sometimes in woodland
far from water. Nocturnal and diurnal;
swims and dives; uses regular runways on
banks. Feeds on terrestrial and aquatic
invertebrates, also small fish, frogs, killed
by venomous saliva. T, ex Ir, Ic. [1]

Bats (Chiroptera). Any of the 20 spp of
bats found in N Europe are likely to be
attracted to water when insects are
emerging in large numbers, but the 2
spp shown here are especially associated
with water. They all fly at dusk or
throughout the night and feed entirely
upon flying insects. Long experience is
necessary before the spp can be identified
with any confidence in flight. When found
at rest the shape and size of the ear, and
especially of the lobe or 'tragus' within
the conch of the ear, are usually
important features for identification.

Daubenton's Bat *Myotis daubentoni*
VESPERTILIONIDAE BL 40–50 mm, FA 33–39
mm. A small bat, dark brown above,
brownish grey below. Tragus narrow and
pointed, half length of ear; ear small,
scarcely reaching tip of nose when folded
forward; feet large, more than half length
of shins. Woodland, often feeding over
water. Roosts in trees and buildings in
summer, sometimes in large colonies; also
in caves in winter. Flies all night,
emerging about half an hour after sunset.
Feeds on small insects caught in flight.
T, ex Ic, nFS. [2]

Pond Bat *Myotis dasycneme* VESPER-
TILIONIDAE BL 55–65 mm, FA 43–48 mm.
Similar to Daubenton's bat but larger.
Upper surface greyer, with light brown
hair-tips; underside greyish white. Ears
longer, extending beyond tip of nose when
folded forward. Feet large as in
Daubenton's. Woodland, esp near water.
Nocturnal; hunts low over surface of
ponds and lakes. Roosts in trees and

buildings, also in caves in winter;
migratory. neFr, Be, Lu, Ne, De, Ge, Po,
Cz, sSw. [3]

American Mink *Mustela vison*
MUSTELIDAE BL 40–60 cm, TL 15–25 cm.
Weasel-like carnivore with long body and
short legs. Uniform dark brown except
for white on chin; many other colours in
ranch animals but these rarely persist in
wild. Makes purring noise in spring.
Banks of rivers and lakes, marshes.
Nocturnal. Swims well but less aquatic
than otter. Feeds on rodents, fish, birds,
crayfishes. (T, feral populations,
originating in escapes from fur farms.)
[4]

European Mink *Mustela lutreola*
MUSTELIDAE BL 35–45 cm, TL 13–15 cm.
Very similar in appearance and habits to
wild type of American mink but with
white on upper lip as well as on chin.
Elusive and little known, probably now
very rare in N Europe. wFr, Po, Fi. [5]

Raccoon *Procyon lotor* PROCYONIDAE
BL 50–70 cm, TL 20–25 cm. Cat-sized,
with distinctive black mask and ringed
tail. [Raccoon-dog *Nyctereutes procyonoides*,
(Ge, Cz, Po, Fi), also has black mask but
tail is uniform.) Mainly woodland, esp
near water, but very adaptable and
tolerant of disturbance. Agile climber.
Nocturnal; den usually in hollow tree.
Omnivorous, feeding on fruit, nuts,
cereal, eggs, frogs, crayfishes. (Lu, neFr,
Be, Ne, Ge, from N America.) [6]

Otter *Lutra lutra* MUSTELIDAE
BL 60–85 cm, TL 35–50 cm. Large, long
slender body, thick tapering tail. Extremely
agile and graceful in water; runs with
bounding gait on land. Voice varied, sharp
whistle and chirp most frequent. Rivers,
lakes, marshes, estuaries, rocky coasts.
Nocturnal; usually solitary. Most easily
detected by characteristic droppings
(spraints) consisting largely of fish bones
and scales, also crab shells on coast,
deposited on rock or tussock near water.
Den in hole in bank or under rocks. Feeds
on fish, also frogs, birds, crayfishes, crabs.
T, ex Ic. [7, 8]

Beaver *Castor fiber* CASTORIDAE
BL 75–90 cm, TL 30–38 cm. Largest
European rodent. Much less elongate than
otter; broad scaly tail unique. (American
beaver *C. canadensis*, (Fi), very similar but
darker, esp on head.) Much more agile
swimmer than other aquatic rodents.
Lakes, slow rivers, with broadleaved
trees on banks. Mainly nocturnal. Nest in
burrow on bank or in elaborate covered
platform (lodge) in pond. Feeds on water-
side vegetation, also by felling small trees
and storing them in water to feed on bark.
Streams may be dammed to adjust water-
level. Ge, FS, (reintroduced nFr). [1, 2]

Coypu *Myocastor coypus* CAPROMYIDAE
BL 50–65 cm, TL 30–45 cm. Much smaller
than beaver but larger than other aquatic
rodents. Tail not flattened; head very
large; incisor teeth prominent, bright
orange. Teats (4–5 pairs) on flanks. Slow
rivers, lakes, ponds with well vegetated
banks; most often seen in water. Diurnal.
Feeds on grass, sedges and reeds, also
root-crops. (Br, E Anglia only, Fr, Ne,
Ge, SC, from S America.) [3, 4]

Water Vole *Arvicola terrestris* CRICETIDAE
BL 15–22 cm, TL 10–14 cm. Much larger
than similar, but more terrestrial, root and
field voles *Microtus* spp, much smaller
than other aquatic rodents. Tail much
shorter than head and body, ears scarcely
projecting above fur. Rivers, lakes, ditches,
salt-marshes; in grassland away from water

in south of region. Commonly diurnal. Feeds mainly on grass, also other water-side vegetation. Preyed upon by otters, mink, herons, pike. T, ex Ir, Ic. [5, 6]

Root Vole *Microtus oeconomus* CRICETIDAE BL 12–15 cm, TL 4–6 cm. Like miniature water vole; difficult to distinguish from field vole *M. agrestis* and common vole *M. arvalis* but larger and tail relatively longer. Marshes, reed-beds. Can swim but not often seen in water. Feeds on grass, sedges. Ne, Ge, Po, FS. [7]

Musk Rat *Ondatra zibethicus* CRICETIDAE BL 30–40 cm, TL 20–27 cm. Similar to water vole but about twice the size and tail flattened from side to side. Voice a sharp whistle. Ponds, marshes, slow rivers with overgrown banks. Expert swimmer, rarely seen out of water. Nocturnal and diurnal. Makes covered surface nests in marshes, also deep burrows in river-banks. Feeds on water-side vegetation. (Fr, Be, Ne, Ge, Po, Cz, Fi, from N America.) [8]

Common Rat *Rattus norvegicus* MURIDAE BL 20–26 cm, TL 17–23 cm. Tail longer, ears more prominent, muzzle more pointed than other aquatic rodents. Banks of rivers, ponds, ditches, salt-marshes, esp where human disturbance, dumping of rubbish. Competent swimmer, easily mistaken for water vole. Makes runways and burrows on banks. Feeds on seeds, invertebrates, refuse. T. [9, 10]

FURTHER READING

The following list gives at least one book per topic in the order of the ecological essay and the field guide.

Freshwater Biology, L. G. Willoughby (Hutchinson, 1976, London)

Peatlands, P. D. Moore and D. J. Bellamy (Elek Science, 1973, London)

Freshwater Ecology, 2nd Edn, T. T. Macan (Longmans, 1974, London)

Ponds and Lakes, T. T. Macan (Allen & Unwin, 1973, London)

The Broads (New Naturalist No. 46), E. A. Ellis (Collins, London)

Biology of Fresh Waters, P. S. Maitland (Blackie, 1978, London)

What is Ecology?, D. F. Owen (Oxford University Press, 1980, London)

Pesticides and Pollution, K. Mellanby (Collins, 1970, London)

The Thames Transformed, J. & P. Harrison, P. Grant (André Deutsch, 1976, London)

The Jarrold Nature Series: *eg Life in our Rivers*, H. Angel (Jarrold Colour Publications, 1976, Norwich)

A Beginner's Guide to Freshwater Algae, H. Belcher and E. Swale (H.M.S.O., 1976, London)

British Water Plants, S. M. Haslam, C. S. Sinker and P. A. Wolseley (Field Studies Council, 1975, London)

River Plants, S. M. Haslam (Cambridge University Press, 1978, Cambridge)

British Mosses and Liverworts, 2nd Edn, E. V. Watson (Cambridge University Press, 1969, Cambridge)

Flora Europaea, 4 vols, T. G. Tutin (ed.) (Cambridge University Press, 1964–72, Cambridge)

The Wild Flowers of Britain and Northern Europe, R. Fitter, A. Fitter and M. Blamey (Collins, 1974, London)

An Atlas of the Wild Flowers of Britain and Northern Europe, A. Fitter (Collins, 1978, London)

The Concise British Flora, W. Keble Martin, 3rd Edn (Ebury Press and Michael Joseph, 1978, London)

A Field Guide to the Trees of Britain and Northern Europe, A. Mitchell (Collins, 1974, London)

Trees and Bushes of Europe, O. Polunin and B. Everard (Oxford University Press, 1976, London)

Flowers of Europe, O. Polunin (Oxford University Press, 1969, London)

Grasses, C. E. Hubbard (Penguin, 1968, London)

The Invertebrate Panorama, E. Smith *et al* (Weidenfeld and Nicholson, 1971, London)

The Oxford Book of Invertebrates, D. Nichols, J. Cooke and D. Whiteley (Oxford University Press, 1976, London)

The Young Specialist looks at Molluscs, H. Janes (Burke, 1965, London)

A Field Guide to the Insects of Britain and Northern Europe, M. Chinery (Collins, 1973, London)

Grasshoppers, Crickets and Cockroaches of the British Isles, D. R. Ragge (Warne, 1965, London)

A Field Guide to the Butterflies of Britain and Europe, L. G. Higgins and N. Riley (Collins, 1970, London)

The Moths of the British Isles, Two vols, R. South (Warne, 1961, London)

Flies of the British Isles, C. W. Colyer and C. O. Hammond (Warne, 1968, London)

Land and Water Bugs of the British Isles, T. R. E. Southwood and D. Leston (Warne, 1959, London)

Beetles of the British Isles, Two volumes, E. F. Linssen (Warne, 1959, London)

Bees, Wasps, Ants and Allied Orders of the British Isles, E. Step (Warne, 1932, London)

Ray Society publications: *eg British Spiders*, G. H. Locket and A. F. Millidge (Ray Society, British Museum, 1951–53, London)

The World of Spiders, W. S. Bristowe (Collins, 1971, London)

Key to the Fishes of Northern Europe, A. Wheeler (Warne, 1978, London)

A Colour Guide to Familiar Freshwater Fishes, J. Čihař (Octopus, 1976, London)

The Fishes of the British Isles and North-West Europe, A. Wheeler (Macmillan, 1969, London)

A Field Guide to the Reptiles and Amphibians of Britain and Europe, E. N. Arnold, J. A. Burton and D. W. Ovenden (Collins, 1978, London)

A Field Guide to the Birds of Britain and Europe, R. Peterson, G. Mountfort and P. A. D. Hollom (Collins, 1974, London)

Man and Birds, R. K. Murton (Collins, 1971, London)

The Atlas of Breeding Birds in Britain and Ireland, J. T. R. Sharrock (Poyser, 1976, Berkhamsted)

A Field Guide to the Mammals of Britain and Europe, F. H. van den Brink (Collins, 1967, London)

The Handbook of British Mammals, G. B. Corbet and H. N. Southern (eds.) (Blackwell, 1977, Oxford)

ACKNOWLEDGEMENTS

Brian Whitton is very grateful to all those who have provided information whilst the essay was being written. Among many valuable conversations were those with Ken Bowler, Hans Golterman, Nigel Holmes, David Sutcliffe and Bryan Wheeler. The following list of authors of papers includes people he knows well and others who are just names in journals.

Denmark : S. Wium-Andersen
Germany : A. Krause
Ireland : B. MacGowran, M. J. P. Scannell
Netherlands : P. Leentvaar, H. Postma, H. van Dam
Norway : T. Dale, E. T. Gjessing,

A. Henriksen, M. Johannessen, H. Leivestad, I. P. Muniz, R. F. Wright
Poland : J. Čihař
Sweden : H. Ackefors, G. Andersson, W. Dickson, S. Erlinge, A. W. Steffan, S. Tejning, T. Willen
U.K. : A. Allison, K. M. Atkinson, D. J. Bellamy, A. J. Brook, R. J. Bryant, J. A. Burton, A. S. Cooke, K. F. Corbett, M. George, C. E. Gibson, S. M. Haslam, S. I. Heaney, D. J. Hibberd, N. T. H. Holmes, B. P. Jupp, I. F. Keymer, E. D. LeCren, C. S. Lloyd, T. T. Macan, C. F. Mason, P. D. Moore, N. C. Morgan, B. Moss, I. Newton, G. L. Phillips, K. Shepherd, G. R. Smith, D. H. Spence, A. W. Steffen, G. Thomas, A. Wheeler, L. G. Willoughby
U.S.A. (Iceland) : R. W. Castenholz

ILLUSTRATION ACKNOWLEDGEMENTS

pages
11, 26, 34, 35, 42 Heather Angel
10 *left* Dr H. Canter-Lund/NHPA
10 *right*, 14, 30 John Clegg
39 Dr J. A. L. Cooke/Oxford Scientific Films
58 Bruce Coleman Ltd
43 Dr John Edington

pages
6 Eric Hosking
31 Oxford Scientific Films
23 Mauri Rautkari/World Wildlife Fund
15, 18 Dr Colin Reynolds
67 Sólarfilma
47, 51, 55 Brian Whitton

INDEX